SISTERS OF THE SPIRIT

Religion in North America
Catherine L. Albanese and Stephen J. Stein, Editors

Mrs. Jarena Lee.
Preacher of the A. M. E. Church.
Aged sixty years.
Philadelphia, 1844.

(From *Religious Experience and Journal of Mrs. Jarena Lee,* Philadelphia, 1849)

SISTERS OF THE SPIRIT

Three Black Women's Autobiographies of the Nineteenth Century

EDITED WITH AN INTRODUCTION BY
WILLIAM L. ANDREWS

INDIANA UNIVERSITY PRESS • BLOOMINGTON

To Nellie,
friend and colleague

Manufactured in the United States of America

Library of Congress Cataloging-in-Publication Data

Main entry under title:

Sisters of the spirit.

(Religion in North America)
Contents: The life and religious experience of Jarena Lee—Memoirs of the life, religious experience, ministerial travels, and labors of Mrs. Zilpha Elaw—A brand plucked from the fire / by Julia A.J. Foote.
1. Lee, Jarena, b. 1783. 2. Elaw, Zilpha, b. ca. 1790. 3. Foote, Julia A.J., 1823–1900. 4. Afro-American evangelists—Biography. 5. Afro-American women—Biography. 6. Afro-Americans—Religion. I. Andrews, William L., 1946– II. Lee, Jarena, b. 1783. Life and religious experience of Jarena Lee. 1986. III. Elaw, Zilpha, b. ca. 1790. Memoirs of the life, religious experience, ministerial travels, and labors of Mrs. Zilpha Elaw. 1986. IV. Foote, Julia A.J., 1823–1900. Brand plucked from the fire. 1986. V. Series.
BV3780.S57 1986 208′.8042 [B] 85-42544
ISBN 0-253-35260-6
ISBN 0-253-28704-9 (pbk.)
2 3 4 5 90 89 88 87

CONTENTS

PREFACE

William L. Andrews here presents the autobiographies of Jarena Lee, Zilpha Elaw, and Julia Foote, three black women whose narratives are remarkable in a number of ways. The memoirs of all three are rich personal documents, casting important light on a series of themes in mid-nineteenth-century black religion and in American religion in general. The deep vein of personal spirituality these narratives reveal is combined with material that heightens our understanding of camp meetings and class meetings as well as interdenominational relationships during the period. Still more, from solidly within the African Methodist Episcopal church and in the shadow of the legendary Richard Allen, the autobiographies point to a protoholiness movement and even a protopentecostalism. Offering a view from the ranks, they provide a perspective not otherwise available on the role of Allen and other key A.M.E. leaders in shaping the Afro-American church.

The spirituality of vision and dream, which abundantly characterizes these recollections, has often been read in the Afro-American context as "counterrevolutionary." Yet here, with uncanny and otherworldly manifestations aplenty, we find visionary strength and support at the core of a radical religious stance. Probably without consciously intending, these women exemplify in their lives a feminism that challenged male leadership and prerogatives, that found in the Spirit an authority transcending the imposing presence of the ecclesial voice. Although this "spiritual feminism" was still in its formative phases, Lee, Elaw, and Foote pointed the way along a path that other American religious women would tread.

Beyond the radical stance of feminism, though, these women moved to a racial radicalism in which they read the Pauline theological affirmation as existing social fact. For the three, slave or free, black or white, were secondary characterizations when placed beside the primacy of the Spirit's call. While each woman was, in her way, keenly aware of racial difference, each practised a kind of spiritual "one-upping" in which charismatic religious authority transcended social station and, indeed, turned sociological tables to insert whites in a new religious order.

The texts of these narratives leave many questions still unanswered. How is it that women with such comparatively feeble formal education could write accounts cast in dramatic and sophisticated prose, as especially in the latinate sentences of Foote? Were these autobiographies ghost-written? Or dictated to an editor? Or heavily manicured in some other way? And what is their relationship to the rest of the black church? Surely the authors paint themselves at the center; but what would have been the view of their contemporaries in the church concerning their respective missions? How may we view their passionate and visionary religious life in the context of the general revival spirituality as well as the black spirituality of the time? William Andrews addresses some of these questions in his helpful and instructive introduction to the volume. Lee, Elaw, and Foote invite additional interpretation now that their accounts are again readily accessible and available. Andrews has helped to make that possible by bringing these forgotten texts once more to light.

CATHERINE L. ALBANESE
STEPHEN J. STEIN, SERIES EDITORS

FOREWORD

The voices of eighteenth- and nineteenth-century black American women are beginning to be heard again, across the barriers of time and the distortions of historical record. A few of these women—Phillis Wheatley, Sojourner Truth, Harriet Tubman, most notably—have long been considered heroines of their race and sex. While it is always good to affirm the influence of such well-known figures, it is equally important to recognize that they were neither isolated nor atypical, but were inheritors of a black female tradition of activism founded on a commitment to religious faith, human rights, and women's struggles. It is this cultural tradition that this volume addresses, bringing to our attention the autobiographical writings of Jarena Lee, Zilpha Elaw, and Julia Foote. Here are black women who found in their faith an impetus to lives of religious social activism.

Nor were the choices and decisions they made easy for them. As the texts illustrate, all three were at first reluctant to acknowledge their evangelical vocations. They well knew the obstacles they would face as women putting themselves forward in an arena where, among the more orthodox, even their speaking aloud in church was considered inappropriate.

These autobiographical accounts provide us with rare and valuable insights into the internal odysseys these women underwent in order to be able to accept the challenge of public ministries. God struggled with them, and they with him, by way of visions, dreams, and mystical experiences, often of the most harrowing sort, before they bowed to the inevitability of his call to them. Once convinced of their destinies, though, they were able to defend themselves against hostility and censure with appeals to biblical and historical feminist precedent, by defining themselves as instruments of God's purpose, and by attributing their presence in the public sphere not to egotism or ambition on their part, but to the mysterious workings of Providence through them.

All three women were widowed before they committed themselves fully to the demands of their ministries. They could easily have retreated to the bosom of family and church, there to lead lives of quiet, if somewhat threadbare, respectability. Instead, it appears they felt themselves largely freed of familial burdens. They were women on their own in the world, no longer sheltered by youthful innocence, but still young enough to see lives of rich possibility ahead. They launched themselves into all but endless rounds of grueling travel and preaching, from tense and dangerous journeys to slaveholding states in the southern United States, to transatlantic trips to proselytize the unsaved in the industrial regions of London and Manchester, England. In 1827, to pick a more or less representative year, Jarena Lee, at the age of forty-four, traveled 2,325 miles and delivered 178 sermons. Much of that distance she covered on foot, the rest by wagon, ferryboat, and carriage. Zilpha Elaw estimated that during her sojourn in Great Britain she preached more than one thousand sermons before every conceivable audience, from family gatherings to outdoor revivals in which her hearers numbered in the thousands.

The portions of these women's stories given over to the reconstruction of their preaching itineraries may strike some readers initially as episodic, even predictable, in their general outline. But even the less personally revealing parts of these autobiographies offer an almost kaleidoscopic rendering of the country's social spectrum illuminated by its spiritual and emotional needs.

Jarena Lee, Zilpha Elaw, and Julia Foote were all pioneers, as women, as writers, and as preachers. At home on the frontiers of women's consciousness, they gravitate toward another kind of "territory ahead": a geography of "the spirit." Through them we discover the topography of a region where women traveled at great sacrifice and risk, and from which they returned with news of the marvels and adventures of a new and unfolding frontier. This remarkable edition of these texts helps to lift a significant element of black intellectual history from generations of obscurity and neglect, and makes available once again the vivid and persistent voices of three black women who wrote about their lives for the edification of their contemporaries and the enlightenment of future generations.

MARILYN RICHARDSON

ACKNOWLEDGMENTS

I wish to thank Catherine L. Albanese, Sargent Bush, and Stephen J. Stein for their helpful criticism and suggestions for the introduction to this book; my student assistants, Calvin Roso and Michael Scherf, for their library spadework on many of the annotations for these autobiographies; and my wife, Charron, for her aid in the proofreading of large portions of this book.

WILLIAM L. ANDREWS

INTRODUCTION

The earliest forms of autobiography in Afro-American literature are the conversion and captivity narratives that began to appear in England and America during the second half of the eighteenth century. Antedating the fugitive slave narrative by almost fifty years, the spiritual autobiographies of James Gronniosaw (1770), John Marrant (1785), and George White (1810) gave the twin themes of the Afro-American "pregeneric myth"—knowledge and freedom—their earliest narrative form.[1] Like the fugitive slave narrator, the black spiritual autobiographer traced his or her freedom back to the acquisition of some sort of saving knowledge and to an awakening of awareness within. The recognition of one's true identity, unfettered by either the slavery of sin or the sin of slavery, set in motion a process by which early black Christians, and later, black slaves, attained spiritual as well as secular freedom.

On reaching their goals, both the spiritual and the slave autobiographer felt obliged to proclaim their respective gospels. Each sought to accrue authority and power via the word; for the spiritual autobiographer, appropriating God's word to his or her individual purposes constituted an especially bold form of self-authorization. Traditionally, the Negro had been considered a kind of "Canaanite, a man devoid of Logos," whose low social status was "a punishment resulting from sin or from a natural defect of soul."[2] Indeed, some apologists for slavery predicated their arguments on the idea that the Negro had not been endowed by his creator with a soul.[3] Before the fugitive slave narrator could hope for success in restoring political and economic freedom to American blacks, the black spiritual autobiographer had to lay the necessary intellectual groundwork by proving that black people were as much chosen by God for eternal salvation as whites. Without the black spiritual autobiography's reclamation of the Afro-American's spiritual birthright, the fugitive slave narrative could not have made such a cogent case for black civil rights in the crisis years between 1830 and 1865.

The priority of the spiritual autobiography to the slave narrative holds true whether we speak of the history of black women's or black men's writing in the United States. The first slave narrative written by a black American woman was Harriet Jacobs's *Incidents in the Life of a Slave Girl* (1861). Jacobs's story of female resistance to and triumph over slavery was unprecedented in many ways, but it was not the first black woman's autobiography to make female self-determination its fundamental theme. Twenty-five years earlier, *The Life and Religious Experience of Jarena Lee, A Coloured Lady* launched black women's autobiography in America with an argument for women's spiritual authority that plainly challenged traditional female roles as defined in both the free and the slave states, among whites as well as blacks. Having become convinced that she had been called by God to preach, Jarena Lee, the widowed mother of two, committed herself to her ministry and wrote of it as a supremely fulfilling experience, though it necessitated occasional separation from her children and put her at odds with men both in and out of the church. Lee's autobiography offers us the earliest and most detailed firsthand information we have about the traditional roles of women in organized black religious life in the United States and about the ways in which resistance to those roles began to manifest itself.

Lee's example was not an isolated one. In 1846 a second black woman evangelist, Zilpha Elaw, born in freedom as Lee had been, published her *Memoirs* in London while preparing for her return to the United States after a five-year preaching mission in England. Elaw's autobiography recounts in detail many kinds of trials that a black woman had to face in order to make herself heard in a world whose institutions were controlled by men. Dauntless and independent, she distinguished herself among the handful of single American women who ventured into the field of foreign missionary work during the antebellum era. Although she was not the first black American female missionary, Elaw seems to have been virtually unique among her female contemporaries in pursuing her calling without the sanction or support of a denomination or a supervisory board such as the American Board of Commissioners for Foreign Missions, founded in 1810 for the purpose of overseeing Protestant missionary work from the United States.[4] Equally unprecedented, from the standpoint of her physical as well as spiritual heroism, were her preaching missions into the slave states, which she undertook knowing that she risked kidnapping or arrest and sale into bondage for her actions. Jarena Lee welcomed Elaw into evangelism as her spiritual sister, happily sharing at least one pulpit with her. Eventually the two women's life stories would prove them literary compatriots as well. Their autobiographies ground the tradition of Afro-American women's autobiography in feminist ideals sanctioned by evangelical Christianity's radical spiritual individualism.

Before the onset of the Civil War, a third free-born black woman published an autobiography in the vein of Lee's and Elaw's. In 1850, Nancy G. Prince's *Narrative* of her spiritual trials and international travels, which led her from Massachusetts to Russia, to Jamaica, and finally back to New York, appeared in Boston.[5] Prince's observations of the czarist court, where her husband served as a man-in-waiting, together with her account of her later work as a teacher in Jamaica among the recently freed slaves, give her *Narrative* both an exotic flavor and historical importance. Her contribution to the black female spiritual autobiography tradition is not as significant as Lee's and Elaw's work, however, because Nancy Prince never felt divinely directed to defy social and religious mores as radically as Lee and Elaw did. Still, all three women's literary efforts, supported by the publication in 1850 of the biography of the most famous black female evangelist of the era, Sojourner Truth,[6] were precedent-setting. They all testified to God's providential care for an independent black woman in a racist as well as sexist society. Furthermore, two of these three autobiographies insisted on God's selection of a black woman to be his spokesperson to the unsaved and the spiritually recalcitrant of the white as well as the black race.

In the latter half of the nineteenth century, the narratives of former slaves and evangelical ministers continued to dominate Afro-American women's autobiography. The view of slavery and the black woman's situation in it that we find in the narratives of Elizabeth Keckley, Silvia Dubois, and Susie King Taylor is increasingly claiming the attention of literary historians and feminist critics.[7] The careers of black women preachers of this era, the most famous of whom was Amanda Berry Smith and the most unusual of whom was Rebecca Cox Jackson, are also being studied by scholars who seek a fresh understanding of the female role in nineteenth-century American religious and social movements.[8] The more we learn about these long-neglected post–Civil War black women, particularly through their own autobiographies, the more we rediscover their historical significance to the evolution of American feminism. Thus the reprinting in this volume of Julia Foote's *A Brand Plucked from the Fire* for the first time since 1886 offers readers of the memoirs of Jarena Lee and Zilpha Elaw clear evidence that spiritual autobiography by black women not only thrived after 1865 but actually became even more outspokenly feminist than is currently believed today.

Like Lee and Elaw before her, Foote's brand of feminist activism within Christianity evolved out of her conviction that salvation made possible the gift of spiritual "sanctification," i.e., a purifying of one's inner disposition to willful sin, a liberation of the soul to follow the indwelling voice of Christ. Foote grew up in western New York's notorious "Burned Over District," where waves of revivalism had left in their backwash numerous sects devoted to the attainment of Christian perfection. Believers in perfectionist doctrines of sanctification launched a "Holiness" movement within and without Methodism in New York and in Ohio during the 1830s and 1840s. Women like Phoebe Palmer, editor of the *Guide to Holiness,* worked in important though unofficial leadership capacities in this movement. Female converts to the cause later became some of the most outspoken social reformers of the age. Besides serving as one of the earliest female Holiness preachers in black American Methodism, Foote demonstrated her sisterhood with feminists touched by mid-nineteenth century perfectionism in her attacks on general evils like racial bigotry and male authoritarianism and on specific social institutions like capital punishment.[9]

The Lives of Lee, Elaw, and Foote

Jarena Lee was born on February 11, 1783, in Cape May, New Jersey, at the southern tip of the state.[10] Her parents were free but apparently hard pressed financially; they hired Jarena out as a servant girl at the age of seven. Little else is known of her childhood.

In 1804, when she was twenty-one, Jarena Lee was converted to Christianity after a lengthy period of distress concerning her soul's ultimate destiny. Three weeks after joining Philadelphia's Bethel African Methodist Episcopal Church, she rose spontaneously to her feet one Sunday morning and, as the minister announced his text, "made confession unto salvation." This was the first time that Lee felt she "had power to exhort sinners."

For four years after her conversion Lee experienced many doubts about her salvation and sometimes felt desperate enough to attempt suicide. Weathering these temptations, she found a way to overcome them permanently when she met a black man named William Scott, who informed her of the doctrine of "sanctification," as construed by the founder of Methodism, John Wesley. Lee became convinced that her conversion had been incomplete, for while she had been both "convicted for sin" and "justified from sin," she had not yet received "the entire sanctification of the soul to God." Resolving to attain this spiritual goal, Lee successfully petitioned God for it some three months after her meetings with Scott.

Around 1811, Jarena Lee first began to feel a call to preach. Disclosing this call to Rev. Richard Allen, the founder and minister in charge of the Bethel Church, she was gently rebuffed. For more than a dozen years, Allen had been engaged in a struggle for the autonomy of the Bethel Church from the control of white Methodism in Philadelphia. Determined that blacks should have the power to incorporate themselves into independent churches, he was, nevertheless, no schismatic in areas of Methodist doctrine. He had once before refused an Englishwoman the right to preach to his congregation on the grounds that such an act by a woman was contrary to the discipline of the Methodist church. Thus, he informed Lee, he did not object to women holding prayer meetings or exhorting congregations after licensed ministers had preached their sermons. But as for recognizing her in some official capacity as a preacher, Allen reiterated his claim that the rules of Methodism simply "did not call for women preachers."[11]

In 1811 Jarena Lee became the wife of Joseph Lee, pastor of a black church at Snow Hill, six miles from Philadelphia. Removal to Snow Hill left Lee discontented and often lonely; here she was beset with a severe "general debility" that robbed her of her energy and greatly hampered her efforts at informal evangelism in her home. Within six years further tragedies struck, as death took five members of her family, including her husband. Jarena Lee was left with two very young children to provide for.

Returning to Philadelphia in 1818, Lee approached Richard Allen, now bishop of the first black denomination in America, the African Methodist Episcopal church, with a request to be permitted to hold prayer meetings in her own house. This time Allen gave his blessing to her appeal. In 1819 she made a bold, public demonstration of her sense of evangelistic calling by interrupting a sermon in Bethel Church and exhorting extemporaneously from the text chosen by the minister in the pulpit. Instead of being chastised by Allen, she received his endorsement of her call. Soon thereafter she commenced her itinerant preaching career, first in the Philadelphia area and later in the Middle Atlantic and Northeastern states, from Baltimore, Maryland, to Rochester, New York, and as far west as Dayton, Ohio. Her audiences were both white and black. Lee's memoirs suggest that, after some initial resistance to her work by the male clergy, her evangelism gained a good deal of acceptance throughout Methodism. Her energy was remarkable. In 1835 she traveled over seven hundred miles and preached almost the same number of sermons. Her relationship to Richard Allen remained cordial; she seems to have found an accommodation with the all-male A.M.E. hierarchy, not as a licensed preacher, but rather as an official traveling exhorter. In 1839 Lee met Zilpha Elaw while both were proselytizing in western Pennsylvania. Lee recalls that they "enjoyed good seasons together" as a temporary preaching team. A year later, Jarena Lee joined the American Antislavery Society, convinced that through abolitionism, "the gospel will have free course to every nation."

Jarena Lee became an autobiographer out of a conviction that the record of God's work in and through her would help lead others to Christ. In 1833 she enlisted the aid of an unnamed editor to reshape a portion of her religious journal into narrative form suitable for publication. Three years later she spent thirty-eight dollars to have a thousand copies of her *Life* printed; she distributed her book at camp meetings, quarterly meetings of the Methodist church, and even on the streets. While in Cincinnati in 1839, she oversaw the reprinting of a second thousand copies of the *Life.* In 1844 Lee tried to secure the support of the A.M.E. church's Book Committee for the publication of a new expanded edition of her autobiography, but the committee refused, stating that it found her manuscript "written in such a manner that it is impossible to decipher much of the meaning contained in it." Despite the fact that the church had already forbidden traveling preachers to publish books or pamphlets without formal approval, Lee financed the printing of her *Religious Experience and Journal* in 1849, carrying the story of her life up to her fiftieth birthday.

In 1850, at the annual meeting of the Philadelphia Conference of the A.M.E. church, a group of women who believed themselves divinely commissioned to preach regardless of whether the church hierarchy chose to license them formed an impromptu organization. Their purpose, in the view of the church's historian, was to make appointments from their ranks to preaching stations in the Philadelphia Conference. Very likely, Jarena Lee was among this group of female ecclesiastical insurgents. Their association did not hold together, however, and in the next General Conference of the church in 1852, a resolution licensing women to preach was defeated by a large majority of the delegates, all of whom were male. Jarena Lee's role in these debates, and in the rising agitation among black women in the A.M.E. church for equality of access to the pulpit, has not been recorded in the standard histories of black Methodism. Indeed, after the publication of her second autobiography in 1849, Jarena Lee's activities are unknown.[12]

Zilpha Elaw was born around 1790 to free parents who brought her up in the vicinity of Philadelphia, Pennsylvania. Elaw's mother died in childbirth when Zilpha was only twelve. Her father then put her to service in a Quaker family, with whom she resided until she reached the age of eighteen. Having been brought up in a pious manner by her parents, Elaw was readily drawn to the Methodists who were actively proselytizing in her region when she was in her midteens. Around the same time, she began to have religious visions in which Jesus Christ appeared to her on several occasions. She was converted soon thereafter and joined a Methodist society in an outlying region of Philadelphia in 1808.

The marriage of Zilpha and Joseph Elaw took place in 1810. Their relationship was strained by differences arising from her zeal for Christ and his nominal attachment to Christianity. A fuller by trade, Joseph Elaw moved to Burlington, New Jersey, in 1811 in response to job openings in the cloth manufacturing industry of that city. His wife accompanied him and bore him a daughter the following year.

In 1817 Zilpha Elaw attended her first camp meeting. Launched first in 1800 by frontier Presbyterians in Kentucky, week-long revival gatherings in rural areas, attended by hundreds who camped, ate, prayed, sang, and worshiped together, became a mainstay of Methodist evangelism in the East as well as the West during the antebellum era. Elaw's description of the physical arrangement, the program of activities, and the group dynamics of camp meetings suggests the importance of this kind of religious gathering to women who had never taken or felt justified in taking a leadership role in the more traditional religious institutions of the time. During the 1817 camp meeting, Elaw fell into a "trance of ecstasy," during which she became convinced that her soul had been sanctified by God. Emerging from the trance, she did her first speaking in public, offering prayers for others at the meeting. Two years later at a second camp meeting, in the midst of a noisy, fervent scene, Elaw was inspired to exhort a congregation "in the presence of a more numerous assemblage of ministers than [she] had ever seen together before." The urging of a number of Christian women who knew her well helped confirm Elaw's intuition that she had been divinely commissioned to preach.

Elaw's *Memoirs* state that the ministers of the Methodist Society of Burlington, New Jersey, endorsed the black woman's preaching aspirations. A large number of white people in the area came to her pulpit debut. Her fellow black Methodists were initially cool to her ambitions, and her husband pleaded with her to give up the idea of a public ministry since he feared that it would make of his wife an object of ridicule. But Elaw maintained that her evangelistic career was God's will, not "self-directed," and therefore could not be circumvented.

In 1823, Joseph Elaw died of consumption. His widow was compelled to employ herself as a domestic and to put her daughter to service as well. Later she opened a school for black children in the city of Burlington, where only whites were admitted into the public schools. Because of growing apprehension about having failed to live up to her divine commission, Elaw closed the school after two years. She then placed her child under the care of a relative and went to Philadelphia to begin her preaching career.

Zilpha Elaw's early itinerancy was self-supported; she preached under no license or denominational sanction. She chose her field of action herself in consultation with her inner spiritual promptings. In the spring of 1828, she felt obliged to carry her message into the slaveholding states, regardless of the very real danger of being arrested or kidnapped and sold as a slave. She visited among and preached to whites and blacks alike in Baltimore; Washington, D.C.; Alexandria, Virginia; and Annapolis, Maryland. She reports being befriended by a number of influential persons, including Commodore John Rodgers, a former United States Secretary of the Navy. After more than a year and a half of proselytizing in the slave states, Elaw returned to her home in Burlington and resumed her travels in the Middle Atlantic and Northeastern states. Her *Memoirs* record considerable success for the black female evangelist during the next five years.

In the summer of 1840, Zilpha Elaw booked passage to London, having been convinced for more than a decade that God had prepared some great work for her to do there. The last section of her *Memoirs* details her travels throughout central England, where she preached, by her own estimate, more than a thousand sermons and met with recurrent opposition from those who felt women's preaching to be either unscriptural or unseemly. The final portion of her *Memoirs* suggests that in 1845 she had made plans to come home, but whether she did return and what she did upon arrival in the United States are unknown.[13]

Julia A. J. Foote was born in 1823 in Schenectady, New York, the daughter of former slaves who purchased their freedom and espoused a strong belief in Christianity. From her parents Julia learned important lessons about "the fruits of slavery" in Methodism, which helped prepare her to preach a social gospel. Barred from sending their daughter to Schenectady's segregated schools, Julia Foote's parents were obliged to put her to service in a white household whose influence could create an opportunity for her to attend a country school outside the city. For two years, between the ages of ten and twelve, the black servant girl studied diligently, applying herself especially to the reading of the Bible. When she was twelve, Julia returned to her parents' home, where she cared for her four younger siblings while her mother worked. Not long thereafter, the family moved to Albany, New York, where Julia was converted at the age of fifteen and joined an African Methodist church. Julia Foote's religious devotion inspired in her a great desire for education, but racial prejudice and economic necessity restricted her opportunities and forced her to become an autodidact. Doubts about her salvation made what she called the "sweet peace" of sanctification a very precious gift, which, despite the skepticism of her parents and pastor, she was convinced that she received about a year and a half after her conversion.

At the age of eighteen Julia married George Foote, a sailor, and went with him to Boston, where she joined the African Methodist Episcopal Zion church and began to proclaim the wonders of sanctification to others in the church. Her husband objected to her activities and threatened to send her back to her parents if she did not desist. When she refused to obey him, he became increasingly alienated from her. She plunged more fervently into her household ministry and soon became convinced that God had called her to a preaching career.

Jehiel C. Beman, minister of the A.M.E. Zion church in Boston, staunchly opposed the movement in certain quarters of his congregation to allow Julia Foote access to his pulpit. When she responded by holding evangelistic meetings in her home, Beman accused her of being a schismatic and saw to it that she was read out of the church. Foote took her case to higher authorities in the A.M.E. Zion church, but her petition was either ignored or rejected.

Soon thereafter, Julia Foote met with several like-minded women in Philadelphia and, after hiring a hall, held a series of religious meetings over which she presided. In Binghamton, New York, where her parents had moved, Foote preached the doctrine of sanctification in similarly unofficial gatherings of believers. Early in 1845 she began to travel in upstate New York, preaching from various Methodist pulpits, often in company with or invited by ministers of the African Methodist Episcopal church.

After carrying her message as far west as Cincinnati, Foote returned to Binghamton to help nurse her father, who died in May 1849. She then resumed her itinerant evangelism in the New England and Middle Atlantic states. In 1850 she crossed the Allegheny Mountains for the second time, preaching in a number of Ohio towns and in Detroit and Canada before settling down, in the fall of 1851, in Cleveland. Beset with a "throat difficulty," Foote was forced to curtail her evangelism severely. The deaths of her mother and her husband in the mid-1850s added personal bereavement to her disappointment. How she supported herself in Cleveland during the 1850s and 1860s is not known. She apparently recovered the use of her throat around 1869 and returned to preaching in the state of Ohio as part of a more general Holiness revival that swept the Midwest in the early 1870s.

Julia Foote's activities during the next twenty-five years are unknown. At some point during that time, she became a missionary for the A.M.E. Zion church. On May 20, 1894, she became the first woman in the A.M.E. Zion church to be ordained a deacon. Before her death on November 22, 1900, she was ordained an elder in the church, only the second woman to hold that high office in her denomination.[14]

Lee, Elaw, and Foote and the Afro-American Spiritual Autobiography Tradition

All spiritual autobiography in the Christian tradition addresses the central question of the fate of the individual soul. Whether written by blacks or whites, American spiritual autobiography chronicles the soul's journey not only from damnation to salvation but also to a realization of one's true place and destiny in the divine scheme of things. The autobiographies of Lee, Elaw, and Foote are structured in accordance with these two stages of the Christian's psychospiritual development. First these women had to become assured that they were the beneficiaries of Christ's atonement and were therefore heirs to his heavenly kingdom. Then they had to confront the problem of what their role should be as Christian women in the earthly realm.

The pattern that all three women impose on their lives from their youth through their conversion and its aftermath is very traditional among spiritual autobiographers, particularly among evangelical writers. None of these women is especially interested in describing her youth or her family in detail; Julia Foote is the only one who alludes pointedly to ethnic factors influencing her growing up. For each of these women her life before conversion was of no real significance except insofar as it could be used as a kind of negative moral object lesson for her reader. Thus each woman extracts from her childhood instances of thoughtlessness, frivolity, or willfulness, which are highlighted to signify an early state of spiritual lostness and hopelessness. Instruction in Christianity was not absent from their homes, and each recalls profound religious impressions in childhood. The conflict between their "worldliness" and their moral training made childhood for Lee, Elaw, and Foote a time of inner distress, guilt, and anxiety about their spiritual welfare. This depiction of childhood was not at all unusual among American spiritual autobiographers.

In many narratives of conversion, a sense of guilt and occasionally paralyzing anxiety troubles the prospective Christian until his or her midteens or early twenties. Such was the case with Lee, Elaw, and Foote; all were converted in adolescence in rather spectacular fashion. Lee and Elaw record marvelous visions that accompanied the experience of conversion itself. Foote recalls a collapse into unconsciousness followed by the hearing of voices that culminated in the song of her redemption. Ample evidence in the Afro-American spiritual autobiography tradition testifies to the fact that these kinds of visionary experiences, arising from intervals when God strikes the convicted sinner "dead" to all but heavenly revelations, were by no means exceptional or exaggerated.[15] For women, the singularity of these experiences, replete with their imagery of special selection and elevated status, had especially far-reaching consequences, for through these visionary moments they saw themselves transformed, inspirited, and, for the first time, chosen for a providential purpose.

The immediate outcome of the conversions of Lee, Elaw, and Foote was their joining a church that satisfied their felt need for spiritual ministration and community. Thereafter a period of trials and challenges to their faith ensued, as it often does in spiritual autobiography. Jarena Lee discusses her many doubts as to whether she had been saved and her consequent backsliding and despair. Zilpha Elaw was untroubled by such inner conflict, but her marriage complicated her spiritual life and introduced her to temptations that were difficult to resolve. Julia Foote was frustrated in her desire to become better educated and was harassed by feelings of continuing powerlessness in her quest to subdue what she perceived as her sinful side. All three women, therefore, had discovered that conversion alone would not magically solve the problems inherent in their lives. They still had to come to terms with the world outside and the self within if their spiritual recovery was to proceed.

Every Christian, of course, had to live in the world, but there were strict biblical prohibitions against being "of the world." "The world" was the spiritual wilderness through which the pilgrim soul had to travel and be tested before attaining ultimate blessedness. The fewer entanglements in the world, the less likely a Christian was to veer from his or her moral and spiritual course. The question was, how radically to break with the world? More specifically, how much could one deny the world's traditional expectations of a Christian woman? Early black women's autobiographies show us a variety of ways that this question was met. For instance, Nancy G. Prince resolved after her conversion to put her trust in God for the future, but her faith did not rule out marriage in her early twenties, devotion of her life to her husband, and, after his death, dedication of her energies to the uplift of Jamaican freedmen. On the other hand, the most extreme separation from the world can be found in Rebecca Jackson's story, in which one discovers the converted black woman choosing a life of celibacy while still married, and later withdrawing into a Shaker community so as to practice "holy living" in the manner she considered appropriate. Neither as conformable as Prince nor as critical as Jackson was vis-à-vis the world's expectations, Lee, Elaw, and Foote lived experimental lives, exploring the possibilities of a deliberately chosen marginal identity that morally and spiritually engaged the world without being socially engulfed by it.

What the conversion experience spurred in all three women, it appears, was a very real sense of freedom from a prior "self" and a growing awareness of unrealized, unexploited powers within. The usual aim of Christian conversion is a realignment of a person's relationship not just with the world but also with the self. Just as the fallen world is the macrocosmic domain of Satan, the individual self, tainted by original sin, is his microcosmic sphere of control. Thus the selfhood of the unsaved person is corrupt and fundamentally resistant to the authority of God until converted from its waywardness and brought into a proper relationship to its creator. After conversion, the self is transformed into a "new creation," free from bondage to sin and fit for service as an instrument of the divine will. Instead of belonging to Satan, the self now belongs to Christ. Freedom from evil comes only through acknowledging Christ as the absolute master of one's life. Temporal fulfillment and heavenly reward depend on the extent to which one subjects oneself to God's will and ignores both the will of the world and the will of the self, regardless of the personal consequences.[16] Theoretically therefore, the more completely a Christian identifies with a divine Self that supersedes both the corrupt will of the fallen world and the deluding will of the fallen individual self, the more authority that believer may accrue to himself or herself, irrespective of custom or tradition. The experience of conversion alone did not endow Lee, Elaw, or Foote with this kind of self-sufficiency. It would evolve, however, as each woman's spiritual quest moved into its second phase, when a growing sense of calling demanded an equally powerful source of authorization.

Christian tradition granted women spiritual gifts such as the power of prophecy and charismatic preaching. The problem for women in nineteenth-century America was, in what sphere would they have the freedom to exercise their gifts? The American "cult of true womanhood" had established woman's proper sphere as her home; any "outside" activity that conflicted with her domestic duties to her children and her husband was suspect. Political agitation and moneymaking pursuits were, of course, "out." On the other hand, because woman was assumed to be "naturally religious," her participation in church work was usually seen as beneficial both to herself and society. The rise of distaff organizations run by and for women, such as women's auxiliaries in Protestant churches, missionary societies, and various agencies for moral reform, was greeted with enthusiasm in most quarters of antebellum America. In these kinds of organizations women could put their faith into practice without overstepping the bounds of proper feminine decorum or overreaching the traditional limits that mainstream Protestantism had placed around female leadership in the church.[17]

The autobiographies of Lee, Elaw, and Foote show that after conversion each tried to fulfill herself in the various subordinate roles that had been assigned to women in the churches they had joined. As married women they initially confined themselves to a "household ministry," i.e., visiting and informal preaching in the home, which would have been considered fitting for women of their status. When Richard Allen told Jarena Lee that women "had done much good by way of exhortation" in the A.M.E. church, she knew that the role he was recommending to her, that of exhorter, had been made available to women partly because it was not empowered with the authority of the licensed ministry.[18] Exhorters occupied the lowest position in the church's preaching hierarchy and had to have permission before addressing individual congregations. They could lead Sunday school classes and prayer meetings, but in formal church services they usually spoke at the sufferance of the presiding minister and only in response to the biblical text that he had selected for the day. As exhorters women remained dependent on the male leadership of the church for access to the ears of a congregation and to the Bible itself, insofar as it could be used to authorize public speaking in church. Lee, Elaw, and Foote could have exercised their speaking gifts and witnessed to their faith as exhorters without incurring the resistance of the male preaching establishment. These women, however, chose to step outside their appointed sphere and seek a new way of defining themselves vis-à-vis the people of God and the people of the world.

The question is, from what source did they derive the sense of authority that emboldened them to challenge the tradition of male leadership in churches, or, in the case of Elaw especially, to become independent evangelists apart from the sanction of any established church? What caused each of these women to reject the pastoral authority of many male ministers in favor of the primacy of their individual perceptions of God's will? Lee, Elaw, and Foote undoubtedly knew that to their critics, their spiritual self-reliance smacked of prideful individualism at worst, womanly waywardness at best. Nevertheless, they portrayed themselves as serenely confident, as a result of their "sanctification" by the Holy Spirit, that they had ample sanction for acts that many, especially men, would judge as rebelliously self-assertive and destructive of good order in the church.

We cannot understand the special sense of empowerment that Lee, Elaw, and Foote discovered in Christianity unless we examine the idea of "sanctification." For each woman, the conversion experience was but a prelude to what Methodists, beginning with John Wesley, had termed the "second blessing." According to Wesley, the Christian life had two focal points: "justification, or the forgiveness of sins, and the ethical regeneration of sanctification." The stages of salvation that Lee, Elaw, and Foote recount as they narrate their conversion stories are: first, repentance as result of the conviction of one's sinfulness; second, justification from the guilt of sin by Christ's atonement and forgiveness; and third, sanctification, or a "new birth," free from the power of sin by virtue of the indwelling of the Holy Spirit. The fully sanctified Christian achieves spiritual perfection, what Foote calls "holiness," evidenced by inward and outward righteousness. This kind of perfection does not prevent the sanctified Christian from making mistakes, nor does sanctification obviate the Christian's obligation always to seek greater growth in grace and in the knowledge and love of God. What the experience of sanctification confers on the believer is the sense of being in total harmony with the will of God, of being perfectly pure in intention and action insofar as his or her acts are determined by individual intention. The sanctified Christian enjoys the inner peace that comes of being convinced that, having been liberated from sin, one is now completely identified with God in thought, word, and deed.[19]

Wesley stresses that in addition to the blessing of inner peace, sanctification brings an increased sense of power to a Christian. "Believe in the Lord Jesus," Wesley bid his followers, "and thou shalt have peace and power together": power "to trample sin under thy feet"; power "to serve [God] with all thy strength"; power "to seek for glory, and honour, and immortality"; power, in sum, to "be called great in the kingdom of heaven." Wesley also promised the sanctified: "thou shalt both do and teach all the commandments of God, from the least even to the greatest: thou shalt teach them by thy life as well as thy word."[20]

The experience of sanctification liberated Lee, Elaw, and Foote from the sense of personal inadequacy that their perception of their own sinfulness had placed upon them. Belief in the Wesleyan version of sanctification freed them to trust the promptings of their innermost selves because of their conviction that what came from within was of the Holy Spirit, not the corrupt ego. Thus, these three women exhibited in their lives and their writing a remarkable sense of self-worth, self-confidence, and power, despite the traditional spiritual autobiography's treatment of the self as a deceiving antagonist. Through sanctification, Lee, Elaw, and Foote believed that they had recovered their true, pristine identity in Christ. It was their religious duty, therefore, to be faithful to that renewed and purified self. If this meant challenging, even disobeying, ecclesiastical or social authorities, then these women were prepared to do so. It is important to recognize, however, that unlike the famous seventeenth-century Puritan Anne Hutchinson, Lee, Elaw, and Foote were not antinomians. They did not believe that their sanctification made them unaccountable to any law but their own intuitive sense of God's will. They felt obliged to cite from the Bible some precedent or verse that would authorize their convention-shattering views or behavior, and, except for Elaw's preaching missions into the slave states, they did not deliberately defy the laws of man. On the other hand, their consciences did not require biblical sanction in order to denounce contemporary injustices, such as slavery, racism, and sex discrimination, wherever these evils seemed to be hindering God's work. Theirs was a gospel of human liberation addressed particularly to the spiritually enslaved. Still, they knew from personal experience how social bonds contributed to spiritual enslavement, and, as if endorsing Julia Foote's statement, their autobiographies record the ways in which they "realized more and more what a terrible thing it was for one human being to have absolute control over another."

The Social Import of the Autobiographies of Lee, Elaw, and Foote

As spiritual autobiographers, Lee, Elaw, and Foote did not feel obliged to discuss the purely secular details of their lives, believing that this aspect was not what made their stories worthy of public perusal. Nevertheless, their autobiographies speak, indirectly as well as directly, to the question of the social significance of the careers of black women activists on the religious front in nineteenth-century America.

From the standpoint of social as well as psychological analysis, the central theme of these three books is the growth of authentic, individually authorized selfhood. For each of these women, religious conversion triggered a profound psychological reorientation as well. As they came to identify ever increasingly with an indwelling spirit of holiness—what Elaw called "the extraordinary directions of the Holy Spirit"—they ceased to regard themselves as "weak and feeble" females who had "neither might, wisdom nor ability to overcome" their spiritual or social enemies.[21] They began to feel empowered, indeed authorized by God, to listen to and act upon their intuitions, their long-suppressed ambitions, their idealized self-images.

Lee, Elaw, and Foote had been brought up to identify with the four major roles accorded to women in the nuclear, social, and ecclesiastical "families" of nineteenth-century America. As daughter, wife, mother, and ultimately spiritual sister in the Christian faith, these women played a succession of subordinate feminine parts in a series of interrelated familial (i.e., patriarchal) institutions, never finding the kind of fulfillment and community they needed.[22] Their stories show that, as a result, they felt compelled first to declare their independence from the constricting patriarchal "families" that disregarded or impugned their growing sense of individual authority. Their autobiographies also testify to each woman's incipient desire to authorize, through her own example, an alternative role for women within communities of the spirit founded on an egalitarian ideal.

The collective example of Lee, Elaw, and Foote suggests strongly that disobedience of external authorities in the name of an internal ideal helped mold in these women the radical spiritual individualism that their autobiographies celebrate. Although trained to be servant girls, they seem to have been temperamentally ill suited to accept orders without question. Before her conversion, Zilpha Elaw's white mistress charged her frequently with "pertness and insolent behavior." After Julia Foote's white mistress whipped her for stealing some pound cakes—a charge the black girl denied—Julia rebelled by chopping up the rawhide so that no one could repeat this indignity upon her. Neither Elaw nor Foote gloried in this behavior, since it did not stem from a Christian motive. But when Foote became convinced that her spiritual welfare depended on her disobeying even so respectable an authority as her mother, she not only did so readily; she recorded the result of this disobedience in the most positive terms in her autobiography. Foote clearly longed for her parents' understanding and approval of her spiritual course, but she would not allow the tradition of daughterly submission to deter her from her individual sense of mission. Lee and Elaw tell us a good deal less about their youth than does Foote, but, judging from the pattern of their later years, it seems unlikely that their resolution of conflicts between the claims of the Spirit and the claims of parents differed markedly from Foote's.

As wives each of these women tried to conform to the marital mores of nineteenth-century American society, which demanded their obedience to their husbands' authority. Jarena Lee moved with her minister husband to an unfamiliar community, away from family and friends. Elaw and Foote also followed their husbands to distant cities, where their marriages soon became embroiled in an escalating battle of wills over the propriety of these women's religious activism. Lee appears to have suffered something like a nervous breakdown as a result of trying to sublimate her own zeal to preach through marriage to a preacher. Only when she became convinced that her ministry had not been permanently frustrated, only postponed, was she able to submit to the restrictions that her marriage placed on her sense of calling. Elaw and Foote had to contend for their careers more openly and assertively.

Neither Joseph Elaw nor George Foote took his wife's spiritual ideals seriously. Nominal Christians, they both feared personal, and very public, humiliation as a consequence of their wives' zealous affirmation of their faith. Each man tried to bring his wife into compliance with what a majority of people at the time would have termed female decorum. Neither man had reason to expect that the woman he had married would defy him. After all, on earlier occasions, Julia Foote had objected to women preaching, and Zilpha Elaw held throughout her adult life to her conservative ideas about the propriety of a wife's submission to the government of her husband—ideas she reiterated in her *Memoirs.* What neither man realized, however, was that the more convinced each woman became of her divine appointment, the more independent she felt of his censure and the more serenely confident she became in judging her behavior by a higher authority than his. As her alienation from her husband grew, Julia Foote found comfort in a verse from the Book of Isaiah, which read, "For thy maker is thine husband." This implied that, regardless of the dissension in her earthly marriage, she did not have to condemn herself as a failed wife since, from a spiritual standpoint, all her actions had been in obedience to the will of Christ, her heavenly husband.

It is conceivable that in some religious quarters, Christian women like Elaw and Foote, whose husbands tried to hamper their exercise of their faith, could very well have received sympathy and support for their breaking of marital convention. Sects like the Quakers, Seventh-Day Adventists, and the various Holiness "denominations" that emerged in the mid-nineteenth century admitted women to leadership positions and did not consider a married woman who had been called to such leadership her husband's spiritual subordinate.[23] However, when a woman's sense of calling put her at odds with not just the institution of marriage, but also that of motherhood, even the more liberal sectarians balked.[24] Nevertheless, the autobiographies of Jarena Lee and Zilpha Elaw record times in each woman's life when she happily exchanged the role of mother for that of traveling preacher, though doing so meant absenting herself from her fatherless child for long periods of time. When Elaw first placed her daughter under another's care so that she could go on a seven-month preaching mission, she did so under financial as well as spiritual exigency. She was in debt, and her evangelistic tour helped restore solvency to her little family. But when, immediately thereafter, she set out on her extended, uninvited, and very risky mission to the slave states, she could not argue that she was making her journey in the best interests of her family. What she did, she did in response to promptings that overruled the prudence and self-restraint that social convention would expect a mother to abide by for the sake of her child.

When Jarena Lee received her first call to preach to a distant congregation, she readily placed her sickly son in the hands of a friend and departed. During the week she was gone she notes that "not a thought of my little son came into my mind; it was hid from me, lest I should have been diverted from the work I had to do, to look after my son." Such a remark might have been read invidiously by those who believed a mother's primary obligation was to look after her children, especially one who was "sickly." To Lee, however, her "work" took precedence over such demands. She clearly did not identify herself as a mother first and foremost, but rather as a worker whose first duty was to her call, her preaching career. For this reason, she would eventually "break up housekeeping, . . . forsaking all to preach the everlasting Gospel."

From the roles of daughter, wife, and mother in their worldly families, Lee, Elaw, and Foote progressed after their conversions to the status of spiritual sister in the family of Christ. In this supposed democracy of saved souls, all men were their brothers, on an equal spiritual standing with them before the Lord. Yet the all-male pastorate of their churches often insisted on an exclusive authority of leadership, which each woman found impossible to accept without compromising her own sense of mission. To resist this authority, each woman first had to give up her almost automatic assumption, to use Foote's words, that her minister was "too good and too wise not to know what was right" for her. A woman like Lee, whose exhorting might overshadow a minister's, or like Foote, whose preaching seemed to rival that of her minister, had to be prepared to incur the censure of churchmen and women alike for being "too forward." Nevertheless, each of these women braved the charge of being indecorous, "unsexed" females in the pulpit, refusing to be deterred by "men whose whims are law" in the church. This was Zilpha Elaw's scornful characterization of her male adversaries in England and America; she dismissed their "ignorant and prejudiced objections" to her calling with comic characterizations of their "august dignity" and "lordly authority and self-importance." Julia Foote's riposte against patriarchalism in the clergy was even more satirically barbed and politically pointed. After narrating her battle with Jehiel Beman and the failure of the A.M.E. Zion church hierarchy to hear her petition against excommunication, she commented: "there was no justice meted out to women in those days. Even ministers of Christ did not feel that women had any rights which they were bound to respect." The latter statement parodies the infamous language of the Supreme Court's Dred Scott decision of 1857, in which Chief Justice Roger B. Taney concluded that black Americans "had no rights which the white man was bound to respect."[25] In this brilliant verbal stroke, Foote drew a parallel between political racism and ecclesiastical sexism, both sanctioned by an authority of power, not of justice. What more effective way could a black woman protest against sexual prejudice in the black church than by linking it to the kind of prejudice that all blacks, male and female, wanted to be free from and to see abolished in American life?

The struggles of Lee, Elaw, and Foote against the subordination of women in nineteenth-century American social and ecclesiastical "families" inspired in all three some serious reflection on liberating communal alternatives. None of these women thought of herself as a social visionary or reformer of social institutions; none put forward any utopian schemes for new communities, Christian or otherwise. Nevertheless, through their autobiographies, all three women implicitly identify themselves with an inchoate community of the Spirit that transcends normal social distinctions in the name of a radical egalitarianism. Their life stories bear witness to a framework of values and a view of experience that not only help to describe the guiding "spirit" of that community but also help to bring it into being by exemplifying its ethos in both the subject matter and the style of their writing.

We find this spirit manifested socially in the communities of women that formed around each of these three women, first inspiring them with a sense of their potential and worth, and later sustaining them in their tribulations brought on usually by condescending or overbearing men. Most of the time, Lee, Elaw, and Foote found in men a "worldly wisdom, self-sufficient reason, and opinionated faith" that militated against the kind of spontaneous, egalitarian community of the Spirit that these female evangelists wished to generate.[26] Rationalistic skepticism was consistently attacked by revivalists in the mid-nineteenth century as an enemy of what Edward Beecher called "Holy Emotion," the true source of individual and societal salvation.[27] Lee, Elaw, and Foote all make it clear that men maintained and actually took pride in such skepticism when faced with extraordinary female religious experiences, while women were usually much more open-minded and open-hearted in their response to the intuitive and emotive character of the Spirit.

Given this state of affairs, Julia Foote's advice to women in her "Word to My Christian Sisters" was probably representative of the convictions of many early female evangelists: "you will not let what man may say or do, keep you from doing the will of the Lord or using the gifts you have for the good of others. How much easier to bear the reproach of men than to live at a distance from God." Undoubtedly, "man" in this case could apply to all mankind, male and female, but in these three black women's experience it was the male half of mankind that dealt most in "reproach" of women like themselves, and it was "the lofty looks of man," especially as he occupied the pulpit of the church, that poisoned the community of the Spirit with "pride and arrogancy," those two "master sins" of mankind, according to Elaw.

These sins against community manifested themselves not only in hierarchies of authority that ignored female inspiration; they also became institutionalized in religious practice that seemed more concerned with "conformity to the politer standards of morals and tasteful delicacy" than with genuine spiritual inspiration for men and women. Thus from the outset of their ministries, Lee, Elaw, and Foote challenged everything in the church that tended to order and regulate people according to what was customary, socially respectable, polite, and proper. Elaw denounced any religious community whose members behaved like so many "automata." She had no use for "high-toned sensibility"; it was just another mask of worldly pride and vanity. What she valued was an unselfconscious genuineness of response to the Spirit, regardless of the suspension of the proprieties and the "excess of emotions" that generally accompanied the revival of the Spirit. Elaw knew that she was less likely to find such genuineness of response emanating from "the whited exterior" of mainstream society, which is why she readily criticized the overly refined "morals of the more cultivated Saxon stock," preferring the "simplicity and want of polish" of black Christians. Similarly, Julia Foote found the "spirituality, and even holiness" of white America "deluded by a spirit of error, which leads them to say to the poor and the colored ones among them, 'Stand back a little—I am holier than thou.'"

In 1831 the first black feminist-abolitionist in America, Maria W. Stewart, told her people: "Never, no never will the chains of slavery and ignorance burst, till we become united as one, and cultivate among ourselves the pure principles of piety, morality and virtue."[28] In this spirit of liberation, from external as well as internal chains, Lee, Elaw, and Foote conducted their preaching careers. These women saw themselves as revivalists in the broadest sense of the word, beginning with the most essential principles, the primary locus of human being, that of the soul. Was this not what another important black feminist-abolitionist, Frances Ellen Watkins Harper, had called for in her essay "Our Greatest Want"? "We want more soul," she wrote in 1859, "a higher cultivation of all our spiritual faculties. We need more unselfishness, earnestness and integrity. Our greatest need is not gold or silver, talent or genius, but true men and true women."[29] The autobiographies of Jarena Lee, Zilpha Elaw, and Julia Foote introduce us to three "true women" of nineteenth-century America, whose indomitable sense of authenticity and strength of purpose helped launch a gradual and as yet incomplete reformation of American social, as well as religious, ideals. Just as importantly, the narratives of Lee, Elaw, and Foote help us recognize these little-known figures as foremothers of the black feminist literary tradition in the United States.

TEXTUAL NOTE

The texts used in this edition are the 1836 edition of *The Life and Religious Experience of Jarena Lee,* the 1846 edition of Zilpha Elaw's *Memoirs,* and the 1879 edition of Julia Foote's *A Brand Plucked from the Fire.* Lee published a second, expanded edition of her autobiography in 1849 under the title *Religious Experience and Journal of Mrs. Jarena Lee.* After reprinting the 1836 narrative in its entirety, Lee added materials from a journal of her ministerial activities, which extended her life story some two decades beyond the conclusion of her 1836 narrative. This journal, however, reads very much like a log of distances traveled, scriptural texts expounded, places visited, and numbers of people converted. Contemporary readers unused to the formulaic character of nineteenth-century ministerial journals and autobiographies are likely to find the added pages of the 1849 edition often tedious reading and rarely if ever revelatory of the inner character of the woman who wrote them. Because the added length of the 1849 edition does not offer us an appreciably expanded self-portrait of Jarena Lee, this volume reprints the first edition of Lee's autobiography. Further comments on her *Religious Experience and Journal* can be found in the introduction to this book.

The *Memoirs of the Life, Religious Experience, Ministerial Travels and Labours of Mrs. Zilpha Elaw* was published at its author's expense in London in 1846, at the conclusion of Elaw's five-year preaching mission in Great Britain. This autobiography has never been reprinted until now.

Julia A. J. Foote financed the publication of two editions of *A Brand Plucked from the Fire,* the first in 1879 and a reprint in 1886, both printed in Cleveland. The edition used in this book is that of 1879, reprinted here for the first time.

In each of these three texts the original spelling, punctuation, paragraphing, and chapter and section divisions have been preserved, except in cases in which there is an inconsistency of spelling within a text, the evident result of a printer's error. Idiosyncrasies of spelling or punctuation regularly employed by each author in her text have been maintained. All footnotes in the texts are provided by the editor. Other bracketed interpolations, e.g., those identifying passages in the

Bible, are also the editor's. The purpose of these interpolations is to locate for the reader quoted passages in each text whose sources are not identified by the author of the text. In other instances of appropriation of biblical words and phrases without quotation, the interpolated references are designed to indicate something of the stylistic debt that these autobiographies owe to the King James version of the Bible.

THE LIFE AND RELIGIOUS EXPERIENCE OF JARENA LEE,

A Coloured Lady,

GIVING AN ACCOUNT OF HER CALL TO PREACH THE GOSPEL.

REVISED AND CORRECTED FROM THE ORIGINAL MANUSCRIPT, WRITTEN BY HERSELF.

Philadelphia:
Printed and Published for the Author,
1836.

And it shall come to pass . . . that I will pour out my Spirit upon all flesh; and your sons, and your *daughters* shall prophecy.

Joel ii. 28

I was born February 11th, 1783, at Cape May, state of New Jersey. At the age of seven years I was parted from my parents, and went to live as a servant maid, with a Mr. Sharp, at the distance of about sixty miles from the place of my birth.

My parents being wholly ignorant of the knowledge of God, had not therefore instructed me in any degree in this great matter. Not long after the commencement of my attendance on this lady, she had bid me do something respecting my work, which in a little while after, she asked me if I had done, when I replied, Yes—but this was not true.

At this awful point, in my early history, the spirit of God moved in power through my conscience, and told me I was a wretched sinner. On this account so great was the impression, and so strong were the feelings of guilt, that I promised in my heart that I would not tell another lie.

But notwithstanding this promise my heart grew harder, after a while, yet the spirit of the Lord never entirely forsook me, but continued mercifully striving with me, until his gracious power converted my soul.

The manner of this great accomplishment was as follows: In the year 1804, it so happened that I went with others to hear a missionary of the Presbyterian order preach. It was an afternoon meeting, but few were there, the place was a school room; but the preacher was solemn, and in his countenance the earnestness of his master's business appeared equally strong, as though he were about to speak to a multitude.

At the reading of the Psalms, a ray of renewed conviction darted into my soul. These were the words, composing the first verse of the Psalms for the service:

> Lord, I am vile, conceived in sin,
> Born unholy and unclean.
> Sprung from man, whose guilty fall
> Corrupts the race, and taints us all.

This description of my condition struck me to the heart, and made me to feel in some measure, the weight of my sins, and sinful nature.

But not knowing how to run immediately to the Lord for help, I was driven of Satan, in the course of a few days, and tempted to destroy myself.

There was a brook about a quarter of a mile from the house, in which there was a deep hole, where the water whirled about among the rocks; to this place it was suggested, I must go and drown myself.

At the time I had a book in my hand; it was on a Sabbath morning, about ten o'clock; to this place I resorted, where on coming to the water I sat down on the bank, and on my looking into it; it was suggested, that drowning would be an easy death. It seemed as if some one was speaking to me, saying put your head under, it will not distress you. But by some means, of which I can give no account, my thoughts were taken entirely from this purpose, when I went from the place to the house again. It was the unseen arm of God which saved me from self murder.

But notwithstanding this escape from death, my mind was not at rest—but so great was the labour of my spirit and the fearful oppressions of a judgment to come, that I was reduced as one extremely ill. On which account a physician was called to attend me, from which illness I recovered in about three months.

But as yet I had not found him of whom Moses and the prophets did write, being extremely ignorant: there being no one to instruct me in the way of life and salvation as yet. After my recovery, I left the lady, who during my sickness, was exceedingly kind, and went to Philadelphia. From this place I soon went a few miles into the country, where I resided in the family of a Roman Catholic. But my anxiety still continued respecting my poor soul, on which account I used to watch my opportunity to read in the Bible; and this lady observing this, took the Bible from me and hid it, giving me a novel in its stead—which when I perceived, I refused to read.

Soon after this I again went to the city of Philadelphia; and commenced going to the English Church, the pastor of which was an Englishman, by the name of Pilmore, one of the number, who at first preached Methodism in America, in the city of New York.[1]

But while sitting under the ministration of this man, which was about three months, and at the last time, it appeared that there was a wall between me and a communion with that people, which was higher than I could possibly see over, and seemed to make this impression upon my mind, *this is not the people for you.*

But on returning home at noon I inquired of the head cook of the house respecting the rules of the Methodists, as I knew she belonged to that society, who told me what they were; on which account I replied, that I should not be able to abide by such strict rules not even one year;—however, I told her that I would go with her and hear what they had to say.

The man who was to speak in the afternoon of that day, was the Rev. Richard Allen, since bishop of the African Episcopal Methodists in America.[2] During the labors of this man that afternoon, I had come to the conclusion, that this is the people to which my heart unites, and it so happened, that as soon as the service closed he invited such as felt a desire to flee the wrath to come, to unite on trial with them—I embraced the opportunity. Three weeks from that day, my soul was gloriously converted to God, under preaching, at the very outset of the sermon. The text was barely pronounced, which was: "I perceive thy heart is not right in the sight of God" [Acts 8:21], when there appeared to *my* view, in the centre of the heart *one* sin; and this was *malice,* against one particular individual, who had strove deeply to injure me, which I resented. At this discovery I said, *Lord* I forgive *every* creature. That instant, it appeared to me, as if a garment, which had entirely enveloped my whole person, even to my fingers ends, split at the crown of my head, and was stripped away from me, passing like a shadow, from my sight—when the glory of God seemed to cover me in its stead.

That moment, though hundreds were present, I did leap to my feet, and declare that God, for Christ's sake, had pardoned the sins of my soul. Great was the ecstasy of my mind, for I felt that not only the sin of *malice* was pardoned, but all other sins were swept away together. That day was the first when my heart had believed, and my tongue had made confession unto salvation—the first words uttered, a part of that song, which shall fill eternity with its sound, was *glory to God.* For a few moments I had power to exhort sinners, and to tell of the wonders and of the goodness of him who had clothed me with *his* salvation. During this, the minister was silent, until my soul felt its duty had been performed, when he declared another witness of the power of Christ to forgive sins on earth, was manifest in my conversion.

From the day on which I first went to the Methodist church, until the hour of my deliverance, I was strangely buffetted by that enemy of all righteousness—the devil.

I was naturally of a lively turn of disposition; and during the space of time from my first awakening until I knew my peace was made with God, I rejoiced in the vanities of this life, and then again sunk back into sorrow.

For four years I had continued in this way, frequently labouring under the awful apprehension, that I could never be happy in this life. This persuasion was greatly strengthened, during the three weeks, which was the last of Satan's power over me, in this peculiar manner: on which account, I had come to the conclusion that I had better be dead than alive. Here I was again tempted to destroy my life by drowning; but suddenly this mode was changed, and while in the dusk of the evening, as I was walking to and fro in the yard of the house, I was beset to hang myself, with a cord suspended from the wall enclosing the secluded spot.

But no sooner was the intention resolved on in my mind, than an awful dread came over me, when I ran into the house; still the tempter pursued me. There was standing a vessel of water—into this I was strongly impressed to plunge my head, so as to extinguish the life which God had given me. Had I have done this, I have been always of the opinion that I should have been unable to have released myself; although the vessel was scarcely large enough to hold a gallon of water. Of me may it not be said, as written by Isaiah, (chap. 65, verses 1,2.) "I am sought of them that asked not for me; I am found of them that sought me not." Glory be to God for his redeeming power, which saved me from the violence of my own hands, from the malice of Satan, and from eternal death; for had I have killed myself, a great ransom could not have delivered me; for it is written—"No murderer hath eternal life abiding in him" [1 John 3:15]. How appropriately can I sing—

"Jesus sought me, when a stranger,
Wandering from the fold of God;
He to rescue me from danger,
Interposed his precious blood."[3]

But notwithstanding the terror which seized upon me, when about to end my life, I had no view of the precipice on the edge of which I was tottering, until it was over, and my eyes were opened. Then the awful gulf of hell seemed to be open beneath me, covered only, as it were, by a spider's web, on which I stood. I seemed to hear the howling of the damned, to see the smoke of the bottomless pit, and to hear the rattling of those chains, which hold the impenitent under clouds of darkness to the judgment of the great day.

I trembled like Belshazzar,[4] and cried out in the horror of my spirit, "God be merciful to me a sinner." That night I formed a resolution to pray; which, when resolved upon, there appeared, sitting in one corner of the room, Satan, in the form of a monstrous dog, and in a rage, as if in pursuit, his tongue protruding from his mouth to a great length, and his eyes looked like two balls of fire; it soon, however, vanished out of my sight. From this state of terror and dismay, I was happily delivered under the preaching of the Gospel as before related.

This view, which I was permitted to have of Satan, in the form of a dog, is evidence, which corroborates in my estimation, the Bible account of a hell of fire, which burneth with brimstone, called in Scripture the bottomless pit; the place where all liars, who repent not, shall have their portion; as also the Sabbath breaker, the adulterer, the fornicator, with the fearful, the abominable, and the unbelieving, this shall be the portion of their cup.

This language is too strong and expressive to be applied to any state of suffering in *time.* Were it to be thus applied, the reality could no where be found in human life; the consequence would be, that *this* scripture would be found a false testimony. But when made to apply to an endless state of perdition, in eternity, beyond the bounds of human life, then this language is found not to exceed our views of a state of eternal damnation.

During the latter part of my state of conviction, I can now apply to my case, as it then was, the beautiful words of the poet:

> "The more I strove against its power,
> I felt its weight and guilt the more;
> 'Till late I hear'd my Saviour say,
> Come hither soul, I am the way."

This I found to be true, to the joy of my disconsolate and despairing heart, in the hour of my conversion to God.

During this state of mind, while sitting near the fire one evening, after I had heard Rev. Richard Allen, as before related, a view of my distressed condition so affected my heart, that I could not refrain from weeping and crying aloud; which caused the lady with whom I then lived, to inquire, with surprise, what ailed me; to which I answered, that I knew not what ailed me. She replied that I ought to pray. I arose from where I was sitting, being in an agony, and weeping convulsively, requested her to pray for me; but at the very moment when she would have done so, some person rapped heavily at the door for admittance; it was but a person of the house, but this occurrence was sufficient to interrupt us in our intentions; and I believe to this day, I should then have found salvation to my soul. This interruption was, doubtless, also the work of Satan.

Although at this time, when my conviction was so great, yet I knew not that Jesus Christ was the Son of God, the second person in the adorable trinity. I knew him not in the pardon of my sins, yet I felt a consciousness that if I died without pardon, that my lot must inevitably be damnation. If I would pray—I knew not how. I could form no connexion of ideas into words; but I knew the Lord's prayer; this I uttered with a loud voice, and with all my might and strength. I was the most ignorant creature in the world; I did not even know that Christ had died for the sins of the world, and to save sinners. Every circumstance, however, was so directed as still to continue and increase the sorrows of my heart, which I now know to have been a godly sorrow which wrought repentance, which is not to be repented of. Even the falling of the dead leaves from the forests, and the dried spires of the mown grass, showed me that I too must die, in like manner. But my case was awfully different from that of the grass of the field, or the wide spread decay of a thousand forests, as I felt within me a living principle, an immortal spirit, which cannot die, and must forever either enjoy the smiles of its Creator, or feel the pangs of ceaseless damnation.

But the Lord led me on; being gracious, he took pity on my ignorance; he heard my wailings, which had entered into the ear of the Lord of Sabaoth. Circumstances so transpired that I soon came to a knowledge of the being and character of the Son of God, of whom I knew nothing.

My strength had left me. I had become feverish and sickly through the violence of my feelings, on which account I left my place of service to spend a week with a coloured physician, who was a member of the Methodist society, and also to spend this week in going to places where prayer and supplication was statedly made for such as me.

Through this means I had learned much, so as to be able in some degree to comprehend the spiritual meaning of the text, which the minister took on the Sabbath morning, as before related, which was, "I perceive thy heart is not right in the sight of God." Acts, chap. 8, verse 21.

This text, as already related, became the power of God unto salvation to me, because I believed. I was baptized according to the direction of our Lord, who said, as he was about to ascend from the mount, to his disciples, "Go ye into all the world and preach my gospel to every creature, he that believeth and is baptized shall be saved" [Mark 16:15–16].

I have now passed through the account of my conviction, and also of my conversion to God; and shall next speak of the blessing of sanctification.

A time after I had received forgiveness flowed sweetly on; day and night my joy was full, no temptation was permitted to molest me. I could say continually with the psalmist, that "God had separated my sins from me, as far as the east is from the west" [Ps. 103:12]. I was ready continually to cry,

> "Come all the world, come sinner thou,
> All things in Christ are ready now."

I continued in this happy state of mind for almost three months, when a certain coloured man, by name William Scott, came to pay me a religious visit. He had been for many years a faithful follower of the Lamb; and he had also taken much time in visiting the sick and distressed of our colour, and understood well the great things belonging to a man of full stature in Christ Jesus.

In the course of our conversation, he inquired if the Lord had justified my soul. I answered, yes. He then asked me if he had sanctified me. I answered, no; and that I did not know what that was. He then undertook to instruct me further in the knowledge of the Lord respecting this blessing.

He told me the progress of the soul from a state of darkness, or of nature, was threefold; or consisted in three degrees, as follows:—First, conviction for sin. Second, justification from sin. Third, the entire sanctification of the soul to God. I thought this description was beautiful, and immediately believed in it. He then inquired if I would promise to pray for this in my secret devotions. I told him, yes. Very soon I began to call upon the Lord to show me all that was in my heart, which was not according to his will. Now there appeared to be a new struggle commencing in my soul, not accompanied with fear, guilt, and bitter distress, as while under my first conviction for sin; but a labouring of the mind to know more of the right way of the Lord. I began now to feel that my heart was not clean in his sight; that there yet remained the roots of bitterness, which if not destroyed, would ere long sprout up from these roots, and overwhelm me in a new growth of the brambles and brushwood of sin.

By the increasing light of the Spirit, I had found there yet remained the root of pride, anger, self-will, with many evils, the result of fallen nature. I now became alarmed at this discovery, and began to fear that I had been deceived in my experience. I was now greatly alarmed, lest

I should fall away from what I knew I had enjoyed; and to guard against this I prayed almost incessantly, without acting faith on the power and promises of God to keep me from falling. I had not yet learned how to war against temptation of this kind. Satan well knew that if he could succeed in making me disbelieve my conversion, that he would catch me either on the ground of complete despair, or on the ground of infidelity. For if all I had passed through was to go for nothing, and was but a fiction, the mere ravings of a disordered mind, then I would naturally be led to believe that there is nothing in religion at all.

From this snare I was mercifully preserved, and led to believe that there was yet a greater work than that of pardon to be wrought in me. I retired to a secret place (after having sought this blessing, as well as I could, for nearly three months, from the time brother Scott had instructed me respecting it) for prayer, about four o'clock in the afternoon. I had struggled long and hard, but found not the desire of my heart. When I rose from my knees, there seemed a voice speaking to me, as I yet stood in a leaning posture—"Ask for sanctification." When to my surprise, I recollected that I had not even thought of it in my whole prayer. It would seem Satan had hidden the very object from my mind, for which I had purposely kneeled to pray. But when this voice whispered in my heart, saying, "Pray for sanctification," I again bowed in the same place, at the same time, and said, "Lord *sanctify* my soul for Christ's sake?" That very instant, as if lightning had darted through me, I sprang to my feet, and cried, "The Lord has sanctified my soul!" There was none to hear this but the angels who stood around to witness my joy—and Satan, whose malice raged the more. That Satan was there, I knew; for no sooner had I cried out, "The Lord has sanctified my soul," than there seemed another voice behind me, saying, "No, it is too great a work to be done." But another spirit said, "Bow down for the witness—I received it—*thou art sanctified!*" The first I knew of myself after that, I was standing in the yard with my hands spread out, and looking with my face toward heaven.

I now ran into the house and told them what had happened to me, when, as it were, a new rush of the same ecstasy came upon me, and caused me to feel as if I were in an ocean of light and bliss.

During this, I stood perfectly still, the tears rolling in a flood from my eyes. So great was the joy, that it is past description. There is no language that can describe it, except that which was heard by St. Paul, when he was caught up to the third heaven, and heard words which it was not lawful to utter.[5]

MY CALL TO PREACH THE GOSPEL.

Between four and five years after my sanctification, on a certain time, an impressive silence fell upon me, and I stood as if some one was about to speak to me, yet I had no such thought in my heart. But to my utter surprise there seemed to sound a voice which I thought I distinctly heard, and most certainly understood, which said to me, "Go preach the Gospel!" I immediately replied aloud, "No one will believe me." Again I listened, and again the same voice seemed to say, "Preach the Gospel; I will put words in your mouth, and will turn your enemies to become your friends."[6]

At first I supposed that Satan had spoken to me, for I had read that he could transform himself into an angel of light, for the purpose of deception. Immediately I went into a secret place, and called upon the Lord to know if he had called me to preach, and whether I was deceived or not; when there appeared to my view the form and figure of a pulpit, with a Bible lying thereon, the back of which was presented to me as plainly as if it had been a literal fact.

In consequence of this, my mind became so exercised that during the night following, I took a text, and preached in my sleep. I thought there stood before me a great multitude, while I expounded to them the things of religion. So violent were my exertions, and so loud were my exclamations, that I awoke from the sound of my own voice, which also awoke the family of the house where I resided. Two days after, I went to see the preacher in charge of the African Society,[7] who was the Rev. Richard Allen, the same before named in these pages, to tell him that I felt it my duty to preach the gospel. But as I drew near the street in which his house was, which was in the city of Philadelphia, my courage began to fail me; so terrible did the cross appear, it seemed that I should not be able to bear it. Previous to my setting out to go to see him, so agitated was my mind, that my appetite for my daily food failed me entirely. Several times on my way there, I turned back again; but as often I felt my strength again renewed, and I soon found that the nearer I approached to the house of the minister, the less was my fear. Accordingly, as soon as I came to the door, my fears subsided, the cross was removed, all things appeared pleasant—I was tranquil.

I now told him, that the Lord had revealed it to me, that I must preach the gospel. He replied by asking, in what sphere I wished to move in? I said, among the Methodists. He then replied, that a Mrs. Cook, a Methodist lady, had also some time before requested the same privilege; who it was believed, had done much good in the way of exhortation, and holding prayer meetings; and who had been permitted to do so by the verbal license of the preacher in charge at the time. But as to women preaching, he said that our Discipline knew nothing at all about it—that it did not call for women preachers.[8] This I was glad to hear, because it removed the fear of the cross—but not no sooner did this feeling cross my mind, than I found that a love of souls had in a measure departed from me; that holy energy which burned within me, as a fire, began to be smothered. This I soon perceived.

O how careful ought we to be, lest through our by-laws of church government and discipline, we bring into disrepute even the word of life. For as unseemly as it may appear now-a-days for a woman to preach, it should be remembered that nothing is impossible with God. And why should it be thought impossible, heterodox, or improper, for a woman to preach? seeing the Saviour died for the woman as well as the man.

If a man may preach, because the Saviour died for him, why not the woman? seeing he died for her also. Is he not a whole Saviour, instead of a half one? as those who hold it wrong for a woman to preach, would seem to make it appear.

Did not Mary *first* preach the risen Saviour, and is not the doctrine of the resurrection the very climax of Christianity—hangs not all our hope on this, as argued by St. Paul? Then did not Mary, a woman, preach the gospel? for she preached the resurrection of the crucified Son of God.[9]

But some will say, that Mary did not expound the Scripture, therefore, she did not preach, in the proper sense of the term. To this I reply, it may be that the term *preach,* in those primitive times, did not mean exactly what it is now *made* to mean; perhaps it was a great deal more simple then, than it is now:—if it were not, the unlearned fishermen could not have preached the gospel at all, as they had no learning.

To this it may be replied, by those who are determined not to believe that it is right for a woman to preach, that the disciples, though they were fishermen, and ignorant of letters too, were inspired so to do. To which I would reply, that though they were inspired, yet that inspiration did not save them from showing their ignorance of letters, and of man's wisdom; this the multitude soon found out, by listening to the remarks of the envious Jewish priests. If then, to preach the gospel, by the gift of heaven, comes by inspiration solely, is God straitened; must he take the man exclusively? May he not, did he not, and can he not inspire a female to preach the simple story of the birth, life, death, and resurrection of our Lord, and accompany it too, with power to the sinner's heart. As for me, I am fully persuaded that the Lord called me to labour according to what I have received, in his vineyard. If he has not, how could he consistently bear testimony in favour of my poor labours, in awakening and converting sinners?

In my wanderings up and down among men, preaching according to my ability, I have frequently found families who told me that they had not for several years been to a meeting, and yet, while listening to hear what God would say by his poor coloured female instrument, have believed with trembling—tears rolling down their cheeks, the signs of contrition and repentance towards God. I firmly believe that I have sown seed, in the name of the Lord, which shall appear with its increase at the great day of accounts, when Christ shall come to make up his jewels.

At a certain time, I was beset with the idea, that soon or late I should fall from grace, and lose my soul at last. I was frequently called to the throne of grace about this matter, but found no relief; the temptation pursued me still. Being more and more afflicted with it, till at a certain time when the spirit strongly impressed it on my mind to enter into my closet, and carry my case once more to the Lord; the Lord enabled me to draw nigh to him, and to his mercy seat, at this time, in an extraordinary manner; for while I wrestled with him for the victory over this disposition to doubt whether I should persevere, there appeared a form of fire, about the size of a man's hand, as I was on my knees; at the same moment, there appeared to the eye of faith a man robed in a white garment, from the shoulders down to the feet; from him a voice proceeded, saying: "Thou shalt never return from the cross." Since that time I have never doubted, but believe that god will keep me until the day of redemption. Now I could adopt the very language of St. Paul, and say that nothing could have separated my soul from the love of god, which is in Christ Jesus [Rom. 8:35–39]. From that time, 1807, until the present, 1833, I have not yet doubted the power and goodness of God to keep me from falling, through sanctification of the spirit and belief of the truth.

MY MARRIAGE.

In the year 1811, I changed my situation in life, having married Mr. Joseph Lee, Pastor of a Coloured Society at Snow Hill, about six miles from the city of Philadelphia. It became necessary therefore for me to remove. This was a great trial at first, as I knew no person at Snow Hill, except my husband; and to leave my associates in the society, and especially those who composed the *band* of which I was one. Not but those who have been in sweet fellowship with such as really love God, and have together drank bliss and happiness from the same fountain, can tell how dear such company is, and how hard it is to part from them.

At Snow Hill, as was feared, I never found that agreement and closeness in communion and fellowship, that I had in Philadelphia, among my young companions, nor ought I to have expected it. The manners and customs at this place were somewhat different, on which account I became discontented in the course of a year, and began to importune my husband to remove to the city. But this plan did not suit him, as he was the Pastor of the Society; he could not bring his mind to leave them. This afflicted me a little. But the Lord soon showed me in a dream what his will was concerning this matter.

I dreamed that as I was walking on the summit of a beautiful hill, that I saw near me a flock of sheep, fair and white, as if but newly washed; when there came walking toward me, a man of a grave and dignified countenance, dressed entirely in white, as it were in a robe, and looking at me, said emphatically, "Joseph Lee must take care of these sheep, or the wolf will come and devour them." When I awoke, I was convinced of my error, and immediately, with a glad heart, yielded to the right way of the Lord. This also greatly strengthened my husband in his care over them, for fear the wolf should by some means take any of them away. The following verse was beautifully suited to our condition, as well as to all the little flocks of God scattered up and down this land:

"Us into Thy protection take,
And gather with Thine arm;
Unless the fold we first forsake,
The wolf can never harm."

After this, I fell into a state of general debility, and in an ill state of health, so much so, that I could not sit up; but a desire to warn sinners to flee the wrath to come, burned vehemently in my heart, when the Lord would send sinners into the house to see me. Such opportunities I embraced to press home on their consciences the things of eternity, and so effectual was the word of exhortation made through the Spirit, that I have seen them fall to the floor crying aloud for mercy.

From this sickness I did not expect to recover, and there was but one thing which bound me to earth, and this was, that I had not as yet preached the gospel to the fallen sons and daughters of Adam's race, to the satisfaction of my mind. I wished to go from one end of the earth to the other, crying, Behold, behold the Lamb! To this end I earnestly prayed the Lord to raise me up, if consistent with his will. He condescended to hear my prayer, and to give me a token in a dream, that in due time I should recover my health. The dream was as follows: I thought I saw the sun rise in the morning, and ascend to an altitude of about half an hour high, and then become obscured by a dense black cloud, which continued to hide its rays for about one third part of the day, and then it burst forth again with renewed splendour.

This dream I interpreted to signify my early life, my conversion to God, and this sickness, which was a great affliction, as it hindered me, and I feared would forever hinder me from preaching the gospel, was signified by the cloud; and the bursting forth of the sun, again, was the recovery of my health, and being permitted to preach.

I went to the throne of grace on this subject, where the Lord made this impressive reply in my heart, while on my knees: "Ye shall be restored to thy health again, and worship God in full purpose of heart."

This manifestation was so impressive, that I could but hide my face, as if someone was gazing upon me, to think of the great goodness of the Almighty God to my poor soul and body. From that very time I began to gain strength of body and mind, glory to God in the highest, until my health was fully recovered.

For six years from this time I continued to receive from above, such baptisms of the Spirit as mortality could scarcely bear. About that time I was called to suffer in my family, by death—five, in the course of about six years, fell by his hand; my husband being one of the number, which was the greatest affliction of all.[10]

I was now left alone in the world, with two infant children, one of the age of about two years, the other six months, with no other dependance than the promise of Him who hath said—"I will be the widow's God, and a father to the fatherless" [Ps. 68:5]. Accordingly, he raised me up friends, whose liberality comforted and solaced me in my state of widowhood and sorrows. I could sing with the greatest propriety the words of the poet.

> "He helps the stranger in distress,
> The widow and the fatherless,
> And grants the prisoner sweet release."

I can say even now, with the Psalmist, "Once I was young, but now I am old, yet I have never seen the righteous forsaken, nor his seed begging bread" [Ps. 37:25]. I have ever been fed by his bounty, clothed by his mercy, comforted and healed when sick, succoured when tempted, and every where upheld by his hand.

THE SUBJECT OF MY CALL TO PREACH RENEWED.

It was now eight years since I had made application to be permitted to preach the gospel, during which time I had only been allowed to exhort, and even this privilege but seldom.[11] This subject now was renewed afresh in my mind; it was as a fire shut up in my bones. About thirteen months passed on, while under this renewed impression. During this time, I had solicited of the Rev. Bishop Richard Allen, who at this time had become Bishop of the African Episcopal Methodists in America, to be permitted the liberty of holding prayer meetings in my own hired house, and of exhorting as I found liberty, which was granted me. By this means, my mind was relieved, as the house was soon filled when the hour appointed for prayer had arrived.

I cannot but relate in this place, before I proceed further with the above subject, the singular conversion of a very wicked young man. He was a coloured man, who had generally attended our meetings, but not for any good purpose; but rather to disturb and to ridicule our denomination. He openly and uniformly declared that he neither believed in religion, nor wanted anything to do with it. He was of a Gallio disposition,[12] and took the lead among the young people of colour. But after a while he fell sick, and lay about three months in a state of ill health; his disease was consumption. Toward the close of his days, his sister who was a member of the society, came and desired me to go and see her brother, as she had no hopes of his recovery; perhaps the Lord might break into his mind. I went alone, and found him very low. I soon commenced to inquire respecting his state of feeling, and how he found his mind. His answer was, "O tolerable well," with an air of great indifference. I asked him if I should pray for him. He answered in a sluggish and careless manner, "O yes, if you have time." I then sung a hymn, kneeled down and prayed for him, and then went my way.

Three days after this, I went again to visit the young man. At this time there went with me two of the sisters in Christ. We found the Rev. Mr. Cornish, of our denomination, labouring with him.[13] But he said he received but little satisfaction from him. Pretty soon, however, brother Cornish took his leave; when myself, with the other two sisters, one of which was an elderly woman named Jane Hutt, the other was younger, both coloured, commenced conversing with him, respecting his eternal interest, and of his hopes of a happy eternity, if any he had. He said but little; we then kneeled down together and besought the Lord in his behalf, praying that if mercy were not clear gone forever, to shed a ray of softening grace upon the hardness of his heart. He appeared now to be somewhat more tender, and we thought we could perceive some tokens of conviction, as he wished us to visit him again, in a tone of voice not quite as indifferent as he had hitherto manifested.

But two days had elapsed after this visit, when his sister came for me in haste, saying, that she believed her brother was then dying, and that he had *sent* for me. I immediately called on Jane Hutt, who was still among us as a mother in Israel, to go with me. When we arrived there, we found him sitting up in his bed, very restless and uneasy, but he soon laid down again. He now wished me to come to him, by the side of his bed. I asked him how he was. He said, "Very ill;" and added, "Pray for me, quick?" We now perceived his time in this world to be short. I took up the hymn-book and opened to a hymn suitable to his case, and commenced to sing. But there seemed to be a *horror* in the room—a darkness of a mental kind, which was felt by us all; there being five persons, except the sick young man and his nurse. We had sung but one verse, when they all gave over singing, on account of this unearthly sensation, but myself. I continued to sing on alone, but in a dull and heavy manner, though looking up to God all the while for help. Suddenly, I felt a spring of energy awake in my heart, when darkness gave way in some degree. It was but a glimmer from above. When the hymn was finished, we all kneeled down to pray for him. While calling on the name of the Lord, to have mercy on his soul, and to grant him repentance unto life, it came suddenly into my mind never to rise from my knees until God should hear prayer in his behalf, until he should convert and save his soul.

Now, while I thus continued importuning heaven, as I felt I was led, a ray of light, more abundant, broke forth among us. There appeared to my view, though my eyes were closed, the Saviour in full stature, nailed to the cross, just over the head of the young man, against the ceiling of the room. I cried out, brother look up, the Saviour is come, he will pardon you, your sins he will forgive. My sorrow for the soul of the young man was gone; I could no longer pray—joy and rapture made it impossible. We rose up from our knees, when lo, his eyes were gazing with ecstasy upward; over his face there was an expression of joy; his lips were clothed in a sweet and holy smile; but no sound came from his tongue; it was heard in its stillness of bliss, full of hope and immortality. Thus, as I held him by the hand his happy and purified soul soared away, without a sign or a groan, to its eternal rest.

I now closed his eyes, straightened out his limbs, and left him to be dressed for the grave. But as for me, I was filled with the power of the Holy Ghost—the very room seemed filled with glory. His sister and all that were in the room rejoiced, nothing doubting but he had entered into Paradise; and I believe I shall see him at the last and great day, safe on the shores of salvation.

But to return to the subject of my call to preach. Soon after this, as above related, the Rev. Richard Williams was to preach at Bethel Church, where I with others were assembled.[14] He entered the pulpit, gave out the hymn, which was sung, and then addressed the throne of grace; took his text, passed through the exordium, and commenced to expound it. The text he took is in Jonah, 2d chap. 9th verse,—"Salvation is of the Lord." But as he proceeded to explain, he seemed to have lost the spirit; when in the same instant, I sprang, as by an altogether supernatural impulse, to my feet, when I was aided from above to give an exhortation on the very text which my brother Williams had taken.

I told them that I was like Jonah; for it had been then nearly eight years since the Lord had called me to preach his gospel to the fallen sons and daughters of Adam's race, but that I had lingered like him, and delayed to go at the bidding of the Lord, and warn those who are as deeply guilty as were the people of Ninevah.

During the exhortation, God made manifest his power in a manner sufficient to show the world that I was called to labour according to my ability, and the grace given unto me, in the vineyard of the good husbandman.

I now sat down, scarcely knowing what I had done, being frightened. I imagined, that for this indecorum, as I feared it might be called, I should be expelled from the church. But instead of this, the

Bishop rose up in the assembly, and related that I had called upon him eight years before, asking to be permitted to preach, and that he had put me off; but that he now as much believed that I was called to that work, as any of the preachers present. These remarks greatly strengthened me, so that my fears of having given an offence, and made myself liable as an offender, subsided, giving place to a sweet serenity, a holy job of a peculiar kind, untasted in my bosom until then.

The next Sabbath day, while sitting under the word of the gospel, I felt moved to attempt to speak to the people in a public manner, but I could not bring my mind to attempt it in the church. I said, Lord, anywhere but here. Accordingly, there was a house not far off which was pointed out to me, to this I went. It was the house of a sister belonging to the same society with myself. Her name was Anderson. I told her I had come to hold a meeting in her house, if she would call in her neighbours. With this request she immediately complied. My congregation consisted of but five persons. I commenced by reading and singing a hymn, when I dropped to my knees by the side of a table to pray. When I arose I found my hand resting on the Bible, which I had not noticed till that moment. It now occurred to me to take a text. I opened the Scripture, as it happened, at the 141st Psalm, fixing my eye on the 3d verse, which reads: "Set a watch, O Lord, before my mouth, keep the door of my lips." My sermon, such as it was, I applied wholly to myself, and added an exhortation. Two of my congregation wept much, as the fruit of my labour this time. In closing I said to the few, that if any one would open a door, I would hold a meeting the next sixth-day evening; when one answered that her house was at my service. Accordingly I went, and God made manifest his power among the people. Some wept, while others shouted for joy. One whole seat of females, by the power of God, as the rushing of a wind, were all bowed to the floor at once, and screamed out. Also a sick man and woman in one house, the Lord convicted them both; one lived, and the other died. God wrought a judgment—some were well at night, and died in the morning. At this place I continued to hold meetings about six months. During that time I kept house with my little son, who was very sickly. About this time I had a call to preach at a place about thirty miles distant, among the Methodists, with whom I remained one week, and during the whole time, not a thought of my little son came into my mind; it was hid from me, lest I should have been diverted from the work I had to, to look after my son. Here by the instrumentality of a poor coloured woman, the Lord poured forth his spirit among the people. Though, as I was told, there were lawyers, doctors, and magistrates present, to hear me speak, yet there was mourning and crying among sinners, for the Lord scattered fire among them of his own kindling. The Lord gave his handmaiden power to speak for his great name, for he arrested the hearts of the people, and caused a shaking amongst the multitude, for God was in the midst.

I now returned home, found all well; no harm had come to my child, although I left it very sick. Friends had taken care of it which was of the Lord. I now began to think seriously of breaking up housekeeping, and forsaking all to preach the everlasting Gospel. I felt a strong desire to return to the place of my nativity, at Cape May, after an absence of about fourteen years. To this place, where the heaviest cross was to be met with, the Lord sent me, as Saul of Tarsus was sent to Jerusalem,[15] to preach the same gospel which he had neglected and despised before his conversion. I went by water, and on my passage was much distressed by sea sickness, so much so that I expected to have died, but such was not the will of the Lord respecting me. After I had disembarked, I proceeded on as opportunities offered, toward where my mother lived. When within ten miles of that place, I appointed an evening meeting. There were a goodly number came out to hear. The Lord was pleased to give me light and liberty among the people. After meeting, there came an elderly lady to me and said, she believed the Lord had sent me among them; she then appointed me another meeting there two weeks from that night. The next day I hastened forward to the place of my mother, who was happy to see me, and the happiness was mutual between us. With her I left my poor sickly boy, while I departed to do my Master's will. In this neighborhood I had an uncle, who was a Methodist, and who gladly threw open his door for meetings to be held there. At the first meeting which I held at my uncle's house, there was, with others who had come from curiosity to hear the coloured woman preacher, an old man, who was a deist, and who said he did not believe the coloured people had any souls—he was sure they had none. He took a seat very near where I was standing, and boldly tried to look me out of countenance. But as I laboured on in the best manner I was able, looking to God all the while, though it seemed to me I had but little liberty, yet there went an arrow from the bent bow of the gospel, and fastened in his till then obdurate heart. After I had done speaking, he went out, and called the people around him, said that my preaching might seem a small thing, yet he believed I had the worth of souls at heart. This language was different from what it was a little time before, as he now seemed to admit that coloured people had souls, whose good I had in view, his remark must have been without meaning. He now came into the house, and in the most friendly manner shook hands with me, saying, he hoped God had spared him to some good purpose. This man was a great slave holder, and had been very cruel; thinking nothing of knocking down a slave with a fence stake, or whatever might come to hand. From this time it was said of him that he became greatly altered in his ways for the better. At that time he was about seventy years old, his head as white as snow; but whether he became a converted man or not, I never heard.

The week following, I had an invitation to hold a meeting at the Court House of the County, when I spoke from the 53d chap. of Isaiah, 3d verse. It was a solemn time, and the Lord attended the word; I had life and liberty, though there were people there of various denominations. Here again I saw the aged slaveholder, who notwithstanding his age, walked about three miles to hear me. This day I spoke twice, and walked six miles to the place appointed. There was a magistrate present, who showed his friendship, by saying in a friendly manner, that he had heard of me: he handed me a hymn-book, pointing to a hymn which he had selected. When the meeting was over, he invited me to preach in a schoolhouse in his neighbourhood, about three miles distant from where I then was. During this meeting one backslider was reclaimed. This day I walked six miles, and preached twice to large congregations, both in the morning and evening. The Lord was with me, glory be to his holy name. I next went six miles and held a meeting in a coloured friend's house, at eleven o'clock in the morning, and preached to a well behaved congregation of both coloured and white. After service I again walked back, which was in all twelve miles in the same day. This was on Sabbath, or as I sometimes call it, seventh-day; for after my conversion I preferred the plain language of the quakers: On fourth-day, after this, in compliance with an invitation received by note, from the same magistrate who had heard me at the above place, I preached to a large congregation, where we had a precious time: much weeping was heard among the people. The same gentleman, now at the close of the meeting, gave out another appointment at the same place, that day week. Here again I had liberty, there was a move among the people. Ten years from that time, in the neighbourhood of Cape May, I held a prayer meeting in a school house, which was then the regular place of preaching for the Episcopal Methodists; after service, there came a white lady of the first distinction, a member of the Methodist Society, and told me that at the same school house, ten years before, under my preaching, the Lord first awakened her. She rejoiced much to see me, and invited me home with her, where I staid till the next day. This was bread cast on the waters, seen after many days.

From this place I next went to Dennis Creek meeting house, where at the invitation of an elder, I spoke to a large congregation of various and conflicting sentiments, when a wonderful shock of God's power was felt, shown everywhere by groans, by sighs, and loud and happy amens. I felt as if aided from above. My tongue was cut loose, the stammerer spoke freely; the love of God, and of his service, burned with a vehement flame within me—his name was glorified among the people.

But here I feel myself constrained to give over, as from the smallness of this pamphlet I cannot go through with the whole of my journal, as it would probably make a volume of two hundred pages; which, if the Lord be willing, may at some future day be published.[16] But for the satisfaction of such as may follow after me, when I am no more, I have recorded how the Lord called me to his work, and how he has kept me from falling from grace, as I feared I should. In all things he has proved himself a God of truth to me; and in his service I am now as much determined to spend and be spent, as at the very first. My ardour for the progress of his cause abates not a whit, so far as I am able to judge, though I am now something more than fifty years of age.

As to the nature of uncommon impressions, which the reader cannot but have noticed, and possibly sneered at in the course of these pages, they may be accounted for in this way: It is known that the blind have the sense of hearing in a manner much more acute than those who can see: also their sense of feeling is exceedingly fine, and is found to detect any roughness on the smoothest surface, where those who can see can find none. So it may be with such as am, who has never had more than three months schooling; and wishing to know much of the way and law of God, have therefore watched the more closely the operations of the Spirit, and have in consequence been led thereby. But let it be remarked that have never found that Spirit to lead me contrary to the Scriptures of truth, as I understand them. "For as many as are led by the Spirit of God are the sons of God."—Rom. viii. 14.

I have now only to say, May the blessing of the Father, and of the Son, and of the Holy Ghost, accompany the reading of this poor effort to speak well of his name, wherever it may be read. AMEN.

MEMOIRS
OF THE
LIFE, RELIGIOUS EXPERIENCE, MINISTERIAL TRAVELS AND LABOURS
OF
MRS. ZILPHA ELAW,
AN AMERICAN FEMALE OF COLOUR;

Together with Some Account of the Great Religious Revivals in America

[Written by Herself]

"Not that we are sufficient of ourselves to think any thing as of ourselves; but our sufficiency is of God." 2 Cor. iii. 5.

London:
Published by the Authoress, and Sold by T. Dudley,
19, Charter-House Lane; and Mr. B. Taylor,
19, Montague-St. Spitalfields.

1846.

DEDICATION

To the Saints and faithful Brethren in Christ, who have honoured my ministery with their attendance, in London and other localities of England.

Grace be unto you, and peace, from God the Father, and the Lord Jesus Christ.[1]

Dear Brethren and Friends,

After sojourning in your hospitable land, and peregrinating among you during these last five years; in the course of which period, it has been my happiness to enjoy much spiritual intercourse with many of you in your family circles, your social meetings, and in the house of God, I feel a strong desire again to cross the pathless bosom of the foaming Atlantic and rejoin my dear friends in the occidental land of my nativity; and, in the prospect of an early departure from your shores, I feel that I cannot present you with a more appropriate keepsake, or a more lively memento of my Christian esteem, and affectionate desires for your progressive prosperity and perfection in the Christian calling, than the following contour portrait of my regenerated constitution—exhibiting, as did the bride of Solomon, comeliness with blackness [Song of Sol. 1:5]; and, as did the apostle Paul, riches with poverty, and power in weakness [2 Cor. 12:9]—a representation, not, indeed, of the features of my outward person, drawn and coloured by the skill of the pencilling artist, but of the lineaments of my inward man, as inscribed by the Holy Ghost, and, according to my poor ability, copied off for your edification.

If, therefore, there is anything in the soul reviving and thrilling Christian intercourse we have enjoyed together in the Spirit of Christ, and in the holy communion with which we have so frequently met together in the house of God, mingled our ascending petitions at the throne of grace, unbosomed our spiritual conflicts and trials to one another, and listened with devotional interest to the messages of gospel mercy, and the unfolding mysteries of divine grace, in times now passed over for ever, worthy of your cherished recollections; and, if the poor and weak instrumentality in the gospel of Jesus, of the coloured female, whose labours and sojourn amongst you are hastening to a close, have rendered her an object, not unworthy of your cherished recollections; receive with cordial and generous courtesy, this small token of an esteem and love, which she will continue to cherish on a far distant shore, in another clime, long as life permits its exercise, and resume, on our mutual recognition in that renewed state of existence, which will be characterised by the eternal developments of elevated holiness, blissful immortality, and transcendant glory.

My dear brethren and sisters in the Lord. I gratefully acknowledge the numerous marks of kindness you have conferred upon me during my residence in your land. I intreat your prayers for my preservation from the perils of the deep, whensoever my path may lie through it; and your continued remembrance of my pilgrim course and ministerial labours, at the throne of grace. I affectionately exhort you to walk worthy of the high vocation wherewith you are called, shunning, carefully, the destructive vices which so deplorably abound in and disfigure the Christian community, in this day of feverish restlessness and mighty movement. Remember, dear brethren, that they who will be rich, fall into temptation, and a snare, and numerous foolish and hurtful lusts, which will eventually drown them in perdition. Cease, therefore, from earthly accumulations; but lay up for yourselves treasures in heaven. Renounce the love of money; for it is the root of all evil [1 Tim. 6:10]. Love not the world; for the love of God is not in those who love the world. Look deep into the principles which form the under current, regardless of the artificial surface-polish of society; and abhor the pride of respectability; for that which is highly esteemed amongst men, is an abomination in the sight of God. Deal not in tale-bearing; neither be busy-bodies in other men's matters. Judge not one another, for your Judge standeth before the door. Be not ambitious, ostentatious, proud, haughty, morose, or wrathful; for God resisteth the proud and haughty scorner. Be ye, therefore, clothed with meekness and humility. Shut not your hearts against the poor, but ever remember them; for blessed is he that considereth them; and very unlike Jesus is he who cherishes a lurking prejudice in his heart against the children of need, and stoppeth his ears at their plaints. Take heed what you read: as a tree of knowledge, both of good and evil, is the press; it ofttimes teems with rabid poisons, putting darkness for light, and light for darkness; extolling earthly grandeur and honour, spurious valour and heroism; fixing reputation and character on a false basis; and frequently appearing as the panegyrist of the rankest principles, and the basest vices. Above all, shun an infidel, obscene or disloyal newspaper press, which is the scavenger of slander, and the harlequin of character; the masquerade of morals, and the burlesque of religion; the proteus of sentiment, and the dictionary of licentiousness; the seminary of libertines, and the hot-bed of sedition. Defile not your eyes with the sight of its columns, nor your heart with its proximity. Remember that you are called to be saints, not politicians and newsmongers. Give your cordial preference, therefore, to the Holy Scriptures; carefully read, study, and digest them, especially the title-deeds of the Christian covenant. Endeavour, as far as in you lies, to do the will of God on earth, as it is done in heaven. Imbibe the sentiments and spirit, the temper, disposition and manner of Christ Jesus, your inestimable pattern. Cautiously, diligently, and habitually observe and obey the directions and statutes of Christ and his apostles, that your foundation may be built not upon the sand of current traditions and prejudices, but upon the prophets and apostles, Christ Jesus being the chief cornerstone [Eph. 2:20], and that you may become His true and finished disciples, perfect and entire, lacking nothing, but complete in all the will of God.

And now, dear brethren, I commend you to God and the word of His grace, which is able to build you up, and give you an inheritance among all those who are sanctified. Amen.

Dear Friends, farewell! May the grace of our Lord Jesus Christ, and the love of God, and the communion of the Holy Spirit be with you all. Amen.

MEMOIRS
of the
Life, Religious Experience, Ministerial Travels, and Labours
of
MRS. ELAW.

I was born in the United States of America, in the State of Pennsylvania, and of religious parents.[2] When about six years of age, my mother's parents, who resided on their own farm, far in the interior of America, at a distance of many hundred miles, came to visit us. My parents had three children then living; the eldest, a boy about twelve years of age, myself, and a younger sister. On his return, my grandfather took my brother with him, promising to bring him up to the business of his farm; and I saw him not again until more than thirty years afterwards.

At twelve years of age I was bereaved of my mother, who died in childbirth of her twenty-second child, all of whom, with the exception of three, died in infancy. My father, having placed my younger sister under the care of her aunt, then consigned me to the care of Pierson and Rebecca Mitchel, with whom I remained until I attained the age of eighteen. After I had been with the above-mentioned persons one year and six months, it pleased God to remove my dear father to the world of spirits; and, being thus bereft of my natural guardians, I had no other friends on earth to look to but those kind benefactors under whom my dear father had placed me.

But that God whose mercy endureth for ever, still continued mindful of me; but oh, what a change did I experience in my new abode from that to which I had been accustomed. In my father's house, family devotion was regularly attended to morning and evening; prayer was offered up, and the praises of God were sung; but the persons with whom I now resided were Quakers, and their religious exercises, if they observed any, were performed in the secret silence of the mind; nor were religion and devotion referred to by them in my hearing, which rendered my transition from home the more strange; and, being very young, and no apparent religious restraint being laid upon me, I soon gave way to the evil propensities of an unregenerate heart, which is enmity against God, and heedlessly ran into the ways of sin, taking pleasure in the paths of folly. But that God, whose eyes are ever over all his handy works, suffered me not unchecked to pursue the courses of sin. My father's death frequently introduced very serious reflections into my mind; and often was I deeply affected, and constrained to weep before God, when no human eye beheld my emotion. But, notwithstanding these seasons of serious contrition, my associations with the juvenile members of the family were too generally marked by the accustomed gaities of a wanton heart. Our childish conversations sometimes turned upon the day of judgment, and our appearance in the presence of the great God on that portentous occasion, which originated in my breast the most solemn emotions whenever I was alone; for I felt myself to be so exceedingly sinful, that I was certain of meeting with condemnation at the bar of God. I knew not what to do; nor were there any persons to whom I durst open my mind upon the subject, and therefore remained ignorant of the great remedy disclosed by the plan of salvation afforded by the gospel, and incapable of religious progress. I was at times deeply affected with penitence, but could not rightly comprehend what it was that ailed me. Sometimes I resolutely shook off all my impressions, and became more thoughtless than before; one instance, in particular, is so riveted on my memory, that I shall never forget it when ever I glance back upon my youthful life. On this occasion I was talking very foolishly, and even ventured to take the name of God in vain, in order to cater to the sinful tastes of my companions; it well pleased their carnal minds, and they laughed with delight at my profanity; but, whilst I was in the very act of swearing, I looked up, and imagined that I saw God looking down and frowning upon me: my tongue was instantly silenced; and I retired from my frolicsome companions to reflect upon what I had said and done. To the praise of divine mercy, that God who willeth not the death of a sinner, but rather that all should turn unto him and live [Ezek. 18:32], did not even now abandon me, but called me by an effectual call through the following dream. It was a prevailing notion in that part of the world with many, that whatever a person dreamed between the times of twilight and sunrise, was prophetically ominous, and would shortly come to pass; and, on that very night, after I had offended my heavenly Father by taking His name in vain, He aroused and alarmed my spirit, by presenting before me in a dream the awful terrors of the day of judgment, accompanied by its terrific thunders. I thought that the Angel Gabriel came and proclaimed that time should be no longer; and he said, "Jehovah was about to judge the world, and execute judgment on it." I then exclaimed in my dream, "Oh, Lord, what shall I do? I am unprepared to meet thee." I then meditated an escape, but could not effect it; and in this horrific dilemma I awoke: the day was just dawning; and the intense horror of my guilty mind was such as to defy description. I was now about fourteen years of age; and this dream proved an effectual call to my soul. I meditated deeply upon it, my spirits became greatly depressed, and I wept excessively. I was naturally of a very lively and active disposition, and the shock my feelings had sustained from this alarming dream, attracted the attention of my mistress, who inquired the reason of so great a change. I related my dream to her, and also stated my sentiments with respect to it: she used every endeavour to comfort me, saying that it was only a dream; that dreams have nothing ominous in them; and I ought not to give myself any more concern respecting it: but she failed in her attempt to tranquilize my mind, because the convictions of my sinfulness in the sight of God, and incompetency to meet my Judge, were immoveable and distressing. I now gave myself much to meditation, and lisped out my simple and feeble prayers to God, as well as my limited apprehensions and youthful abilities admitted. About this time, the Methodists made their first appearance in that part of the country,[3] and I was permitted to attend their meetings once a fortnight, on the Sabbath afternoons, from which I derived great satisfaction; but the divine work on my soul was a very gradual one, and my way was prepared as the dawning of the morning. I never experienced that terrific dread of hell by which some Christians appear to have been exercised; but I felt a godly sorrow for sin in having grieved my God by a course of disobedience to His commands. I had been trained to attend the Quaker meetings; and, on their preaching occasions, I was pleased to be in attendance, and often found comfort from the word ministered by them; but I was, notwithstanding, usually very much cast down on account of my sins before God; and in this state I continued many months before I could attain sufficient confidence to say, "My Lord and my God." But as the darkness was gradually dispelled, the light dawned upon my mind, and I increased in knowledge daily; yet I possessed no assurance of my acceptance before God; though I enjoyed a greater peace of mind in waiting upon my heavenly father than at any previous time; my prayer was daily for the Lord to assure me of the forgiveness of my sins; and I at length proved the verification of the promise, "They that seek shall find" [Luke 11:9]; for, one evening, whilst singing one of the songs of Zion, I distinctly saw the Lord Jesus approach me with open arms, and a most divine and heavenly smile upon his countenance. As He advanced towards me, I felt that his very looks spoke, and said, "Thy prayer is accepted, I own thy name." From that day to the present I have never entertained a doubt of the manifestation of his love to my soul.

Yea, I may say further than this; because, at the time when this occurrence took place, I was milking in the cow stall; and the manifestation of his presence was so clearly apparent, that even the beast of the stall turned her head and bowed herself upon the ground. Oh, never, never shall I forget the scene. Some persons, perhaps, may be incredulous, and say, "How can these things be, and in what form did He appear?" Dear reader, whoever thou art, into whose hands this narrative may fall, I will try to gratify thee by endeavouring to describe his manifestation. It occurred as I was singing the following lines:—

"Oh, when shall I see Jesus,
And dwell with him above;
And drink from flowing fountains,
Of everlasting love.
When shall I be delivered
From this vain world of sin;
And, with my blessed Jesus,
Drink endless pleasures in?"[4]

As I was milking the cow and singing, I turned my head, and saw a tall figure approaching, who came and stood by me. He had long hair, which parted in the front and came down on his shoulders; he wore a long white robe down to the feet; and as he stood with open arms and smiled upon me, he disappeared. I might have tried to imagine, or persuade myself, perhaps, that it had been a vision presented merely to the eye of my mind; but, the beast of the stall gave forth her evidence to the reality of the heavenly appearance; for she turned her head and looked round as I did; and when she saw, she bowed her knees and cowered down upon the ground. I was overwhelmed with astonishment at the sight, but the thing was certain and beyond all doubt. I write as before God and Christ, and declare, as I shall give an account to my Judge at the great day, that every thing I have written in this little book, has been written with conscientious veracity and scrupulous adherence to truth.

After this wonderful manifestation of my condescending Saviour, the peace of God which passeth understanding was communicated to my heart; and joy in the Holy Ghost, to a degree, at the last, unutterable by my tongue and indescribable by my pen; it was beyond my comprehension; but, from that happy hour, my soul was set at glorious liberty; and, like the Ethiopic eunuch,[5] I went on my way rejoicing in the blooming prospects of a better inheritance with the saints in light.

This, my dear reader, was the manner of my soul's conversion to God, told in language unvarnished by the graces of educated eloquence, nor transcending the capacity of a child to understand.

The love of God being now shed abroad in my heart by the Holy Spirit, and my soul transported with heavenly peace and joy in God, all the former hardships which pertained to my circumstances and situation vanished; the work and duties which had previously been hard and irksome were now become easy and pleasant; and the evil propensities of my disposition and temper were subdued beneath the softening and refining pressure of divine grace upon my heart.

In the year 1808, I united myself in the fellowship of the saints with the militant church of Jesus on earth; and I can never forget that memorable evening on which I went up formally to present my hand to the brethren, and my heart for ever to the Lord.

I was received by the travelling preacher, the Rev. J. Polhemos. After sermon, he conducted the class; in the course of which he inquired if there were any persons present who desired to join the society: I then arose from my seat, and replied, "Yes, bless the Lord, here is one." He fixed his eyes upon me for a short time, and said, "Well, this seems a bold champion indeed." He then asked me the reason of my hope in Christ; if I enjoyed the evidence and witness of the Holy Spirit; if I calculated that I should be able to hold out to the end; and many very important questions besides; cautioning me against the deceptive imagination that the testimony I had given before the brethren, which had been witnessed by angels, or my union with the church, would alone be sufficient for my salvation. He then inquired if there existed any objections against my admission as a member of the Methodist Episcopal Society; and there being none, he entered my name into the class book of the society. I then returned home, meditating on that which I had heard and done, and praying that God would bestow on me sufficient grace to enable me to perform all his righteous will. Truly, in those days, my peace flowed as a river, and the light of God's countenance continually shone upon me; my path grew brighter and brighter, and my soul was stayed upon his gracious word and promises.

But, notwithstanding this tide of divine comforts so richly replenished my soul, Satan, my great adversary, frequently assailed me with various trials and temptations, and the young folks often derided me as being a Methodist: it was my happiness to be such, and I thanked God who counted me meet to be a partaker of the heavenly calling. I sometimes met with very severe rebukes from my mistress,[6] and I endured her reproofs without the exhibition of my former resentments and saucy replies: whatever storm arose, I was hid in the cleft of the rock until it was blown over. How vast a source of consolation did I derive from habitual communion with my God; to Him I repaired in secret to acquaint Him with all my griefs, and obtained both sympathy and succour. At such times, an overflowing stream of love has filled my soul, even beyond my utmost capacity to contain, and I have thought, when in such ecstacies of bliss, that I should certainly die under them, and go to my heavenly father at once, from an earthly to an heavenly transport; for I could not imagine it possible for any human being to feel such gusts of the love of God, and continue to exist in this world of sin.

But it was with me as with the great apostle of the Gentiles; when I was a child I thought as a child, I spake as a child, I understood as a child; but when I attained to maturity, I put away childish things [1 Cor. 13:11]. For as an earthly father pitieth his children, so does our Heavenly Father pity those who fear Him; they who serve Him in the time of peace, He will not abandon in the times of war and conflict, which in our probation here it behoves us to pass through. He has promised to carry the young Lambs in His bosom [Isa. 40:11]; and He verified that promise, in my experience, in the day of my trouble. Many were the tears which overflowed my eyes, and indicated the sorrows of my heart, and which none but God was the witness of. There were no persons in the house in which I resided, to whom I could at any time open my mind; for the knowledge of God was possessed by none in that family with the exception of my master, and amongst them I dwelt as a speckled bird; but the want of suitable associates, and the singularity with which I was treated, drove me to God my refuge, and proved very congenial to increased intimacy of communion with Him.

Prior to my experience of the life and power of godliness, my mistress frequently charged me with pertness and insolent behaviour; but after I had imbibed somewhat of the meekness and gentleness of Jesus, and had been instructed by his religion not to answer again when chided, then she frequently charged me with sullenness and mopishness. This treatment often sent me to the throne of grace, to seek the sympathy of Him who is touched with the feeling of our infirmities. I now felt, bitterly, the loss of my dear mother, whose earthly remains had long since been consigned to the house appointed for all living, and her spirit made meet for the inheritance of the saints in light, in which I hope to meet her at the right hand of God. Oh, how often do I think of the advantages enjoyed by many young people, who are blessed with devout and godly parents, and of the little estimation they are held in by too many perverse and giddy children, who, instead of greatly prizing the grace conferred upon them, resent the kind restraints of family worship and attendance at the house of God. Some of them, perhaps, may ultimately be led as I was, when their parents are gathered to the generation of their fathers, to pine after the privileges which they had once despised and finally lost. See ye to it, ye careless, giddy, perverse young folks, while the light of parental godliness yet illumines the house; prize it, imbibe it, conform yourselves to and profit by it, that the fervent petitions of your pious parents, in your behalf, may be prevailingly successful, by the production of a spirit of prayer in yourselves, and the bowing of your souls to God.

Before I knew the power of real religion, I was timid and fearful when alone in the dark; and if I had recently heard of the death of any person, even if it had occurred at a distance of twelve miles, I durst not go out of doors at night alone, from the superstitious dread of seeing their apparition, and to pass a grave-yard alone was terrible indeed; but when the Lord had spoken peace to my soul, by the manifestation of Christ, my fear was removed; and my heavenly Father instructed me in reference to departed spirits, that if they slept in Jesus they would have no desire again to visit this world of sorrow; and if, on the other hand, they had died under the power and dominion of Satan, he would surely retain them safely in his custody, and not allow of their enlargement. I thus was freed from the terror by night, and dwelt secure under the protection of the Almighty.

The place of meeting for the class I was connected with, was two miles distant from the abode, and my way thither lay near two grave-yards; but, thanks be unto God, I had no dread upon my mind as I passed them continually on my way to and return from the class meeting; and I counted this as strong evidence of a great privilege to a heart renewed by divine and omnipotent grace; to God be all the praise! It is to be considered that a two miles journey in the more rural territories of the United States, is very different from the same distance along the streets or well frequented roads of England: across the lonely fields, and through the dark and hazy woods at night, the way is awfully silent and frightfully wild; but these nocturnal walks were to me seasons of sweet communion with my God: I went on my way rejoicing; fervent prayers and heavenly meditation were to me the very elements of life; my meat and drink by day and night. My delights were to follow the leadings and obey the dictates of the Holy Spirit, and glorify with my body and spirit my Father who is in heaven. I enjoyed richly the spirit of adoption: knowing myself to be an adopted child of divine love, I claimed God as my Father, and his Son Jesus as my dear friend, who adhered to me more faithfully in goodness than a brother: and with my blessed Saviour, Redeemer, Intercessor, and Patron, I enjoyed a delightsome heavenly communion, such as the world has never conceived of.

Thus I passed three happy years after my conversion, growing in grace and in the knowledge of God. At the commencement of my religious course, I was deplorably ignorant and dark; but the Lord himself was graciously pleased to become my teacher, instructing me by his Holy Spirit, in the knowledge of the Holy Scriptures. It was not by the aid of human instruments that I was first drawn to Christ; and it was by the Lord alone that I was upheld, confirmed, instructed, sanctified, and directed.

The persons who become members of the Methodist societies in America are first introduced to the class, which they attend for six months on probation; at the expiration of which, if their conduct has been consistent with their professions, they are baptised, and accounted full members of the society. After I had completed my six months probation, I was baptised by the Rev. Joseph Lybrand; and I shall never forget the heavenly impression I felt on that joyfully solemn occasion. Truly the one Spirit of Jesus doth by means of His ministers, baptise us into the one body of Jesus. 1 Cor. xii. 13. When he said, "I baptise thee into the name of the Father, Son, and Holy Ghost, Amen," I was so overwhelmed with the love of God, that self seemed annihilated: I was completely lost and absorbed in the divine fascinations. The Rev. Divine then added, "Be thou faithful unto death, and thou shalt receive a crown of life; and 'Whatsoever thy hand findeth to do, do with all might' [Eccles. 9:10]; for this is the will of God in Christ Jesus concerning you." I was now accounted a full member of the society, and privileged with the communion of the Lord's Supper. In this happy home I continued nearly seven years, and only parted from it when I left my situation.

In the year 1810, I surrendered myself in marriage to Joseph Elaw, a very respectable young man, in the general acceptation of the term, but he was not a Christian,—that is, a sincere and devoted disciple of Christ, though nominally bearing His name. Oh! let me affectionately warn my dear unmarried sisters in Christ, against being thus unequally yoked with unbelievers. In general your lot would be better, if a millstone were hung about your necks, and you were drowned in the depths of the sea, than that you should disobey the law of Jesus [Matt. 18:6], and plunge yourselves into all the sorrows, sins, and anomalies involved in a matrimonial alliance with an unbeliever. This mischief frequently emanates from the delusive sentiments in which the female portion of the Christian community is steeped. Young ladies imagine themselves their own mistresses before they are able to shift for themselves; and especially when they attain the legal maturity fixed by the civil law. Pride, consequential haughtiness, and independent arrogance in females, are the worst vices of humanity, and are denounced in the Scriptures as insuring the severest retributions of God. Isaiah iii. 16–24. The laws of Scripture invest parents with the trust and control of their daughter, until the time, be it early or late in life, when the father surrenders her in marriage to the care and government of a husband; then, and not till then, the guardianship and government of her father over her ceases; and then formed as she is by nature for subordination, she becomes the endowment and is subject to the authority of her husband. The boastful speeches too often vented by young females against either the paternal yoke or the government of a husband, is both indecent and impious—conveying a wanton disrespect to the regulations of Scripture: the fancied independence and self-control in which they indulge, has no foundation either in nature or Scripture, and is prolific with the worst results both to religion and society. That woman is dependant on and subject to man, is the dictate of nature; that the man is not created for the woman, but the woman for the man, is that of Scripture [1 Cor. 11:9]. These principles lie at the foundation of the family and social systems; and their violation is a very immoral and guilty act. These remarks will not, I trust be out of place here. I now observe, in reference to the marriage of a Christian with an unbeliever, that there is not, there cannot be in it, that mutual sympathy and affectionate accordance which exists in the marriage lives of devoted Christians, when both parties are cordially progressing on the king's highway. How discordant are the sentiments, tastes, and feelings of the Christian and unbeliever, when unequally, and I may say, wickedly allied together in the marriage state. The worldly man displays his settled aversion to the things of religion, and especially against the sincerity and tenacity with which his believing partner adheres to them; and on the other hand, the believer displays his settled abhorrence of the things of the world, to which he is crucified and dead: nor can the strength of any carnal attachment betwixt the parties, or the utmost stretch of courtesy on both sides, ever reconcile the radical opposition of their principles. If the saint winks at the worldly course pursued by his partner, he evidences the weakness of Christian principle in himself, is unfaithful to his profession, and perfidious to the King of Kings; if he reproves it, he involves the household in strife, his own soul in vexation, and perils it by wrath. Besides, the wife is destined to be the help-meet of her husband;[7] but if he be a worldly man, she cannot, she dare not be either his instrument or abettor in worldly lusts and sinful pursuits; if he be a saint, and she a child of wrath, she is not his help-meet, but his drawback and curse; and in either case she possesses the title or name of a wife without the qualification, viz. that of a help-meet. By the Jewish law, the marriage of a Jew with a woman of a prohibited nation, was not accounted marriage, but fornication, Ezra x. 11, Hebrews xii. 16;[8] and it is a very serious impropriety also under the Christian dispensation. I am aware that when once the carnal courtship is commenced, the ensnared Christian fondly imagines that he shall soon be able to persuade his unregenerate companion to think as he does, and also to love and serve God with him; and on the other hand, the carnal suitor accounts religion as mere whimsy and pretence, and flatters himself that he shall soon divert the object of his desire from so melancholy and superstitious a pursuit; and thus both of them are miserably deceived, and miss of that happiness they so fallaciously had dreamt of. I am sorry to say, I know something of this by experience. My dear husband had been a member of the society to which I belonged, and had been afterwards disowned by them; but I could not regard him as a backslider from religion, for I am of opinion that he had never tasted of the pardoning love of God through the atonement of Jesus Christ. He made me many promises that he would again unite with the Church, and try to devote his life to the service of God; but they were never fulfilled. After we had been married about a year, he resolved to use every means to induce me to renounce my religion, and abolish my attendance at the meeting-house. It was then that my troubles began, and grew so severe, that I knew not what to do; but that God who is a present help in every time of need was with me still, and enabled me to endure every trial with meekness; and when suffering his keenest chidings for my attendance at the meeting-house, I kept my mouth as with a bridle, and sinned not with my tongue. He was passionately fond of music and dancing, and determined to introduce me to such amusements; thinking that I should be as delighted as himself with the merriments of the world, and hoping thereby to accomplish his object: but that God whom I served night and day, preserved me in the hour of temptation, and shielded me from harm. We resided about twenty miles from Philadelphia, a city of great note in America, and which I had never yet seen. An opportunity at length was presented for us to repair thither; and my dear husband projected my introduction to his favourite resort—the ball-room, on our visit to this great city. We accordingly travelled to Philadelphia; and after we had been there for a few days, we went to take a walk and view the different edifices and parts of the city: he then conducted me into a place which I quickly recognized as a ball-room; for the violin struck up, and the people began to caper the merry dance, and take their fill of pleasure. The tones of the music and the boundings of the people were to me like awful peals of thunder; and all I could do was to weep before God. I often think and say,

> "Where'er I am, where'er I move,
> I meet the object of my love."

Although I was then in a ball-room, I think that I never heard a sermon that preached more impressively to me than the display I witnessed there, in the din and scenery of that vapourish bubble of worldly gaiety and pleasure. Well might the wise man exclaim, "all is vanity and vexation of spirit!"[9]

From the ill success of this wretched experiment, my dear husband found his expectations disappointed, and he never after urged me to accompany him to such places,—to God be all the praise! We soon returned home; and I continued on my course, blessing and praising God for his kind preserving care of me in the perilous hour of temptation.

My husband was a fuller by trade; and when the embargo was laid on British vessels, all traffic ceased betwixt the two nations;[10] the cloth manufacturers in the States enlarged their business very extensively, and the demand for hands was urgent. By this turn of affairs we were induced to remove our place of residence to the city of Burlington, in the state of New Jersey, which was to me a happy removal indeed; and I plainly read the indications of the Lord's goodness in it: for the class assembled at a house but a few doors from mine; the chapel was also near, and I more plentifully enjoyed the means of grace, and grew thereby. Highly did I prize these precious privileges, for I grew in grace daily, and in the knowledge of the truth as it is in Jesus. With cheerful gratitude and paramount peace could I sing these lines—

> "How happy every child of grace,
> Who knows his sins forgiven;
> This earth, he cries, is not my place,
> I seek my rest in Heaven."

I am compelled to omit much interesting and important matter relative to my religious experience and life, and pass to the more strikingly eventful points, lest I should swell these pages beyond my present limited means for the press.

In the year 1817, I attended an American camp-meeting.[11] Oh, how I should like our dear English friends to witness some of our delightful camp-meetings, which are held in the groves of the United States. There many thousands assemble in the open air, and beneath the overspreading bowers, to own and worship our common Lord, the Proprietor of the Universe; there all arise and sing the solemn praises of the King of majesty and glory. It is like heaven descended upon an earthly soil, when all unite to

> "Praise God, from whom all blessings flow."

The hardest hearts are melted into tenderness; the driest eyes overflow with tears, and the loftiest spirits bow down: the Creator's works are gazed upon, and His near presence felt around.

In order to form a camp-meeting, when the place and time of meeting has been extensively published, each family takes its own tent, and all things necessary for lodgings, with seats, provisions and servants; and with waggons and other vehicles repair to the destined spot, which is generally some wildly rural and wooded retreat in the back grounds of the interior: hundreds of families, and thousands of persons, are seen pressing to the place from all quarters; the meeting usually continues for a week or more: a large circular inclosure of brushwood is formed; immediately inside of which the tents are pitched, and the space in the centre is appropriated to the worship of God, the minister's stand being on one side, and generally on a somewhat rising ground. It is a scaffold constructed of boards, and surrounded with a fence of rails.

In the space before the platform, seats are placed sufficient to seat four or five thousand persons; and at night the woods are illuminated; there are generally four large mounds of earth constructed, and on them large piles of pine knots are collected and ignited, which make a wonderful blaze and burn a long time; there are also candles and lamps hung about in the trees, together with a light in every tent, and the minister's stand is brilliantly lighted up; so that the illumination attendant upon a camp-meeting, is a magnificently solemn scene. The worship commences in the morning before sunrise; the watchmen proceed round the inclosure, blowing with trumpets to awaken every inhabitant of this City of the Lord; they then proceed again round the camp, to summon the inmates of every tent to their family devotions; after which they partake of breakfast, and are again summoned by sound of trumpet to public prayer meeting at the altar which is placed in front of the preaching stand. Many precious souls are on these occasions introduced into the liberty of the children of God; at the close of the prayer meeting the grove is teeming with life and activity; the numberless private conferences, the salutations of old friends again meeting in the flesh, the earnest inquiries of sinners, the pressing exhortations of anxious saints, the concourse of pedestrians, the arrival of horses and carriages of all descriptions render the scene portentously interesting and intensely surprising. At ten o'clock, the trumpets sound again to summon the people to public worship; the seats are all speedily filled and as perfect a silence reigns throughout the place as in a Church or Chapel; presently the high praises of God sound melodiously from this consecrated spot, and nothing seems wanting but local elevation to render the place a heaven indeed. It is like God's ancient and holy hill of Zion on her brightest festival days, when the priests conducted the processions of the people to the glorious temple of Jehovah. At the conclusion of the service, the people repair to their tents or other rendezvous to dinner; at the termination of which prayers are offered up, and hymns are sung in the tents, and in the different groups scattered over the ground; and many precious souls enter into the liberty of God's dear children. At two o'clock, a public prayer-meeting commences at the stand, and is continued till three, when the ministers preach again to the people. At six o'clock in the evening, the public services commence again as before; and at the hour of ten, the trumpet is blown as a signal for all to retire to rest; and those who are unprovided with lodgings, leave the ground. On the last morning of the camp-meeting, which is continued for a week, a solemn love feast is held; after which, all the tents are struck and everything put in readiness for departure; the ministers finally form themselves in procession and march round the encampment; the people falling into rank and following them. At length the ministers turn aside from the rank, stand still, and commence singing a solemn farewell hymn; and as the different ranks of the people march by, they shake hands with their pastors, take an affectionate farewell of them, and pass on in procession, until the last or rear rank have taken their adieu. This farewell scene is a most moving and affecting occasion. Hundreds of Christians, dear to each other and beloved in the Spirit, embrace each other for the last time, and part to meet no more, until the morning of the resurrection; and many a stout-hearted sinner has been so shaken to pieces at the pathetic sight, as to fall into deep conviction of his depravity before God, which has ended in genuine repentance and saving conversion to Christ. I, for one, have great reason to thank God for the refreshing seasons of his mighty grace, which have accompanied these great meetings of his saints in the wilderness. It was at one of these meetings that God was pleased to separate my soul unto Himself, to sanctify me as a vessel designed for honour, made meet for the master's use. Whether I was in the body, or whether I was out of the body, on that auspicious day, I cannot say; but this I do know, that at the conclusion of a most powerful sermon delivered by one of the ministers from the platform, and while the congregation were in prayer, I became so overpowered with the presence of God, that I sank down upon the ground, and laid there for a considerable time; and while I was thus prostrate on the earth, my spirit seemed to ascend up into the clear circle of the sun's disc; and, surrounded and engulphed in the glorious effulgence of his rays, I distinctly heard a voice speak unto me, which said, "Now thou art sanctified; and I will show thee what thou must do." I saw no personal appearance while in this stupendous elevation, but I discerned bodies of resplendent light; nor did I appear to be in this world at all, but immensely far above those spreading trees, beneath whose shady and verdant bowers I was then reclined. When I recovered from the trance or ecstasy into which I had fallen, the first thing I observed was, that hundreds of persons were standing around me weeping; and I clearly saw by the light of the Holy Ghost, that my heart and soul were rendered completely spotless—as clean as a sheet of white paper, and I felt as pure as if I had never sinned in all my life; a solemn stillness rested upon my soul:

> "The speechless awe that dares not move,
> And all the silent heaven of love."

Truly I durst not move, because God was so powerfully near to me; for the space of several hours I appeared not to be on earth, but far above all earthy things. I had not at this time offered up public prayer on the camp ground; but when the prayer meeting afterwards commenced, the Lord opened my mouth in public prayer; and while I was thus engaged, it seemed as if I heard my God rustling in the tops of the mulberry-trees. Oh, how precious was this day to my soul! I was after this very frequently requested to present my petitions to the throne of grace in the public meetings at the camp; and to my astonishment, during one of the services, an old gentleman and his wife, whose heads were blanched by the frost of time, came to me, fell upon their knees, and desired me to pray for them, as also many others whom I expect to meet in a happier world:[12] and before the meeting at this camp closed, it was revealed to me by the Holy Spirit, that like another Phoebe,[13] or the matrons of the apostolic societies, I must employ myself in visiting families, and in speaking personally to the members thereof, of the salvation and eternal interests of their souls, visit the sick, and attend upon other of the errands and services of the Lord; which I afterwards cheerfully did, not confining my visits to the poor only, but extending them to the rich also, and even to those who sit in high places in the state; and the Lord was with me in the work to own and bless my labours. Like Enoch,[14] I walked and talked with God: nor did a single cloud intervene betwixt God and my soul for many months after.

But Satan at length succeeded in producing a cloud over my mind, and in damping the delightful ardours of my soul in these blessed labours, by suggesting, that I ought not to make so bold a profession of an entire sanctification and holiness of spirit, lest I should be unable at all times to maintain it; and to this evil suggestion I sinfully acceded, and dilated chiefly in my visits on the goodness of God; and much ceased to enforce that high attainment, and to witness to the indwelling presence and superintending sway of the Holy Spirit in a clean and obedient heart, which I had so powerfully experienced; but alas! I soon proved that to God must be cheerfully ascribed the glory, or he will not vouchsafe to us a continuance of the happy enjoyment.

I write this as a warning to others who may be attacked with the same temptation, that they may be careful not thus to grieve the Holy Spirit of God: but ever remember, that we are witnesses of that gracious passage of Scripture, "This is the will of God, even your sanctification" [1 Thess. 4:3]. "For this the Saviour prayed on behalf of his disciples, 'Sanctify them by thy truth, Thy word is truth'" [John 17:17]: and Peter says, "Ye have purified your souls in obeying the truth through the spirit" [1 Pet. 1:22]: and "As he which hath called you is holy so be ye holy in all manner of conversation" [1 Pet. 1:15]. As therefore, this blessed doctrine is most certainly beloved by us Methodists, it is both our high privilege and bounden duty to manifest it to those around us; and, in default thereof, we shall bring clouds of darkness upon our souls.

I shall here narrate a very extraordinary circumstance which occurred in the family of Mr. Boudinot, one of the richest gentlemen in the city of Burlington. The Lord bade me repair to this gentleman's residence, and deliver a gospel message to him. I was astounded at the idea of going to such a man, to talk to him of the condition of his soul; and began to reason with myself as to the propriety thereof. Satan also suggested that a man of his rank and dignity would not listen to such a poor, ignorant creature as myself. I therefore concluded, that possibly I might be mistaken about this message, and that it might have arisen in my imagination merely, and not have come from God. I accordingly decided in my mind that I would not go to him. But oh! how soon did my heavenly Master show me that I had disobeyed his high commands, given me by the impression of his Spirit upon my heart; for I habitually enjoyed so clear an illumination of the divine presence and glory upon my soul, a conscience so pure, and an eye so single, that the slightest omission would produce the intervention of a cloud and an obscuration of the divine ray upon my spirit; and thus I felt on this occasion, being deprived of the divine ray, and of the peculiar zest and nearness of divine intercourse I had hitherto enjoyed with my heavenly Father. I endeavoured to search out and ascertain the reason, why the lustre of my Father's countenance was obscured upon my soul; for so manifest was the gloom on my spirit, that even my class leader said, "Why, how is this Zilpha, that you appear less lively than you did a week or two since?" yet I still remained ignorant of the cause thereof; but on the next class evening, one of the itinerating ministers presided, and he gave forth the following lines to be sung—

"Jesus, the hindrance show,
Which I have feared to see;
And let me now consent to know,
What keeps me back from Thee."

While singing these lines, I was led to discover that I had not obeyed the call of the Lord, by refusing to go to Mr. Boudinot's, as I had been directed.

"In me is all the bar,
Which God would fain remove;
Remove it; and I shall declare,
That God is only love."

I then laid open my case before my dear minister; and I shall never forget the kind and excellent advice he gave me upon that occasion. I never durst take any important step without first consulting my superiors; and having informed him of the painful exercises of mind I had passed through, and of the disregard I had paid to my heavenly direction, he advised me [the] means, to go whither I had been directed, and no more confer with flesh and blood; but proceed in the course of duty and obedience, leaving the event to God, before whose judgment-seat we shall all stand to give an account of our stewardship. Upon this, I again sought my heavenly Father at the throne of grace, promising that I would go in his name, whither he had sent me, if He would be pleased to restore to me the light of his countenance and Spirit; and He graciously favoured me with the request of my heart.

I then went to the residence of Mr. Elias Boudinot, and had access to all who were in his house; and it was a day for ever to be remembered; for such an outpouring of divine unction took place, as I never witnessed in all my life. All other matters were laid aside but that of religion; and little was to be seen but weeping and mourning. Some of us were occupied in praising the Lord, but most of the household were weeping the penitential tear for their sins. There were company visiting at the house at the time, and when dinner was ready, there were none to come and partake of it; we had quite a search to find, and some trouble to induce them to come to dinner. One lady, who was then on a visit there, had shut herself up in her apartment to read the New Testament; another was shut up in another apartment; one of the servants had locked himself up in the pantry, and there he cried aloud upon God for mercy. It was a day of wonders, indeed! Oh, that so gracious a visitation might come upon thousands of families in England! How sweet is the path of obedience! God will bless while man obeys; "for what his mouth hath said, his own almighty hand will do." I again enjoyed a full measure of the Holy Spirit, and kept that sacred, hallowed fire alive in my soul; to God be all the praise!

I thus attended to my Master's business in this and similar spheres of effort for the space of five years; during which period much good resulted from the attempts of so simple and weak an instrument as myself; because directed by the wisdom, and sustained by the mighty power of God. Five happy years, on the whole, were they indeed to me; notwithstanding that I had many sorrows and grievous trials to endure and contend with.

"Trials must and will befal;
But with humble faith to see,
Love inscribed upon them all,
This is happiness to me."

The bitters of my cup were continually sweetened by the smiles of Jesus; and all things went on easy, because my heavenly Father took the heaviest end of the cross and bore it with me; thus the crooked was made straight, and the rough became smooth.

In 1816, I had a presentiment on my mind of a speedy dissolution; and felt so confident in this expectation, that, when in the class-meeting, I could not forbear from speaking in a strain which implied my speedy departure. My leader inquired if I was about to leave Burlington? Upon which, I opened my mind to him, and the train of my feelings; he made no comment upon it at the time; and in the week following I accidentally met with a severe fall, by which I was so injured internally, as to allow no presage of recovery; my medical attendant pronounced it impossible that I could live, and my friends for many days looked to see me breathe my last; but God ordered it otherwise to every expectation.

While I was thus lying with but one step betwixt me and death, a dear lady, who was a preaching Quakeress, came to see me, and take a last farewell, not expecting to see me again in this life, as she was about taking a religious tour in the country. She affectionately told me she hoped that all would be well with me, and that we should again meet in a better world, though we might meet no more in the flesh. But though my recovery was very gradual indeed, yet it pleased God to raise me up again; and then, with what renewed pleasure did I sit under the sound of the glorious gospel of our Lord and Saviour Jesus Christ, and resume the work of my heavenly Master, going forth in his great name from day to day, and holding sweet converse with my God, as a man converses with his friend. This family or household ministry, as I may call it, was a particular duty, a special calling, which I received from the Lord to discharge for the space of five years; at the expiration of which, it was taken from me, and consigned to another sister in the same class with myself. How wonderful are the works of the Almighty, and his ways past finding out by the children of men! I was often so happy in this work as to be quite unable to contain myself; sometimes I cried out, "Lord, what wilt thou have me do?" for it seemed as if the Lord had yet something more in reserve for me to undertake.

I had at this time but one sister living, who resided in Philadelphia, about twenty miles distant from Burlington; she was the only sister, who with myself arrived at years of maturity; a very pious woman, and she conducted herself very strictly and exemplarily in all her movements: she was so sanctified and devoted a Christian, that some persons have informed me, that they have sat with her in their meetings, and received much edification from beholding the earnest devotedness of mind she manifested in the House of God; thus, "as iron sharpeneth iron, so doth the countenance of a man his friend" [Prov. 27:17].

This dear sister of mine was at length attacked with a mortal disease, and intelligence of her illness was communicated to me. I therefore repaired to Philadelphia; and, on entering the room, I found her so emaciated and altered in appearance, that I scarcely knew her; but in so happy a frame of mind, that the body seemed almost unable to detain so heavenly a spirit. As I stood by her bed-side weeping, she said,

> "I'll take my sister by the hand,
> And lead her to the promised land."

Thus I found her; and after staying with her a few days; thus I left her, and returned home to Burlington. But being pressed with concern for her, I could not long rest at home; I therefore arranged my affairs there, and taking my little daughter with me, set off again for Philadelphia. When I arrived at the house of my brother-in-law, I went directly into the chamber where my sister was lying; and the first thing she said to me was, "My dear sister, I am going to hell." I had not either spoken or sat down in the house; but upon hearing this, I kneeled down and tried to pray; but she instantly exclaimed, "Oh, do not pray, for you will only send me the sooner to judgment!" My astonishment was immense at finding her in such an altered condition of mind; for only a fortnight previously she was exulting in the high praises of God, completely weaned from all things of an earthly nature, and longing to depart to the world of spirits. Many kind brethren and sisters visited her, and prayer was made day and night unto God for her, that her soul might be released from the bonds of darkness; but she remained in this horrible state for nearly a week after my arrival. Some of the ministers bade me not to be discouraged on her account; saying that for they had witnessed others who had been in a similar condition, and had afterwards experienced a most powerful deliverance. I had never before heard of such a case, much less witnessed one; and it was equally as surprising as it was afflictive to me; but the Spirit of God at times whispered in my heart, "Be of good cheer, thou shalt yet see the glory of God." My faith and hope were thereby strengthened; yet the sorrowful sight of my poor dear sister opposing every effort of the friends to pray with and for her, did not a little, at intervals, object and cast me down. Thanks be unto God, the hour at last arrived when he was pleased to burst through the gloom, and set the captive free. A number of the friends had assembled in the house, and we joined in prayer together; after several friends had prayed, in a moment such a spirit of prayer came upon me, as seemed to shake the whole place, as at the memorable apostolic prayer-meeting. Acts v. 31. I immediately commenced praying; and while thus engaged, my dear sister exclaimed aloud, "Look up, children, the Master is coming!" and she shouted, "Glory to God in the highest, and on the earth peace; for I again have found Jesus, the chiefest among ten thousand. Honour and glory, and majesty and power, be given to Him for ever and ever." "Now," said she, "turn me round, and let me die in the arms of Jesus; for I shall soon be with Him in glory." We then turned her over on her other side, as she requested, and awaited the event; she then swooned away, and lay for some time to all appearance dead.

What will infidelity say to this? It surely will not attempt to charge a sincere and godly Christian on her death-bed with hypocrisy; nor can it be consistently attributed to fanaticism. The antagonising conflicts of Christian faith, and its triumphs through the aids of the Holy Spirit over the powers of darkness, as exemplified on such occasions, are very remote from the whimsical vagaries of an over-heated and incoherent imagination; such experience, under certain circumstances, is the natural cause and effect of exercise of Christian faith, in collision with forces asserted by the gospel to be engaged in hostile action to it; and it is a fact worthy of extensive observation, that the vast variety of mental exercises and religious experiences of all true and lively Christians, in every grade of society, in all ages, and in all denominations and sections of the Christian Church, are of too uniform and definite a character to be ascribed to the wild and fluctuating uncertainties of fanaticism: so widely spread an uniformity as that which exists in the genuine pilgrim's progress of Christian experience, can never be philosophically shewn to be an attribute of fanaticism; an uniformity, like that of the human constitution, admitting of the greatest variety of individual features, yet all governed by the same laws; and it may be retorted also, that stubborn facts continually prove, in other countries as well as in modern Gaul, that no fanaticism is more luxuriant, bewitching, and arrogant, than that which inscribes on its ensign—"The Age of Reason," and roots itself in the soil of infidelity.[15]

After my dear sister had laid in a swoon for some time, she revived, and said, amongst other things which I could not remember, "I have overcome the world by the kingdom of heaven;" she then began singing, and appeared to sing several verses; but the language in which she sung was too wonderful for me, and I could not understand it. We all sat or stood around her with great astonishment, for her voice was as clear, musical, and strong, as if nothing had ailed her; and when she had finished her song of praise, (for it was indeed a song of praise, and the place was full of glory,) she addressed herself to me, and informed me, that she had seen Jesus, and had been in the society of angels; and that an angel came to her, and bade her tell Zilpha that she must preach the gospel; and also, that I must go to a lady named Fisher, a Quakeress, and she would tell me further what I should do. It was then betwixt one and two o'clock in the morning, and she wished me to go directly to visit this lady, and also to commence my ministry of preaching, by delivering an address to the people then in the house. I cannot describe my feelings at this juncture; I knew not what to do, nor where to go: and my dear sister was pressingly urgent for me to begin and preach directly; and then to go and see the above-named lady. I was utterly at a loss what to say, or how to move; dear heart, she waited in silence for my commencing, and I stood in silence quite overwhelmed by my feelings. At length, she raised her head up, and said, "Oh, Zilpha! why do you not begin?" I then tried to say something as I stood occupied in mental prayer; but she said, "Oh! do not pray, you must preach." I then addressed a few words to those around me, and she was very much pleased with the attempt: two of the sisters then took me by the arm, and led me into another room; they there informed me they expected to see me sink down upon the floor, and that they thought my sister was perhaps a little delirious. The next day when I was alone with her, she asked me if that hymn which she had sung on the previous night was not beautiful; adding, "Ah, Zilpha! angels gave it me to sing; and I was told that you must be a preacher; and oh! how you hurt me last night by not going where I told you; but as soon as you moved, I was released." She continued in this happy frame of mind until her soul fell asleep in Jesus. The whole of this sick-bed scene, until its termination in death, was as surpassingly wonderful to me, as a Christian, for its depths of religious experience and power, as it was afflictively interesting to me as a relative. I have, however, since learnt that some other Christians have occasionally been known, when in the very arms of death, to break forth and sing with a melodious and heavenly voice, several verses in a language unknown to mortals. A pure language, unalloyed by the fulsome compliment, the hyperbole, the tautology and circumlocution, the insinuation, double meaning and vagueness, the weakness and poverty, the impurity, bombast, and other defects, with which all human languages are clogged, seems to be essential for the associations of glorified spirits and the elevated devotions of heaven, are, doubtless, in use among the holy angels, and seems to be a matter of gracious promise on the part of Jehovah, on behalf of his redeemed people. Zephaniah iii. 9.

I have been very careful, and the more minute in narrating the experience of my dear sister during her illness and death, in hope that it may possibly meet the cases of others tempted in a similar manner; that they may take encouragement from her happy and triumphant end. She had evidently grieved the Holy Spirit in some way or other, and He had withdrawn from her His comforting presence for a time; but He returned to her again with abundant mercy and comforting grace. After receiving a little refreshment, the last words she spoke were, "Now I want a good prayer;" her husband then commenced prayer; and during the exercise, her happy spirit bade adieu to the frailties and sorrows of this mortal life, prepared for, and assured of, her title to a jointure in the ever-blooming glories of the inheritance of the saints in light.

Notwithstanding the plain and pointed declaration of my sister, and though the Scriptures assert that not many wise, rich, and noble are called; but God hath chosen the foolish things of this world to confound the wise, and the weak things of the world to confound the mighty [1 Cor. 1:27], I could not at the time imagine it possible that God should select and appoint so poor and ignorant a creature as myself to be his messenger, to bear the good tidings of the gospel to the children of men. Soon after this, I received a visit from a female who was employed in the work of the ministry, who asked me if I did not think that I was called by the Lord to that work? to which I replied in the negative; she then said, "I think you are; now tell me, do not passages of Scripture often open to thy mind as subjects for public speaking and exposition? Weigh well this matter and see; for I believe that God has provided a great work for thy employment."

But still I could not believe that any such line of duty was enjoined upon me. Though one intimation came after another, and I had warning after warning, to prepare me for and urge me to it, I went on from one degree to another, without seriously and earnestly entertaining the subject; yet I often reflected on that which had been expressed by this kind friend, and especially on what had fallen from the lips of my dear sister Hannah but a short time previously to her death; but I kept these things very reservedly to myself, and pondered them in my heart, as did Mary the mother of Christ. Besides all this, I continually endured such sore trials from my poor unconverted husband, as powerfully operated to deter me from the thought of such an undertaking; but on the other hand, when I had been contemplating the wonderful works of creation, or revelation of the mind and truth of God to man, by the inspiration of his prophets, I have been lost in astonishment at the perception of a voice, which either externally or internally, has spoken to me, and revealed to my understanding many surprising and precious truths. I have often started at having my solitary, contemplative silence thus broken; and looked around me as if with the view of discovering or recognising the ethereal attendant who so kindly ministered to me, Heb. ii. 14; not, indeed, with the slightest alarm, though with much wonder; for I enjoyed so intimate and heavenly an intercourse with God, that I was assured He had sent an angel to instruct me in such of His holy mysteries as were otherwise beyond my comprehension. Such communications were most gratifying and delightful to me; yet I had not sagacity sufficient to discern, that, gifted with such an aid as this, I had a sufficiency from God for the proclamation of his gospel. 2 Cor. iii. 5. Every thing failed to convince me that God had destined me for the ministry; intimation and qualification were alike unheeded by my unbelieving ignorance of the will and ways of God; and thus I continued for several years after my sister's death, unmindful of the allurements as well as the precepts of God.

As all other means had failed to move me to proceed upon my appointed duties, the Lord used other means to move me; for when gentle means do not answer, the rod must be applied to bring us into subjection to our Master's will. In 1819, it pleased God to lay me upon a bed of affliction, with a sickness which, to all appearance, was unto death; an internal inflammation wasted my body, in defiance of all the means and remedies which were resorted to; and I grew worse and worse. The medical gentleman who attended me said, he could do no more for me; he was a very pious Christian, and his visits were very precious to me; for we often held much sweet counsel together about the things of God. Real religion is very seldom to be found amongst the medical profession; but thanks be to God, there are some to be met with, occasionally, who can administer comfort to the soul while relieving the ailments of the body; and thus it was with him.

I had many persons come from far and near to visit me, because God was with me; my soul was preserved in great peace and tranquillity; but, on one occasion, when in conversation with my husband about my death, which seemed to be fast approaching, I could not forbear from weeping, from the thought of leaving behind me, in this evil and stormy life, my poor little girl who was then about seven years of age. It then occurred to my mind, that this natural anxiety which I felt, did not comport with an absolute submission to the will of God; and evinced the inordinate strength and force of those ties by which I was still bound to this earth. I then, in prayer, pledged myself afresh to God, begging that he would effectually wean me from all the excesses of nature's ties; and that my affections and will might be brought into due submission to the will of my heavenly Father. I wrestled in prayer against my insubordinate affections, for about two hours, and the Lord graciously bestowed upon me the victory; and I became so dead to this world, that I felt no anxiety to give any directions as to what should be done for the child after my decease. I was perfectly resigned to the will of God, and willing either to live or die as he thought best; though I could rather have preferred to depart and be with Christ, which is far better. While thus awaiting the divine disposal, my doctor came in one morning, and said, "There is but one thing more that I can try for you, and it is a very severe operation; nor can I say how it will affect you; but if you wish to try it, I will apply it in the name of God;" adding, "that it is our duty to try every means for the restoration of health, leaving the event to God." I therefore consented to submit to the operation, which was, to have my side burnt with caustic, and have an issue inserted therein. I complied, and the thing was done; but it well nigh proved the breaking asunder of the slender thread of life. The kind Quaker lady, who much visited and attended to me during my illness, being unable to witness the operation, was absent from me on that day: when she came on the morrow, I had scarcely power left me sufficiently to recognise her; and my exhaustion was so extreme, that I could not even raise my hand. I was many weeks ere I recovered from this painful operation, and my debility was long protracted; but at times the presence of the Holy Spirit was so powerful within me, that I seemed quite invigorated and strong; and in this illness, I received another striking communication in reference to my future employment in the ministry; it occurred after the renewed dedication of my soul to God as above related. About twelve o'clock one night, when all was hushed to silence, a human figure in appearance, came and stood by my bedside, and addressed these words to me, "Be of good cheer, for thou shalt yet see another camp-meeting; and at that meeting thou shalt know the will of God concerning thee." I then put forth my hand to touch it, and discovered that it was not really a human being, but a supernatural appearance. I was not in the least alarmed, for the room was filled with the glory of God, who had permitted the veil to be removed from my mortal vision, that I might have a glimpse of one of our heavenly attendants,—of one who had a message to deliver to me from God. There are many sceptical persons who conceitedly, rashly, and idly scoff at the idea of apparitions and angelic appearances; but they ignorantly do it in the face of the most extensive experience, instinct, belief, and credible testimony of persons of every nation, and of all ages, as well as the inspired statements of the Scriptures. The universal belief of mankind in the separate existence of the soul after death, is sustained, not by fanciful speculations, but by matters of fact; from facts of this class, this belief derives more substantial support and confirmation than from all the cold deductions of metaphysical ratiocination. Ocular proof is its own demonstration, and commands a far more extensive currency than logical influence. Seldom do the juries of our criminal courts establish their verdicts on evidence equally abundant and express, with that which is furnished by every locality to facts of this description; and the number of such facts in the possession of the present generation of mankind, or even of each hamlet or parish in the world, is astonishingly greater than ever meets the ear of the public, or enters into the conceptions of the headstrong, heroic, and unreasoning sceptic. From that moment I was assured of my ultimate recovery; nor could any human assurances or arguments have persuaded me to the contrary. Soon after this, one of our ministers having heard of my illness, and of the happy frame of my mind, travelled a distance of several miles to see me; he informed me, that he longed to be in such a situation as mine—so near to the gate of heaven. I replied, "Brother, it seemeth to me that I shall yet see another camp-meeting." He then addressed me in a manner that implied, that in his judgment it was quite impossible, and out of the question. But from the very hour in which the kind celestial messenger delivered to me that comforting and assuring announcement, I began to amend; though my recovery was very gradual, and it was a long time ere I was able to sit up. Thanks be unto the Lord, my sickness was not unto death, but for the glory of God. So sturdy had been my unbelief, that my merciful and indulgent God was thereby induced to adopt more severe and extraordinary means to bring me into subjection to his holy will. My spirit and temper were now subdued, and resigned to do the will of God, which I was desirous to ascertain, but my hour was not yet come; I therefore waited patiently until the time when it was to be revealed to me, often, in the mean time, saying, "Lord, what wilt thou have me to do? whatever seemeth good unto Thee, give me the ability, and I will do it."

Eight months had passed away since I had been permitted to attend in the sanctuary of God; but the happy day arrived at last, when I was sufficiently recovered to repair thither again. My kind friends came to assist me to go to the chapel, by supporting me on each side; and I arrived there very comfortably. A minister occupied the pulpit on that occasion, who was unknown to me, and preached on the nocturnal visit of Nicodemus to Jesus [John 7:50]. He spoke with much power, and the glory of God filled the house; the people shouted for joy, and the whole place seemed in motion. Glory for ever! Glory be to God! for his presence was manifested on earth. After an interval of fifteen months from the time when I received the angelic announcement, I heard it published in the meeting, that there was to be a camp-meeting in five weeks from that time. At the moment when I heard the notice proclaimed, I felt a sensation as if I had received a blow on the head, or had sustained an electric shock. So singular a feeling surprised me, and gave rise to much thought; but I could not account for, or explain its cause.

The spot where the camp-meeting was announced to be held, was at a great distance from my home; and as my long indisposition had borne heavily on my earthly resources and entirely exhausted them, I knew not how I should be furnished with sufficient means to undertake such a journey. My poor husband was extremely hostile to religion, and had an extravagant prejudice against camp-meetings; the bare mention of them usually irritated him, excited him to treat me with much bitterness, and urged him to denounce them as pregnant with all manner of evil. However, on my return home, I informed him of the projected camp-meeting, and of my desire to be present at it; and contrary to my expectations, he spoke not a word in reply. I was surprised at this, but I regarded it as springing from the restraining power of that God, who, on one occasion, would not permit even a dog to move his tongue against the children of Israel as they passed by [Exod. 11:7].

I had been ill nearly two years, and was even then unable to help myself; nor had I any apparel suitable for me to go into the grove with; and much clothing was requisite for such an occasion. I knew not therefore what to do; it would have been useless to have applied to my husband for assistance for such a purpose: go without more apparel I could not; I was therefore quite at a stand to know how to proceed. But God took the cause in hand, and made the way plain and pleasant; for my dear old master Mitchel, under whom I had been brought up, had heard a year back that Zilpha was very sick; and though he had received no subsequent intelligence as to whether she lived or died, yet he thought if she was living, she must by this time be in need of some pecuniary assistance; he had been inclined, therefore, to send her a supply of money, but knew not how to effect it from want of opportunity. However, in the month of August, the Society of Friends hold their quarterly meetings in Burlington, New Jersey; and they are in the practice of taking long journeys to attend these meetings; so he encouraged his son and daughter to come over to the meeting at Burlington; desiring them when there, to search after and if possible find out the residence of Zilpha, present his kind love to her, and hand her a donation which he committed to their care. When the quarterly meeting of the Friends came on in our city, to my great astonishment who should come to see me, but William and Achsah

Mitchel, the former companions of my youthful days, with whom I had been reared; and as we [had] not seen each other for several years, it was indeed a happy meeting; and they came to me with presents, as did the wise men who came to the infant Jesus and his mother, and presented them with frankincense and myrrh; to God be all the praise! Then I might have said with Job's friend, "The Almighty has been my defence; and now I have plenty of silver" [Job 22:25]. Being thus supplied, I was enabled to make preparations for going into the mount of God, to hear his holy word; and during all my preparations, my husband, contrary to his usual manner, preserved a perfect silence. Thus all went on easily and calmly, it being the Lord's doing, and it was marvellous in my eyes.

As the time drew near, we ascertained that a considerable number of coloured people were about going thither from our parts; and the members of our class arranged for all of them to sojourn together in one tent.[16] But we were as yet unprovided with one, nor did we know where or how to procure it. My heavenly Father then put it into my heart to go to a friend of mine, and ask for the loan of his tent, and I obtained it at my request without the least hesitation; and thus all things were provided in readiness for the projected journey.

I have been particular in narrating these circumstances, to show the ever-mindful care of God for us; and how he disposes our matters even when we are unable to discern any possible way, or to provide for the exigencies which clog up and embarrass our paths. How remarkable was it that my dear father Mitchel, who had brought me up from my childhood, should, after an absence of ten years, be stirred up in his mind to send me such a timely relief; and the more especially as it was the first favour of the kind that I received from him. Oh! let all the powers within me unite in fervent adoration of the God I love.

At length the auspicious morning arrived for us to proceed on our journey to the holy mount of God; the carriage soon drove up to my door, and I bade farewell to my dear husband. We started off, and it being a delightful day, we had a very pleasant journey, and arrived on the camp ground in the afternoon of the same day. I was very cordially received by the dear friends, and the dear brethren in the ministry joyfully hailed my appearance on the camp ground; and I was promptly handed to a seat to take refreshments after my journey. There were thousands already assembled; but the best of all was, God was there; and much good was accomplished in the name of Jesus. Friday and Saturday were two heavenly days indeed; the mighty power of God was greatly displayed, and His ministers were like a flame of fire; so animated with godly zeal. I never saw so much godly effort and evangelic exertion displayed in all my life as on that occasion. On the Lord's-day morning, the presiding Elder stepped forth in the might of the Holy Spirit, like Joshua, when he went to meet the angelic captain of the Lord's hosts, and said, "Let this day be entirely spent in holiness to the Lord; let no table be spread; but let us abstain as much as possible from food, and see what the Lord will do for us this day; for this is the great day of battle against the old dragon and the powers of darkness." Oh! what a memorable day was this. The public prayer-meeting commenced at seven o'clock in the morning; and at half-past eight o'clock, dear Mr. Potts preached a powerful sermon, under which many souls were awakened to a concern for their eternal interests. At ten, the trumpet sounded again for preaching, and the presiding Elder preached from 2 Cor. v. 20. "Now then we are ambassadors for Christ; as though God did beseech you by us; we pray you in Christ's stead, be ye reconciled to God." When he came to the application of his discourse, there seemed not to be one person on the spot, whose eyes were not suffused with tears; both high and low, rich and poor, white and coloured, were all melted like wax before the fire. In every part of that vast concourse, the number of which was estimated at seven thousands, there were heaving bursts of penitential emotion, with streaming eyes; and the mighty action of the Holy Spirit, and the quickening energy of God was so obvious and exhilirating, that all the sons of God shouted for joy. At the conclusion of this lively and interesting meeting, the people returned to their tents to pray with, and direct and comfort those who were in the distresses of godly sorrow. A number of persons were collected in our tent, who were in great distress, earnestly imploring the mercy of God. We engaged in fervent prayer with and for them; and a great noise being made from the mingling of so many voices, and of such various tones of sorrow and rejoicing, of despair and exultation, of prayer and praise hundreds were attracted to the place, and came round to witness the scene, and ascertain what was going forward. One of the brethren manifested some uneasiness and dissatisfaction at the eagerness with which the people came rushing into our tent; and I said to him, "Oh, never mind, my brother: let them come in and see the wonderful works of God;" and I was in the act of pressing through the crowd to open the back part of the tent, which I was just about to do, when I felt, as it were a hand, touch me on the right shoulder; and a voice said to me, "Go outside of the tent while I speak with thee." I turned myself round to see from whom the voice proceeded; but there were none near me but those of our own company; and not any of them were addressing me. I immediately went outside and stood at the door of the tent; and in an instant I began as it were involuntarily, or from an internal prompting, with a loud voice to exhort the people who yet were remaining near the preacher's stand;[17] and in the presence of a more numerous assemblage of ministers than I had ever seen together before; as if God had called forth witnesses from heaven, and witnesses on earth, ministers and members, to witness on this day to my commission, and the qualifications He bestowed on me to preach his holy Gospel. How appropriate to me was the text which had been preached from just before, "Now, then, we are ambassadors for Christ." Our dear ministers stood gazing and listening with wonder and astonishment; and the tears flowed abundantly down their cheeks while they witnessed the wonderful works of God. After I had finished my exhortation, I sat down and closed my eyes; and there appeared a light shining round about me as well as within me, above the brightness of the sun; and out of that light, the same identical voice which had spoken to me on the bed of sickness many months before, spoke again to me on the camp ground, and said, "Now thou knowest the will of God concerning thee; thou must preach the gospel; and thou must travel far and wide." This is my commission for the work of the ministry, which I received, not from mortal man, but from the voice of an invisible and heavenly personage sent from God. Moreover, this did not occur in the night, when the dozing slumbers and imaginative dreams are prevalent, but at mid-day, between the hours of twelve and two o'clock; and my ministry was commenced in the midst of thousands who were both eye and ear witnesses of the fact. Oh, adorable Trinity! dispose me to do thy holy will in all things. This was my experience on the Lord's day on the camp ground; a day wherein the energies of the Holy Spirit were amazingly exerted, and His presence circulated; and on which, hundreds drank into, and were filled with the Spirit. It was such a day as I never witnessed either before or since. On the Monday came the solemn parting time, of bidding farewell to the brethren and sisters, who were about to proceed to their different stations and places of residence, never to meet again until they meet before the throne of Jesus. Many hundreds of them have doubtless, since then, gone to their final rest; and will sing the praises of their Redeemer in that world of immortality to which we are all hastening; may we then hail their happiness; and with them share the bliss of the blood-bought myriads around the glorious throne in heaven. Having taken our farewell of the dear friends on the camp ground, we started for Burlington; and happily and safely returned home more spiritual and heavenly minded, and stronger in the Lord, than when we came. On my arrival at home, I found all well, and things peaceful and quiet; and for a short time, I went on my way rejoicing.

But Satan, my unwearied adversary, did not suffer me long to remain exempted from conflict and trouble. Soon after my return, I laid my case in reference to my call to the work of the ministry before the ministers; and they greatly encouraged me to proceed, and to preach wherever and whenever opportunities offered. They saw no impropriety in it, and therefore advised me to go on and do all the good I could. I first broached the subject to Mr. John Potts, the beloved brother who preached at the camp-meeting on the morning of the day on which the heavenly commission was delivered unto me; and I obtained the approbation and sanction of all the ministers and of the society. But some of the members of our class soon began to betray a little jealousy, lest I should rise into too great estimation; for a prophet is not without honour, save in his own country [Matt. 13:57]; and they began to discover many faults and imperfections in me; for three years previously there had not been a single jarring string amongst us; and nothing could be done without my opinion being first given; in every thing I suited them exactly, and we were a very loving and happy band; but after I commenced the work of the ministry, I was a person of no account, and ever had been; and I became so unpopular, that all our coloured class abandoned me excepting three. Like Joseph, I was hated for my dreams; and like Paul, none stood with me.[18] This treatment, however painful, by no means damped my ardour in the work to which I had been called. I still continued in my Master's work, and great crowds assembled every Lord's day to hear me: the Lord was with me and strengthened me in my feeble labours; the number of white brethren and sisters who flocked to my ministry increased daily; the work prospered amazingly; and thus I had gone on for two months before my husband knew any thing about it; for he never went to a place of worship. At last the tidings came to his ears, and were tauntingly disclosed by one who said to him, "Josh, your wife is a preacher:" this important announcement he met with a direct negative; but when he returned home, he asked me if it was true; and I informed him that it was. "Well," said he, "I'll come and hear you, if I come barefoot:" at these words my heart leaped for joy; and I indulged in sanguine hopes that he might thereby be converted to God. He came according to his word; and I think that conviction of the sinfulness of his state strongly fastened on his conscience, for he became much troubled in mind: he was also apprehensive that I should become a laughing-stock for the people; and this also grieved him considerably: sometimes he said to me, "Now child, we are undone:" it appeared to him so strange and singular a thing, that I should become a public speaker; and he advised me to decline the work altogether, and proceed no further. I was very sorry to see him so much grieved about it; but my heavenly Father had informed me that he had a great work for me to do; I could not therefore descend down to the counsel of flesh and blood, but adhered faithfully to my commission; and very soon after, all my friends who had forsaken me, returned to me again, for they perceived that God was with me; and many were added to our numbers, whom I hope to meet in the realms of immortality.

My poor husband's health about this time began visibly to decline; and his disorder soon settled into an intractable consumption: the amount of care which now devolved upon me was very great; I was compelled to work very hard to keep my little family and household comfortable in this time of affliction; and it was frequently with great difficulty that I balanced my income and expenditure; but thanks be to God, he opened my way before me, comforted, cheered, and strengthened me, and conducted me through all my difficulties far beyond my expectations: it is true, I diligently used every means in my power, and my exertions were sanctified and blessed by the Lord. The worst feature of this affliction was that my dear husband yet remained a stranger to the precious blood of atonement, and to the Lamb of God who taketh away the sins of the world [John 1:29]. A short time prior to his death, he indicated a better state of mind than formerly: he even confessed the misconduct with which he had behaved towards me; requested my forgiveness, and expressed his hope of meeting me in the better world; he acknowledged that my behavior had ever been irreproachable; and hoped that the Lord would ever sustain me: many other things he uttered of much importance; and his countenance assumed such a calmness and sweetness, that the neighbours who visited him observed the change, and spake of it with great satisfaction. Glory be to God, who doeth all things well; who is too wise to err, too good to be unkind.

"Above the rest this note shall swell,
My Jesus hath done all things well."

The fatal hour came at last when the brittle thread of life snapped asunder, and his spirit fled to an invisible world. This mournful event took place on the 27th day of January, 1823. It was a day never to be forgotten. Although my poor husband had suffered under so protracted an illness, and I had had so much time to prepare for the solemn hour, I found my strength very inadequate to sustain the awful scene; my strength, alas, was perfect weakness; but God was my strong tower and my refuge in the day of distress. Some kind friends came forward, and offered to undertake the interment of the corpse and defray the expenses of his funeral; but as it was the last thing I could do for him, I declined their generous offer, and chose rather to do it myself; and though it involved me in considerable expense, my creditors waited patiently, until by the Lord's blessing I was enabled to pay it all off to the uttermost farthing; to God be all the praise!

After my dear husband was buried, and I had become a little settled, instead of submitting myself in all things to be led by the Spirit, I rather leaned to my own understanding, and procured a situation of servitude for my little girl, and another for myself, judging these the best means I could adopt for the liquidation of my debts; and I remained in service until my health was so impaired that I was compelled to relinquish it; nor did the blessing of my heavenly Father appear to prosper this course; for I was constantly obliged to be under medical treatment, and yet grew worse and worse. I therefore left my situation, and went back to my house, which I had still reserved in case I should want it. I then opened a school, and the Lord blessed the effort, and increased the number of my pupils, so that I soon had a nice little school; many of the [S]ociety of [F]riends came and visited it, and assisted me with books and other necessaries for it. They were also much pleased with the improvement of the children; and when any strangers came to visit Burlington, they introduced them to me; and it was gratifying to many of them to see a female of colour teaching the coloured children, whom the white people refused to admit into their seminaries and who had been suffered formerly to run about the streets for want of a teacher. The pride of a white skin is a bauble of great value with many in some parts of the United States, who readily sacrifice their intelligence to their prejudices, and possess more knowledge than wisdom. The Almighty accounts not the black races of man either in the order of nature or spiritual capacity as inferior to the white; for He bestows his Holy Spirit on, and dwells in them as readily as in persons of whiter complexion: the Ethiopian eunuch was adopted as a son and heir of God; and when Ethiopia shall stretch forth her hands unto him [Ps. 68:31], their submission and worship will be graciously accepted. This prejudice was far less prevalent in that part of the country where I resided in my infancy;

for when a child, I was not prohibited from any school on account of the colour of my skin. Oh! that men would outgrow their nursery prejudices and learn that "God hath made of one blood all the nations of men that dwell upon all the face on the earth." Acts xvii. 26.

But my mind was not long at rest in this situation; for the remembrance of the commission which I had received from the Lord very strongly impressed me; and as the Lord had said, "Thou must preach the gospel, and thou must travel far and wide," so He was about to bring it to pass, but I knew not in what manner. I was not as yet out of debt; and with an empty exchequer, I felt myself but ill adapted to set out on an excursion for preaching the gospel. I was not as yet sufficiently broken in nor bent enough to the discipline of heaven, entirely to live and walk in the Spirit; but projected many schemes and ways for the Lord to act by; yet He did not stoop down to my wretched conceptions, nor avail Himself of my short-sighted plans: for He hath said, "I am God, and besides me there is no Saviour" [Isa. 43:11]. "For as the heavens are higher than the earth, so are my ways higher than your ways, and my thoughts than your thoughts." Isaiah lv. 9. I appointed many opportunities in my own mind, on which to venture on a journey into the country to preach the gospel in far distant places, if the Lord would beforehand furnish me with the necessary supplies for such an undertaking; but I thought it a sin to undertake such a journey while I remained indebted to any man. And here Satan bound me down for two years; at the expiration of which, I possessed no more accumulation of funds than before; and notwithstanding that my school was greatly improved, yet I was hedged up on every side; as it is written. "Cursed is every one that continueth not in all things written in the book of the law to do them" [Gal. 3:10].

I then began to question the reality of my call to the ministry; and endeavored to bring it to the test by laying my heart before the Lord, and solemnly praying to the God of my salvation, that if it were His will for me to go out to preach the gospel, He would give me a token thereof by opening my way before me at the end of three months; and, if otherwise, that He would remove from my mind the weighty impression, which clogged me with care, kept me as a prisoner on parole, and blighted every other prospect in life. I accordingly waited very quietly until the time was nearly expired, watching carefully the signs of the time: but all was still dark; and not only so, I was also attacked with a severe fit of sickness and rendered unable to attend to my school. I then concluded that I had been mistaken, and endeavoured to attribute my past impressions to the zeal of imagination; for I thought, if it had really been the design of God to send me forth to preach His gospel, He would have disposed my affairs so as to open my way, and suitably replenish my purse for the journey; but instead of this being the case, my situation became more and more irksome, and hemmed in with difficulties. Oh! how amazingly difficult is it for the Christian, when decoyed by erratic gleams, or delusive principles, he misses his way, wanders from his proper compass point, and flounders amongst the marshy reeds of worldly principles and proprieties, to detect his error, espy the gospel beacon, and regain his path: thus it was with me; and in prayer I said to my heavenly master, in reference to my ministry, "Now I know that I am mistaken; and I am not going out at all."

I had no sooner uttered these words, than a dreadful and chilling gloom instantaneously fluttered over, and covered my mind; the Spirit of the Lord fled out of my sight, and left me in total darkness—such darkness as was truly felt; so awful a sensation I never felt before or since. I had quenched the Spirit, and became like a tormented demon. I knew not what to do, for I had lost my spiritual enjoyments; my tongue was also silenced, so that I was unable [to] speak to God: and though my congregation continued to meet every Lord's day, I had no power whatever to preach to them. The members of the class inquired why I did not preach to the people? "You see," said they, "how the people flock to hear you, and yet you do not preach to them." This went like a dagger to my heart; for it was evident to all that I had displeased my God, and therefore He had withdrawn His Holy Spirit from me; nor had I any life or power whatever in prayer. I then laid my case before some of the church; but none of them could administer any comfort to me. I also consulted some of the Society of Friends, but they could give me no instructions, because my business was not with mortal man, but with the living God. The anguish of my soul continually increased; every thing went contrary with me, and I fretted and repined, and found fault when there was no occasion, except in myself. I shall never forget the reproof I received from my little daughter on account of the irritability of my temper. She looked at me one day, and said, "Mother, what does ail thee? why, I never saw thee so before; I believe thou art going to be like some of the queer old women." I received this reproof as sent from God, who, I believe, had put it into the mind of the child to utter it; and, from that day, I solemnly pledged myself to the Lord, that if He would again bestow on me the aids of His Holy Spirit, I would go forth in His ministry just as I was, not waiting for any further provision or preparation, but trusting alone in His holy words; and I prayed that He would enable me again to preach to my people in Burlington; and that on such and such day of the month, I would obey His holy commands, whatever might become of me. The Lord accepted of my proposition; and on the next Lord's day, my tongue was set at liberty, and my heart was enlarged; and I was enabled to preach with more fluency and copiousness than ever before. I then informed my audience, that I must leave them, and go out into the vineyard of the Lord; and announced to them on what day I should preach my farewell address to them. It was a Bochim [Judg. 2:5], a day of weeping indeed with them, but they said, "the will of the Lord be done."

I had been under this dark cloud for more than three weeks; and the time appeared to me more than three months; but it now retired, and my captivity vanished. Heaven again opened to my eyes and ears, because I was at last led to discern the path of obedience, and hearken to the counsel of the Almighty, saying, "This is the way; walk ye in it." The chastisement of God is often more profitable than His indulgence would be; His correction is kindness, and His severity mercy.

My peace again flowed as a river on a calm summer's day; and I began to draw my school to a close. About three weeks prior to the time appointed for the dismission of my scholars, some friends who resided in the direction my mind was disposed to take, and with whom I had been previously acquainted, came to Burlington; and they, together with some of my dear people thought it advisable for me to accompany them on their return; but I saw no possibility of doing this, because they were about to take their departure before I could arrange my affairs, and receive the accounts due to me at the end of the current quarter. I therefore informed my kind friend that I should not be ready to go with him; but he insisted upon it, and enforced it with many arguments. I replied, "It is utterly impossible for me to be ready to go with you;" at which he seemed somewhat offended; and his wife then said, "Why, Zilpha, if thou feelest that thou art bound to go, and if it is thy wish to go, and if thou canst not get ready at this time, never mind, go as soon as thou canst, and thou wilt get along somehow, and thou wilt hardly understand how; if thou art sent, He that sends thee will take care of thee." This filled my heart with tenderness, and my eyes with tears, and I replied, "Oh, neighbour Hull, this is a word of consolation indeed now I will return home and weep before the Lord, and all will be well." I returned home, and my little daughter seeing the tears flowing down my cheeks, said to me, "Now, mother, what is the matter?" for she was aware of the great anxiety of mind I had so long been labouring under, and said all she could to comfort me; and added, "If I were you, I should not mind what any person said, but I should go just as I had arranged to go, and do not think any thing about me, for I shall do very well." By this time my scholars had gathered, and the school business commenced; and for the Bible class, the lesson was in the Psalms; one of the little boys commenced the 125th Psalm, which begins thus, "They that trust in the Lord shall be as Mount Zion, which cannot be removed, but abideth for ever." While the psalm was being read, it seemed as if I had never seen it before; but the Almighty had sent it as a special message from heaven to me; those words so filled my heart, that all my tears were dried away and I could only exclaim, "Glory be to God!" My soul rejoiced in God my Saviour, yea, the God of my salvation. No more foreboding fears assailed me; every circumstance readily converged to its proper point, and all things were prepared exactly to the appointed hour. I took my little girl, and placed her under the care of a dear relative of mine, and proceeded on my way to the City of Philadelphia, commenced my Master's business, and strange to relate, when I arrived in that large city, every one appeared to be acquainted with my situation. I preached in a great many chapels, and every congregation voluntarily made a collection for my aid; and every person at whose house I visited, gave me something for my journey. Oh! how astonishing was this to me. I had been for several years striving to provide myself with necessary supplies for my Master's work, and without success; nor did I ever think of obtaining any money in my travels. It never occurred to me that I should receive a single penny in this work; but when I was willing, I ought to say—made willing to go just as I was, as the apostles of old, without purse or scrip, then the Lord made my way straight before me, and dealt bountifully with me; then was that blessed promise verified, "Seek ye the kingdom of God, and His righteousness, and all other things shall be added unto you" [Matt. 6:33]. In the first three weeks I obtained every particle that I wanted, and abundance of silver to proceed on my journey with. Oh! what mercy and what goodness was manifested to such a poor, unbelieving, weak, and unworthy instrument as me. How often have I said, "Lord! send by whom thou wilt send, only send not by me; for thou knowest that I am ignorant: how can I be a mouth for God!—a poor, coloured female: and thou knowest we have many things to endure which others do not." But the answer was, "What is that to thee? follow thou me."

Thus I left my child and ventured on my journey, not knowing whither I should go. From Philadelphia I started for New York; and on my journey passed within three hundred yards of my own home, yet did not call there, but pursued my journey and arrived in New York; and there the Lord rendered my ministry a blessing to many precious souls—glory be to His name. I was absent from home seven months; and when I returned I was able to meet my creditors and pay my debts, which was an unspeakable indulgence. Hallelujah. Praise the Lord.

I returned home in April, 1828, and remained there a few days. During my stay at home, I was one day exercised with devout contemplations of God, and suddenly the Spirit came upon me, and a voice addressed me, saying, "Be of good cheer, and be faithful; I will yet bring thee to England and thou shalt see London, that great city, and declare my name there." I looked round to ascertain from whence and from whom the voice proceeded, but no person was near me; my surprise was so great that my very blood seemed to stagnate and chill in my veins: it was evidently the Spirit of the Lord whose I am, and whom I serve, who had spoken to me; and my soul responded to His word, saying, "The will of the Lord be done in and by me on earth, as it is by His servants in Heaven." My mind was at this time very much perplexed as to what was the will of God concerning me: I was in doubt as to what I ought to do; but, after a few days, I took my journey again to Philadelphia, with the intention of visiting the southern or slave-holding states of America; here I saw my dear daughter, and remained with my friends during some few weeks; but the confusion of my mind still continued, and whenever I opened a Bible, wherever I visited, as well as at my apartments, the book of the prophet Jonah was perpetually presented before me. I mentioned to my friends the uncertainty of my mind as to what the Lord required me to do, the propriety of a voyage to England, and my repeatedly opening in the Bible at the book of Jonah; and they assured me that if it was God's will that I should then visit England, He would make it appear, and smooth the way for me in His own good time. I therefore rested upon this assurance; and while I yet abode in Philadelphia, I dreamed one night, that I saw two ships cleared out of the docks there, bound for England, and I was not on board either of them. I then concluded that the time for my journey to England had not yet come; and being now satisfied on this matter, I started off for the southern territories of the United States, where slavery is established and enforced by law. When I arrived in the slave states, Satan much worried and distressed my soul with the fear of being arrested and sold for a slave, which their laws would have warranted, on account of my complexion and features.[19] On one occasion, in particular, I had been preaching to a coloured congregation, and had exhorted them impressively to [ac]quit themselves as men approved of God, and to maintain and witness a good profession of their faith before the world, &c. I had no sooner sat down, than Satan suggested to me with such force, that the slave-holders would speedily capture me, as filled me with fear and terror. I was then in a small town in one of the slave states; and the news of a coloured female preaching to the slaves had already been spread widely throughout the neighbourhood; the novelty of the thing had produced an immense excitement and the people were collecting from every quarter, to gaze at the unexampled prodigy of a coloured female preacher. I was sitting in a very conspicuous situation near the door, and I observed, with very painful emotions, the crowd outside, pointing with their fingers at me, and saying, "that's her," "that's her;" for Satan strongly set before me the prospect of an immediate arrest and consignment by sale to some slave owner. Being very much alarmed, I removed from my seat to a retired part of the room, where, becoming more collected, I inquired within myself, "from whence cometh all this fear?" My faith then rallied and my confidence in the Lord returned, and I said, "get thee behind me Satan, for my Jesus hath made me free." My fears instantly forsook me, and I vacated my retired corner, and came forth before all the people again; and the presence and power of the Lord became greatly manifested in the assembly during the remainder of the service. At the earnest request of the friends, I consented to preach there again on the following Lord's-day morning, which I accordingly did. Some of the white brethren in connexion with the Methodist Society were present on that occasion; at the conclusion thereof, they introduced themselves to me, and wished me to preach for them in the afternoon; to which I agreed; and they obtained permission of the authorities to open and use the courthouse; and therein I obtained a very large auditory; and God gave forth proofs that my ministry was from Him, in giving me many seals to it on that day; thus was I relieved from my fearful forebodings, and pursued my course with increased energy, rejoicing in the prosperity and success with which the Almighty crowned my efforts.

After this, I visited Baltimore in the State of Maryland and attended a conference of the coloured brethren, by whom I was very kindly received; a large field of labour was provided, and a great and effectual door of utterance opened to me by the Lord. After labouring there for some weeks, I proceeded to the City of Washington, the capital of the United States, and the seat of government: here also I laboured with much success; many souls obtaining the knowledge of salvation by the remission of their sins, with the gift of the Holy Spirit, through the instrumentality of so feeble an earthen vessel. I continued my travels southward into the State of Virginia, and arrived at the City of Alexandria, where the Lord rendered my labours effectual to the conversion of many from darkness to light, and from the power of Satan unto God. I abode there two months, and was an humble agent, in the Lord's hand, of arousing many of His heritage to a great revival; and the weakness and incompetency of the poor coloured female but the more displayed the excellency of the power to be of God. There were some among the great folks whom curiosity induced to attend my ministry; and this formed a topic of lively interest with many of the slave holders, who thought it surpassingly strange that a person (and a female) belonging to the same family stock with their poor debased, uneducated, coloured slaves, should come into their territories and teach the enlightened proprietors the knowledge of God; and more strange still was it to some others, when in the spirit and power of Christ, that female drew the portraits of their characters, made manifest the secrets of their hearts, and told them all things that ever they did.[20] This was a paradox to them indeed: for they were not deficient of pastors and reverend divines, who possessed all the advantages of talents, learning, respectability and worldly influence, to aid their religious efforts; and yet the power of truth and of God was never so manifest in any of their agencies, as with the dark coloured female stranger, who had come from afar to minister amongst them. But God hath chosen the weak things of the world to confound the mighty. Divine goodness raised me and honoured me as an angel of God; yet my bodily presence continued weak; the passions, frailties and imperfections of humanity abounded in my own consciousness; the union of such meanness and honour rendered me a riddle to myself. I became such a prodigy to this people, that I was watched wherever I went; and if I went out to tea with any of the friends, the people would flock around the house where I was; and as soon as they judged that the repast was finished, they came in and filled the house, and required me to minister to them the word of life, whether I had previously intended to preach or not. The people became increasingly earnest in their inquiries after truth; and great was the number of those who were translated out of the empire of darkness into the Kingdom of God's dear Son.

At this place, resided a gentleman named Abijah Janney, belonging to the [S]ociety of [F]riends, at whose house I spent many delightful hours.[21] One day he requested to speak with me alone; and having accompanied him to another apartment, when we were seated, he said to me, "Now Zilpha, I perceive that thy visit to this place will be attended with much good, if thy deportment amongst the whites and especially amongst the slaves, be prudently conducted, for there seemeth in reference to the great topics of thy ministry to be much interest felt by the people generally." This was a well-timed and salutary caution, and most prudent advice to me, situated as I was in connexion with two distinct communities, so opposite in condition, so contrasted in intelligence, and so antipodal in their feelings and prejudices. These words at such a time were to me as apples of gold in pictures of silver.

During my continuance in this city, I had a very severe attack of the fever which is endemial in that climate; but I was attended by a physician of first rate eminence, and by several most kind and anxious nurses; and the Lord was pleased speedily to raise me up again; most kind and affectionate were this people to me: before I was able to sit up an hour, Mr. Janney sent his carriage morning and evening to take me out, that I might be benefited by the refreshing breezes, and be regaled by the sweet zephyrs which gently fan over the verdant plains of that genial clime. It was the Lord's doing; and to him be all the praise.

On my recovery, I again resumed my Divine Master's work; and going to my physician to discharge his demands for his skilful care and kind attendance upon me during my illness, he refused to receive any remuneration, assuring me, the reflection that he had been instrumental, through the blessing of God, of contributing towards my recovery, afforded him much pleasure; that it was his desire his past services to me should be free of cost; and expressed his hope that I might long be spared to do the will and work of the Lord.

Although I had been sick and laid aside for a time, I lost nothing, except the dross of earthly affections: it was merely a furnace, in which my heavenly father saw the necessity of my being placed for a time; and I believe that I was thereby weaned still more from the world, separated to my God and purified in holiness. The Methodist preacher at that station, Mr. J. Gess, behaved to me with very great kindness; he much promoted my labours in that neighbourhood, and I proceeded throughout the vicinity of Alexandria, preaching the gospel with the happiest results. On one occasion, I took an excursion with some ladies, a few miles into the country, to preach at a distant farmhouse occupied by a Mr. Marifield; and as is usual with the farmers there to keep very savage dogs for the protection of their premises, this gentleman had three of those animals; very fierce and ferocious creatures, which met us at the door; but, as the family were present, without giving us any molestation; yet as the people soon came flocking to the meeting, the inmates were concerned on account of the ferocity of the dogs, and tried to fasten them up, but could not succeed; but God restrained the savage beasts and they were very quiet, though the assemblage was so large, that we were compelled to resort to the orchard, and hold our meeting beneath the spreading apple trees. When I took my position, the three dogs came and laid down, one on each side, and the other behind me; and there they remained till the conclusion of the service; and as the people shook hands with me and bade me adieu, they rose, wagged their heads, and brushed me as if to welcome my visit there. It was a most interesting and profitable season; and the presence and power of God were greatly manifested; there were several youth in attendance, who were reputed to be very wild and giddy, but they appeared to be struck with awe at the religious fervour manifested, and conducted themselves with reverence and solemnity.

I had also another engagement, arranged by some friends, for me to go into another part of the county, about twelve miles distant, and preach in the grove; but I was prevented by heavy rains from fulfilling it for three Lord's days successively: at length, the weather becoming more favourable, I was published to preach there on the following Lord's day: as the time drew near, I was in much perplexity through inability to fix on any passage of Scripture as a text to preach from, or rather, because the Lord had not as yet presented a passage to my mind or fastened one upon my spirit; but as I was speaking to the dear friend at whose house I was then visiting, of the dilemma I was in, the following passage powerfully flashed upon my mind, "Set thine house in order, for thou shalt die and not live" [2 Kings 20:1]. In meditating upon this passage, my soul was barren. I was oppressed by a complete dearth of suitable ideas, and unable to obtain any spiritual opening or discernment of this text; I then foolishly endeavoured to abandon it; and as if I possessed the right of self direction, or liberty to select what messages I pleased, searched the Scriptures for another text; but to no purpose; for every other was sealed up from me, though I continued my search until twelve o'clock on the Saturday night, and resumed it in the morning at the dawning of light; but I learned that when the Lord impresses a text on the minds of His servants, that He will not be tempted by our solicitations to have another one substituted. Having such a distance to go, we started off at nine o'clock in the morning; and I went as reluctantly as a criminal goes to the bar: as we approached within a few miles of the selected spot, we observed the people from every direction over the face of the country repairing thither; which rendered the distress of my mind the more poignant. It is a weighty matter for a well-furnished preacher to address a numerous auditory in the name of the Lord of Hosts; but to go as I then did, destitute of a topic whereon to preach, was a mental affliction indeed. When we arrived at the place, it was already like a camp-meeting; the platform was erected, hundreds of persons assembled, and all things in readiness. I directly ascended the stand, and read forth a hymn, which was sang by the congregation, offered up prayer, and gave out another hymn. Whilst the congregation were singing, I was anxiously searching for a text to preach from; but no other could I find than that which had been given me. When, therefore, the singing was finished, I arose and read the passage before referred to, which I had no sooner done, than my mind took a comprehensive grasp of the subject; a region of truths were unfolded to my view, such as I had never previously conceived of; and it occupied me an hour and a half to exhaust the fund of sentimental treasure, which the Divine spirit poured into my mind. It was, indeed, a time of refreshing from the presence of the Lord.

At the conclusion of my discourse, I inquired if there were any ministers present; intimating, that if this was the case, an opportunity was offered them of further addressing the audience; and a minister being present from George Town, who had arranged to preach a funeral sermon at a neighbouring spot, and the relatives of the deceased being all present, it was agreed that he should preach it there from the platform; and it constituted an appropriate sequel to my sermon; we enjoyed quite an heavenly day in the grove, and returned home in the evening in peace.

Among the number of persons who were introduced into the fold of our God, in the city of Alexandria, was Miss Butts, a young lady who found peace with God through our Lord Jesus Christ, and manifested remarkable piety. In the correspondence with which she subsequently favoured me, she indicated an affectionate desire to see me again in the flesh; and assured me of the happiness and freedom she enjoyed in the service of the Lord. The work of the Holy Spirit was greatly manifested in this city; both high and low, rich and poor, white and coloured, all drank out of the living streams which flowed from the City of our God. Every day brought me tidings of souls newly born of God. Even the angels in heaven rejoice over the repenting sinner, and much more should the redeemed on earth! Oh, the depth both of the riches and knowledge of God! How unsearchable are His judgments, and His ways past finding out! [Rom 11:33]

Before I took my leave of this city, Lady Hunter, the wife of Major Hunter, came to Alexandria; being a member of the Methodist Society, she invited me to spend a few days at her house, and preach on the Lord's day. I accepted the invitation, and enjoyed my visit greatly. The Major was not a religious man; and as the ministers frequently visited his Lady, he was in the habit of attacking them with controversial cavils against their faith. As he displayed but little respect to persons, when he came home from the city, accompanied by several other gentlemen, the Bible was produced, the family summoned to evening prayers, and I was required to officiate as chaplain. As I prayed, read, and commented upon the Scriptures he mustered his interrogatories, and produced his objections. I had no more desire for a mental collision than ambition for or prospect of a triumph in a contest for intellectual pre-eminence with such an antagonist; but as He who sent me, helped my infirmities, and was ever ready to succour me, I was enabled to reply to all his questions and quibbles, and maintain the truth. Indeed, he appeared highly gratified that my answers were such as in no way put the cause of religion to the blush before his friends, who had been introduced for the purpose of testing my poor feminine abilities. The Lord directed his servants on such emergencies, to take no thought or premeditation for the framing of their speech; and promised them a suitable inspiration of his Holy Spirit; and he richly assisted me on this occasion; to Him, therefore, be all the renown!

Taking my departure, amidst the regrets of many, from Alexandria, I returned to Washington; my visits were very numerous there among the people; and my company was desired by many of the great folks, even by the friends and associates of the President of the United States. Some religious gentlemen, friendly to the cause of missions, proposed for me to go out to Africa, and labour among the native tribes; but I declined their proposal; telling them, my heavenly Father had given me no such direction; and I dared not go thither unless sent by his Divine Majesty; but if God had required me to go thither, I should not have ventured on a refusal: they therefore urged this matter no further. I was continually visited by ladies from all parts of the city and its vicinity; many of them informed me they had heard their friends relate, with most lively interest, the astonishing wonders of divine grace and power, which had attended our meetings in the groves; and what seasons of refreshing and spiritual edification they had experienced at those meetings. When on a visit at the residence of General Van Esse, I was invited by Lady Lee, the wife of General Lee,[22] to a visit at her residence; and to preach at a chapel the ladies had erected at Green-leaf point, for the use of the missionaries who came thither. On the day appointed, her carriage came for me, and I went accordingly: after tea, a great number of her friends met there, who were going to the meeting; and among them was Commodore Ro[d]gers and his Lady,[23] with many others who came from a distance. When the time came, Mrs. Lee and myself went on first; and she took the opportunity to caution me against the supposition that the bulk of those ladies and gentlemen were religious persons; assuring me they were merely coming from motives of curiosity to hear what I might say, and witness my performance. If I had gone confiding in my own poor abilities, this information would, doubtless, have utterly disconcerted me; but I depended on the faithful promise of my Master, that he will be with me even unto the end; nor was I disappointed. A large congregation assembled, composed of persons of all grades of society. I commenced the service by reading a portion of the Scriptures; when I gave forth my hymn, the ladies assisted to sing it, and the service was thus far sustained with propriety. I based my discourse on the Gospel of St. John v. 25. The Lord was pleased to give efficacy to the word of His grace, and to apply it with saving power to the mind of Lady Ro[d]gers. I perceived in the course of my sermon, that she was greatly interested and powerfully affected by it: indeed a mighty religious awe and solemnity rested upon the entire assembly. During the service, and for several days afterwards, the spiritual welfare of Mrs. Ro[d]gers was a theme, which, as it were, involuntarily occupied a very prominent interest in my mind; and I felt strongly assured that the Lord would endow her with the rich blessings of his salvation. In a few days after, I proceeded on my travels, and heard nothing further of the results of this meeting.

My next visit was to Baltimore, and from thence I went to Annapolis, where I continued during a great part of the winter. Here, also, the Lord gave forth to the people His gracious attestations that my ministry was from Him; for my speech and my preaching were not with enticing words of man's wisdom, but in demonstration of the Spirit, and in power: it was mighty through God, to the pulling down of strongholds; and became the power of God to the salvation of many. On one Lord's-day evening in this place, I was led by the Spirit to discourse very impressively on mortality and death; so much so, that my sermon might have been well suited to a funereal occasion; I was succeeded in the pulpit by a local preacher, a coloured brother and a slave; this poor brother seemed to manifest an undue anxiety for his freedom. Certainly, freedom is preferable to bondage, as saith the apostle Paul, 1 Cor. vii. 21; who bade the Christian brethren in bondage to be unconcerned about it, unless an opportunity arrived of their attaining freedom; in which case, they were to avail themselves thereof. This poor brother in bonds, however, was very impatient of slavery, and anxiously sighed for liberty. Alas! his life and spirit, his body, his bones, and his blood, as respects this life, were legally the property of, and at the disposal of his fellow man. But his sighs were heard in heaven by Him who looseth the prisoners, and the time of his release arrived. In that same week he was taken ill, and finally fell asleep in Jesus, departing to be "where the wicked cease from troubling, and the weary are at rest. There the prisoners rest together; they hear not the voice of the oppressor; the small and great are there, and the servant is free from his master." Job iii. 17–19. His interment was a remarkably afflictive occasion: his corpse was brought into the chapel during the time of service, and the wailings of the congregation grew so intense, that the officiating minister was unable to proceed with the service. The suddenness of the stroke was surprising; and the loss of their beloved minister appeared to his sorrowful flock more like a dream than a fact. Oh, the abominations of slavery! though Philemon be the proprietor, and Onesimus the slave,[24] yet every case of slavery, however lenient its inflictions and mitigated its atrocities, indicates an oppressor, the oppressed, and the oppression. Slavery in every case, save those of parental government, criminal punishment, or the self-protecting detentions of justifiable war, if such can happen, involves a wrong, the deepest in wickedness of any included within the range of the second table.[25]

In the Slave States of America the law sanctions the arrest of any person of colour, within their territories; and unless such person can produce the most unexceptionable papers in proof of his freedom, the legal officers may sell him on behalf of the State, into perpetual captivity. Blessed for ever be the Lord, who sent me out to preach his gospel even in these regions of wickedness, He preserved me in my going out and my coming in; so that the production of the documents of my freedom was not once demanded during my sojourn on the soil of slavery. While staying at Annapolis, I was engaged to preach at a place some miles distant in the country, and while proceeding thither in a one horse chaise, we were obliged to cross a river and were about to get into the ferry-boat, together with our horse and chaise, when the horse fell down and put us in danger of drowning; but by the dexterity of the men who assisted us, and the blessing of God, we safely landed on the other side, still further in the interior of the Slave States. On another occasion, I went from Annapolis to preach on the Lord's-day at another station in the country. Many hundreds were collected together, to whom I preached from these words, "Behold the Bridegroom cometh; go ye out to meet him" [Matt. 25:6]. An elderly gentleman sat in a very conspicuous seat just before me, greatly agitated; the restraint of his emotions was evidently a matter of great difficulty, for his soul had deeply adopted the prayer of the publican, "God be merciful to me a sinner" [Luke 18:13]. When I retired from the pulpit the people rushed eagerly forward to salute me; they appeared to be quite overpowered by their penitential feelings, and in an agony of self-abasement. The multitude of repenting sinners on that occasion doubtless exhilirated many an angel-mind, and caused heaven itself to thrill with joy. That my mission was from God was manifest to them by His communication of the Holy Spirit, through my ministry, to those who received my testimony; the power of the Lord was present, indeed, to pull down some of the strongholds of Satan, and to set up Christ in the hearts of the people. On my return to Annapolis, I was thrown out of my chaise and so much injured that I was unable to preach in the evening, in the city. I was very ill in consequence for some time, but the Lord raised me up again and restored me to health. On my recovery I resumed my work; and being on a visit at the house of one of our ministers, I heard tidings of Lady Ro[d]gers of Washington, through the medium of a minister who had recently been there. Being on a visit to Commodore Ro[d]gers, the latter inquired if he knew anything of the preaching woman, adding, that he hoped God would bless every lane of her life; for that his wife was become a very pious woman through attending a meeting held by her, at Green-leaf's point; and further, if she would come and reside in that neighbourhood, he would make a suitable provision for her subsistence. A gentleman residing in the city of Annapolis, offered to give me a house and a plot of ground on condition of my residing there; but it was not meet for me to depart from my Master's work, from considerations of worldly interest. I dared not, like Demas, forsake my itinerating ministry, to love this present world:[26] nor was filthy lucre the object I had in view in the service of the gospel. The cheerful liberality of grateful affection is one of the evidences of sincere discipleship to Jesus; but the love of mammon has no place in the hearts of his true ministers, who love the flock rather than the fleece.

Before I left Annapolis a gentleman, named Watson, residing in the city, one of the local preachers, earnestly desired me to accompany him to Mount Tabor, about ten miles distant, and preach for him in his appointment; I had no desire for this journey on account of my remaining weakness, and the severity of the season, it being winter: but as he would take no denial, coming repeatedly to solicit my compliance, I reluctantly consented, and a dreary journey we had; the cold being intensely rigorous, the roads bad, and travelling dangerous. On our arrival I found that the people had not been apprised of my coming, but Mr. Watson ascended the pulpit and introduced me to the audience; he then retired and I occupied his place, very much to the astonishment of the people. A young man was present who behaved very indecorously, and as the people came in he pointed with his finger to me, tittering and laughing. Poor young man; before that meeting was terminated, his laughter was turned to weeping. This place was on that day a Mount Tabor indeed, not celebrated by the visit of Moses, but blest with the presence of Christ.[27] After the service the brethren requested me to preach for them again on the 25th day of December, commonly called Christmas day; but Mr. Watson thought it best to decline another journey in so inclement a season; it was therefore arranged that I should abide at the house of Mr. Beard, one of the trustees of the chapel, till after the 25th instant; and I accordingly returned with him and his family to their house to dinner. At this place I was still further in the interior of the Slave States, and now left without an earthly protector. During the dinner time, the young man above referred to formed the topic of conversation. It appears that he was a slave-driver, accounted the most profligate drunkard in that vicinity, and habituated to every vice; and it was remarked that he had never been previously known to evince so much serious attention to a sermon as he had paid to my discourse, in the morning: and that his kneeling during the concluding prayer was a matter of surprise to them; however, my mind was greatly moved with evangelic interest for this young man: and, like Paul for the Galatians, I travailed in birth for him [Gal. 4:19].

On the appointed morning of the 25th instant, I said to one of Mr. Beard's sons, who was a member of the society, "Now, brother, let us go to meeting, having our swords sharpened, and who knows but God will give us this young man?" "Oh!" he replied, "he is far enough off from here by this time, and has swallowed many bowls of drink ere now." On hearing this, I gave up all expectation of seeing him; but when we entered the chapel, to my great surprise he was there, clothed, and in his right mind. I preached that morning from Luke ii.10; and, under the sermon, every heart was melted, nor was one person to be found in the entire assembly, whose eyes were not suffused with tears. The gallery of the chapel was occupied by the slaves, and the body of the building with proprietors; and all were alike affected. Mr. Beard requested the congregation to restrain the expression of their feelings; but the powerful operation of the Holy Spirit disdained the limits prescribed by man's reason, and bore down all the guards of human propriety and order. The presence of the Holy Ghost filled the place, and moved the people as the wind moves the forest boughs. Mr. Beard's cautions were unavailing; the coloured people in the gallery wept aloud and raised vehement cries to heaven; the people below were also unable to restrain their emotions; and all wept beneath the inspirations of the Spirit of grace. I was obliged to stop in my discourse, and give vent to my own feelings, and leave it to God to preach in His own more effectual way. Oh, what a memorable day was this! Saints and angels poured their little current of holy and benevolent sympathies into the volume of mercy, love, and grace, which streamed from the compassions of the Infinite Eternal into our little earthly sanctuary, to staunch the bleeding heart, remove its guilt, reform its character, and give new impulse to its powers. At the conclusion of the service, several of the gentlemen present collected a sum of money amongst themselves, which they presented to me, with great expressions of gratitude for the faithful and warning discourse I had preached to them in reference to their spiritual interests; the brethren, also, cordially invited me to come again, offering me the use of the chapel whenever I thought fit to come and occupy it: they wished me God's speed, and we took our farewell of each other, probably to meet no more until the gospel dispensation and its ministry is closed for ever.

I then returned to Annapolis, and received the kind welcome of my dear friends there; and from thence I proceeded on my journey homeward, through Baltimore and Philadelphia, to Burlington; and thus closed with me the year 1829, amid scenes of usefulness and godly revivals and conversions to Christ, the memory of which will be cherished with the most lively interest by thousands of persons.

I will mention, in this place, that many months after my visit to Mount Tabor, I received a letter from the young man whose conversion is above narrated; in which he earnestly desired me to come and visit them again, offering to defray all the expenses of the journey; but the Lord had directed my steps in another direction and kept my conscience tender and fearful of offending Him; so that I durst not step aside from the path of His guidance for any private interest, personal gratification, or earthly gain. Whatever of sorrow or difficulty I met with in the paths of the Lord, I was enabled to sustain, and cheerfully to bear the cross after my loving Lord and Master; but the privilege of self-direction the Lord did not permit so ignorant and incompetent a servant as I was, to exercise. It was one of the crying provocations of ancient Israel, that "they did every man that which seemed right in the sight of his own eyes" [Deut. 12:8], and "walked after the imagination of their own hearts" [Deut. 29:19]. May I ever be preserved to "trust in the Lord with all my heart, and not lean to my own understanding" [Prov. 3:5]. Lord! ever teach me the way wherein I should go.

"Oh, may thy Spirit guide my feet,
In ways of righteousness;
Make every path of duty plain
And straight before my face.
Since I'm a stranger here below,
Let not my path be hid;
But mark the road my feet should go,
And be my constant guide."

When I was a child, I thought as a child; and often wondered how the ancient servants of the Lord knew the will of God in reference to their movements in life; and how they understood when and whither the Lord required them to go; but when I had fully dedicated myself to the service of the Lord, I experienced "the secret of the Lord to be with them that fear him" [Ps. 25:14]. When our souls are in a right position before God, the will of the Lord, in reference to our future movements, is always made manifest and plain to us in the Lord's own time. It is only when we are carnal, wayward, neglectful, and disobedient, that our mental vision becomes obscure, and we fail of reading the Lord's indications, or that he ceases to bless us with His guidance. In all the errands on which the Lord has been graciously pleased to send me for the proclamation of His gospel, my work has been attended with the witness of His Spirit, and He hath given seals to my ministry, and souls for my hire.

My mind was at this time directed to the northern States of America; and I accordingly took my daughter with me, and went to New York, where I abode some few weeks, and then went, accompanied by many of the brethren, to Oyster Bay, to attend a camp-meeting held there, which proved a very blessed season to many hundreds of persons; and numbers were, on that occasion, savingly converted to God. On the second time of my appearing in public at that place, I preached from Deut. v. 29, "Oh, that there were such an heart in them, that they would fear me, and keep all my commandments always, that it might be well with them and with their children for ever;" and under this discourse, it pleased God to capture my own daughter in the gospel net; she cried out aloud, during the service, and exclaimed, "Oh, Lord! have mercy upon me, for I can hold out no longer. Oh, Lord! have mercy upon me." This occurred in the midst of listening hundreds, and it produced a most thrilling sensation upon the congregation; for, said they, "It is her own daughter!" and their emotions of sympathy were still more excited, when they learnt that she was my only child. Many a mother strongly felt with me on that occasion; and though my position would not allow me to leave the pulpit, to go and pour the oil of consolation into her wounded spirit, yet, thank God, there were abundance of dear friends present who were ready for every good word and work. The conversion of a soul is not to be effected by the mere effort of man; none but God can communicate a full pardon to the guilty soul; but, ere that meeting dissolved, the glorious work was accomplished, and Christ, the chiefest of ten thousand and the altogether lovely, was manifested in her heart, the hope of glory; thus she experienced the knowledge of salvation by the remission of her sins, being called out of darkness into God's marvellous light; the Spirit of adoption was imparted to her; she rejoiced in the Lord with all her soul; and His love was shed abroad in her heart by the Holy Ghost.

We then returned to New York, where I apprenticed her to the dress-making business; and taking my leave of her and the friends there, I departed for Newhaven, in the State of Connecticut, being richly replenished by Him who hath said, "I will never leave thee nor forsake thee" [Josh. 1:5]; and as I went to and fro in the earth, from place to place, embracing a scope of space and effort too vast for minute detail, the Lord blessed my labours wherever I went, to the conversion of sinners and the edification of saints; but I was not wholly exempted from those trials and persecutions, which are the common lot of the servants of Jesus. The principalities and powers of evil spirits, (Ephes. vi. 12) which Christians have to contend against, which Christ despoiled, (Colos. ii. 15) and which constitute the strength of the empire of darkness, the world of evil spirits, the right hand of the prince of the power of the air, (Ephes. ii. 2) who is the god or deity of this world, (2 Cor. iv. 4); these principalities occasionally obstructed me much; and, by blinding and infatuating the sons of men, inspired them with a hostile zeal against me. This was particularly the case at Hartford; in which city some of the most influential ministers of the Presbyterian body greatly opposed me; and one of them, a Mr. House, resolutely declared that he would have my preaching stopped; but he, like Sanballat,[28] imagined a vain thing; for the work was of God, who made bare his arm for the salvation of men by my ministry. Thanks be unto God who always caused me to triumph in Christ; and made manifest the savour of his knowledge by me in every place.

While the opponents of my ministry were pursuing their plans of opposition, it happened that I was sent for one day to visit a Mr. Freeman, who was dangerously ill; I accordingly went to see him: and while occupied in praying with him, his medical attendant, a physician of the first eminence, and moving in the highest rank in society, came into the chamber; he waited patiently until my supplications were concluded, and I had withdrawn; he then inquired into the condition of his patient, and finding him much better, he exclaimed with surprise, "It is the woman who has made you better." No, dear reader, it was not by my power or holiness that the sick man was benefitted, but the power of God through faith in the name of Jesus; for the Scriptures say, that "the prayer of faith shall save the sick" [James 5:15]. On my departure from the house, the doctor inquired who I was, and from whence I came; and expressed his wish to hear me himself, desiring them to inform him when and where I should next preach. It appeared that he had previously heard many reports respecting me, for my ministry had been attended by persons of every rank in life.

The time soon arrived for my appearance again in the pulpit, and many of the great folks were present, and amongst them, the physician; and the Spirit of the Lord was there also, to direct and bless and own his word, or the efforts of a poor weak female would have been feeble and insipid indeed: but on that occasion a very great interest was excited in the minds of the audience, for greater and mightier is He that is in us, than the spirit which directs the world; and the more we live and walk in the Spirit, the more the might of God dwells in us and breathes in our words. The doctor then visited his minister, the Rev. Mr. House, the very gentleman who had declared that he would stop me from preaching in that city, and spoke of me to him in such terms as induced the clergyman to exclaim, "Well, if God has sent her, I bid her God's speed." The work of the Lord spread throughout the city, and amongst people of every denomination; and such a revival took place as filled the city with astonishment; and Mr. House, my former opponent, seeing the wonderful works of God, exhorted his congregation to be sober and stand at their posts, "for," said he, "I perceive that God is about to do a great work in this city, therefore be ye still, and know that it is of God." Being encouraged by the smiles of my heavenly Father, and animated to increased zeal in his holy cause, I went from house to house and preached Christ and Him crucified to the people; I even ventured into houses of ill fame, and exhorted the debased inmates to repent of their sins and turn to Jesus Christ: and many of these unfortunate females became the genuine disciples of Jesus. I also penetrated into the alleys and courts, and the different outskirts of the town, where vice and immorality abounded; and it pleased God to effect a mighty change in the morals and habits of the people, especially in the south quarter of the town. I met with many persons here, who called themselves Universalists; but they might more properly be named Deistical Sceptics; they pretended to believe that the whole human family would eventually be saved, irrespectively of their principles and conduct. Many of these gentlemen came to hear me preach, at the house of a friend, in the skirts of the city, to which I had been invited, but very little to their satisfaction; they much approved of my prayers, because my intercessions included all the human family: but they were unable to reconcile them with my preaching, in which I insisted on salvation by the remission of sins, through genuine faith in the crucified Redeemer; described the lost condition of mankind, and exhorted men to flee from the wrath to come. Blessed be the Lord, there were several of these very persons who believed and turned to Him with all their heart; and among them was Mrs. Spring, a lady connected with the third Presbyterian chapel in the city, who attended at that meeting with three of her daughters; they were attired in mourning for another daughter, who had recently died: and, as I was expatiating, on the attendance of kind angels on the death bed scenes of the saints, I observed these ladies weeping with great emotion. In a few weeks afterwards, I was again invited to spend a few days at the same house; and I was then informed that this lady and her three daughters had, from that evening, evinced a saving conversion to God, having been under that sermon convinced of sin, of righteousness and of judgment to come. Mrs. Spring stated that she felt more under that discourse, in reference to the death of her daughter, than she did at the time of her decease: and from that time they had no rest until they obtained the assurance of peace with God, through our Lord Jesus Christ: they were soon after introduced to me, and I received much kindness from them.

I met with a young woman in the course of my ministry in Hartford, who was very unsteady and depraved in her habits; her mother was a member of the Methodist Society, and at that time ill; she wished me to be sent for to visit her, but the daughter insisted that I should not come there; or, if I did, she threatened to swear and dance in my presence during my visit, and to treat me with all possible disrespect. However, this young woman was by some means or other induced to come and hear me preach; and the Lord was pleased to open her heart, that she attended unto the things that were spoken; at the conclusion of the service, she came to me and invited me to come and visit her mother; and the next morning she called upon me again. I exhorted her, prayed with and for her, and she became so attached to me, that my company was continually sought by her; she was soon after admitted into the household of faith and I afterwards preached in their cottage: thus one of my enemies became my child in the gospel, and my sister in the Lord.

Intending to take my departure from this city, I went to the coach office, and paid my fare, was booked as a passenger for the next day, leaving directions for the coach to call for me on the following morning; but so eager were the people for my further stay amongst them, that some of the brethren went and took up my fare at the coach office, and would not listen to any proposition for my departure. I therefore resumed my labours among them, being constantly engaged by day and night in the work of the Lord, without an intervening cloud, for the space of three months, preaching in the chapel on the Lord's-day, and on one evening in the week.

On one occasion, a number of persons, amounting to between twenty and thirty, presented themselves in the chapel, in great distress and deep penitence on account of their sins. The excess of their emotions were such, that the order of worship was suspended; for some were calling upon the name of the Lord, some were groaning to receive the atonement of Jesus, while others were rejoicing in his salvation and giving glory to God. Our services were not unfrequently interrupted by scenes of this description; for the operation of the Holy Ghost can no more be circumscribed within the limits of man's arrangement, than the wind and rain and sunshine can be restricted to man's times and opportunities. Order in divine worship and in the house of God is graceful and appropriate; but the life and power of religion is not identified with, nor in proportion to, the polish of the minister, the respectability of the congregation, or the regularity and method of its services: the most abrupt and extraordinary vicissitudes of weather are frequently productive of more benefit than the nicest graduated scale of temperature; and had it not been for some of these instances, in which the Almighty displayed the wonders of his victorious grace, even though the accustomed proprieties and regularity of divine service were at the time abruptly trenched upon and suspended, there are many churches now lively and flourishing, which, notwithstanding the exactness of the order of their worship, and the beauty of their arrangements, would now be but little more than so many religious automata. Our duty is humbly to submit to, rather than attempt to limit, the Holy One of Israel; and when God is at work, though the ark may seem to rock with irregular motion, let not men pretend to more wisdom than their Creator, lest, like Uzzah, they fall themselves in their attempts to direct His energies, and regulate His movements.[29]

My mental hemisphere soon after this became obscured and cloudy, and my mind became exceedingly heavy and sorrowful; satanic spirits also gained access to my soul and harrassed me much, and I seemed oppressed with fearful forebodings of some impending evil: I knew not any cause in myself for this reverse of my spiritual condition, and was wholly unable to account for, and comprehend the reason thereof. The following words constantly ran through my mind during this affliction:

> "Lord, what are all my sufferings here,
> If thou but make me meet,
> With that enraptured host to appear
> And worship at thy feet."

I waded through much gloominess and sorrow; the dial of my spirit was beclouded with great darkness, and I wept much and frequently; but the cause was beyond my comprehension.

The chapel in which I had been preaching was called an union chapel, and was not the property of any particular sect of Christians; but the majority of the persons worshipping therein were Presbyterians; and by them, at length, a great jealousy against me was excited, fostered and hatched under the influence of the rulers of the darkness of this world, professedly on account of my being a Methodist. The chapel was to some extent involved in debt; and this Presbyterian faction came forward before the managers with a proposition to procure a minister to supply the pulpit for three months free of expense; requesting, at the same time, that I might not be informed of their proposal: the volunteer preacher was accordingly introduced and tendered his services to supply the pulpit every Lord's-day; and as the chapel was in debt, the proposition was accepted, and the matter arranged and settled. Upon this, one of our friends came and informed me, that it had been arranged by the managers, that Mr. A. should preach on next Lord's-day, in the morning, myself in the afternoon, and Mr. B. in the evening: this somewhat enlightened my understanding into this mystery of iniquity. I attended the morning service on the next Lord's-day, and heard Mr. A. preach; and in the afternoon, as I was proceeding to the chapel, one of the managers met me and informed me he had learnt that Mr. C. was appointed to preach there on that afternoon, and advised me not to enter the pulpit: thus instructed, I took my seat with the congregation: soon afterwards the deacons entered the chapel, and seeing me setting in a private seat, they came and desired me to ascend the pulpit according to the recent arrangements: I then related to them what the manager had said to me; they assured me his statement was untrue, and urged me to take the pulpit; having been informed of all the circumstances, when I appeared in the pulpit I was obliged to vent my feelings in a shower of tears, before I could utter a word; and my dear flock were very much affected at the sight; but we afterwards enjoyed a very blessed meeting. In the evening, I went again and heard the Rev. Mr. B.; there were many of the officials present; and on the conclusion of the service the congregation still kept their seats, none offered to leave, but maintained a profound silence, and the eyes of many of them were fixed in expectation upon me; I felt called forth by the assembly, and rising to my feet, I said, If there are any present who feel anxious about their souls, and will come forward, we will hold a prayer-meeting. A great number then came forward; and when they were seated, the preacher descended from the pulpit, and with the official gentlemen present, without deigning the least notice of me, went and conferred with the persons who were seeking the salvation of their souls, and instructed them in the way of life; after which, they announced that their minister would preach again on Wednesday evening, and closed the meeting, without giving me an opportunity of saying a word: this conduct seemed much like gospel rivalship, a thing which unhappily too greatly prevails amongst Christians: the apostle Paul intimated that some in his day preached Christ of contention [Phil. 1:16], for the purpose of increasing his affliction; and I cannot but think that this treatment was intended for my affliction; it was too plainly marked to be mistaken; for they all sat waiting in mute silence, until I had invited the inquiring souls to come forward; and then coolly obtruded their grave admonitions on those who had been pricked in their hearts, and were become impatiently violent to grasp the kingdom of heaven; shutting me out entirely, and concluding with a notice that their new minister would preach on the following Wednesday evening, and the next Lord's-day; directing those who wished for further instructions to apply to them at their several residences. My affections were, however, very strongly attached to my little flock; and on the Wednesday evening, I went again to hear the new minister; but the Lord said unto me, "It is enough; I will take thee away from them, and I will put bands upon thee, and thou shalt not go out amongst them; and I will make thy tongue cleave to the roof of thy mouth, that thou shalt be dumb, and shalt not be a reprover to them, for they are a rebellious house. But when I speak unto thee, I will open thy mouth, and thou shalt say unto them, Thus saith the Lord God, He that heareth, let him hear; and he that forbeareth, let him forbear: for they are a rebellious house." Ezek. iii. 25–27. Thus it was partly with me, for on that very night, I was suddenly attacked with a very severe fit of illness, and confined by it for five weeks, so that I became dumb to them indeed. After I had been ill three weeks, the Rev. Mr. Moffit, one of our principal Methodist preachers,[30] came to Hartford; and, under his ministry, the revival which the Lord had began by my instrumentality was renewed again; the chapel became completely deserted, the new minister became discouraged, and shortly withdrew altogether.

Mr. Moffit spent several weeks in Hartford, and preached every evening in the week for the greater part of the time; the people flocked, from every part of the town, to his ministry; and many people were turned unto the Lord. Many of the Methodists and many of my congregation also experienced, under him, a great revival of the work of the Lord in their souls. Before he left the city, it pleased God to raise me up and enable me to go and hear him, and render my thanksgivings to God for His great goodness and tender care towards me in my illness: before I was able to go abroad, those very persons who had treated me so unhandsomely called to inquire after my health; and expressed their hope that God would bless and restore me to health, that I might soon resume my labours among them again, saying, that I had already effected much good to many souls; but as the Lord had said unto me, "when I speak, thou shalt hear: and I will put words in thy mouth and thou shalt speak;" on my recovery, I left the city for a short time; when I returned again, these people were extremely anxious for me to preach to them, and by the grace of God, I resumed my former station and continued my labours amongst them for some time without interruption; the Lord having made it increasingly manifest that He had sent me, and that my ministry was from Him.

A few weeks before I finally left this city, I learnt that Mrs. Adams, the wife of a gentleman in the legal profession, had been dangerously ill for a long time, and had expressed a great desire to see me; I, therefore, without an invitation, called at her residence, but I was so weak at the time, that when I arrived there I fainted, and was taken to bed; when I recovered, I was conducted into her chamber, where Mr. Adams, and all the family were collected, expecting to see her breathe her last; she had been ill so long a time, and wasted so much, that her skin had been broken through by the pressure of her bones. After a little conversation, I inquired if I should pray with her; consent being given, I bowed down before God, and lifted up my heart in supplication on her behalf. It was a time of much power; and all the family were bathed in tears. Mrs. Adams' sister accompanied me to the door on my retiring, and asked me if I did not think her sister was very near her end. I said, 'no: I think she will recover, for God showed me this in the time of prayer.' She then sent one of the servants to lead me home; the next morning I was so ill as to require medical aid; and the physician who attended Mrs. Adams was sent for. He seemed much pleased to communicate to me the intelligence that Mrs. Adams was vastly better; and before I left the city, she was down stairs, at the head of the family. This circumstance made a great impression on the inhabitants of the city, who thought it strange, indeed, that God, in answer to my prayer, should heal the sick: the intelligence flew from street to street, that Mrs. Adams was recovered; and those reverend gentlemen, who had so strenuously exerted themselves to silence my ministry, were themselves completely disconcerted, and their objections silenced. I might add many more of the kind and condescending corroborations, the Lord was pleased to manifest on my behalf in that city; but I forbear narrating any further instances, and leave them to be further revealed in the disclosures of another life.

The wonderful revivals of the work of God, some of which I have attempted to describe, were not done in a corner; but extended throughout the greater part of the vast territory of the United States: many were the labourers, zealous and devoted their spirits, and indefatigable their exertions, whom the Lord raised up, and sent forth to achieve these blessed conquests, the reports of which have long since reached the ears even of British Christians, and excited amongst them some searchings of heart, and some curiosity to have further information respecting them; insomuch that I have understood that men of high repute for learning and wisdom, have been sent over to ascertain the nature, as well to investigate the means and extent of those great transatlantic revivals: what report of the good land they returned with, I have not been informed, but generally I have found that the wise and learned have seldom experienced much of the heavenly discipline of God's Holy Spirit; "the world by wisdom knew not God" [1 Cor. 1:21]; and though many Christians are at immense pains to acquire the wisdom of this world, God bringeth it to nought, and taketh them in their own craftiness; He hideth His counsel from the "wise and prudent, and revealeth it to babes" [Matt. 11:25]. The man who would judge of so high a matter as a revival of the kingdom of heaven upon earth, must be spiritual (he need not be learned) himself; for the spiritual man judgeth all things; yea, even the deep things of God, yet he himself is judged of no man, for no man can fathom the sacred Urim and Thummim, or as St. John says, the holy anointing or unction which abides in his soul.[31]

I left Hartford for Boston, in the state of Massachusetts, in company with a lady, who was from the latter city: and the Lord went before me and cleared up the way; for, in the city of Boston, many doors were opened for my reception; and the Lord wrought wonderfully among the people. Many of the brethren were going to a camp-meeting at Cape Cod, about sixty miles from Boston, and invited me to go with them, which I did with great pleasure, and we had very pleasant weather. Many thousands attended at that meeting, and the Lord manifested forth his glory and his grace. Hundreds came to that camp-meeting, to make sport and derision of the saints, and of their worship, who returned home themselves rejoicing in God their Saviour. A band of young gentlemen, connected with the highest families in the town of Lynn, chartered a large vessel, brought their tent, provisions, and every other necessary for a week's sojourn on the camp ground, with the wicked intention not only of greatly annoying us, but of dispersing the camp-meeting altogether: the manner in which they approached the encampment rendered it but too evident what kind of persons they were, and for what purpose they came. When these wanton young gentlemen arrived upon the ground, they went from tent to tent and appeared to be greatly struck with astonishment at the novel appearance of the scene: for the Lord had set the hearts and consciences of the people in motion; some of them were weeping with godly penitence; others were rejoicing in the salvation of Christ, manifested to their souls; in the public services, the ministers were as a flaming torch, and their words as a two edged sword [Heb. 4:12]; and the powerful discourses they preached from the platform, made a wonderful impression on these giddy young men, and their conduct became greatly altered. On the Thursday, between twelve and two o'clock, matters were so changed that they prepared their tent for religious service, and sent for me to come and preach to them; I went accordingly, and commenced the meeting, and some of our ablest preachers followed soon after and assisted me, and the Lord owned and blessed our message, and many of these young gentlemen became deeply affected, and cried to God for mercy. The ministers evinced the greatest attention and tender care of them; but they more particularly desired to hear, "the woman:" and the next day I was sent for to preach to them again; after which, we all attended the prayer meeting at the preachers' stand; and many of them found mercy with God. When the camp-meeting broke up, all of them with the exception of four, together with many others both white and coloured, manifested the triumphs of redeeming grace, and evinced a saving conversion to God; and the happy result of that meeting was that, in a short space of time, in the town of Lynn alone, upwards of two hundred persons were added to the Methodist Episcopal Church.

The brethren residing at the Cape having strongly solicited me to tarry for a time with them, I consented, and instead of returning with the brethren to Boston, went home with the Cape friends, and travelled with the itinerating preachers on the different circuits of the Cape district, and with great success; for the glorious camp meeting we had just before attended, had laid the foundation for an extensive and continuous revival: the fields were indeed white, already to harvest; and we went to reap them, and receive the rich wages of souls for our hire.

In the course of my excursions, I went into the Haverich circuit, and entered one of their chapels. After the service had commenced, I observed a young man in the assembly who appeared to idolise himself, and to soar very high into the regions of self-conceit; his excessive self-complacency very much attracted my attention, and I felt a desire to have some conversation with him; not suspecting that there was any probability of its coming to pass; but God overrules and arranges matters for His people, that they may glorify His name. It happened that we went that day to dine with this very young gentleman's father-in-law; and during the time of dinner he came in. Some one at the table then asked him if there were many persons in attendance at the meeting in the morning; to which he replied, no; adding, that he was a fool in going, for it was complete folly to attend those meetings. These words came very painfully to my heart; but as I was to preach in the afternoon, and required much self-composure, I passed over his remarks in silence; when the service of the afternoon was over, I returned to tea with the family, and being now at liberty, having no sermon before me to preach, I was not indisposed for a colloquy with him; he was also desirous of having some conversation with me, and had prepared himself for that purpose; after tea, he came again, and brought many others with him to witness his feats of prowess: so he promptly commenced an attack upon me, worked himself into a great fury, and spouted away for a time; but his ammunition was quickly exhausted; his creed, if he had any, was that of modified deism; looking for a future paradise to be enjoyed by all men indiscriminately; he was, however, deplorably ignorant of the Scriptures; I replied to him according to the ability the Lord gave me; and conviction of the truth went with the word, so that he became of the number of believers in Christ, and subsequently behaved to me with very great kindness—to God be all the praise for ever and ever.

My ministry every where, on the Cape, was very numerously attended: there were but few buildings that could contain the numbers who flocked to hear the word of the Lord; as I journied from place to place, many an open waggon became my pulpit, from which I preached in the open air to listening multitudes, the candidates for immortality, and directed them to the Lamb of God who taketh away the sins of the world [John 1:29]. My own soul was filled with heavenly hope, which maketh not ashamed; my affections were set upon things above; my treasure was in heaven; my hope bloomed with the glories of immortality and eternal life; it was the anchor of my soul, sure and steadfast; I rejoiced in hope of the glory of God; and in my ministry, I determined to be conversant with no other topic, to know nothing amongst men but Jesus Christ and him crucified [1 Cor. 2:2]. The divine treasures which God imparted into my earthen vessel I freely poured out; and the Lord constantly replenished me with more; so that I was always being exhausted, and ever being filled with the heavenly treasures of divine knowledge; and became more and more able to bring out of the good treasure in my heart things new and old. The Lord enabled me to keep my heart with all diligence; and having my own soul right with God, I was enabled to set others right also. I affectionately press it upon the attention of every minister of the gospel, who really desires that his ministry may be effectual to convert and sanctify men, to attend to himself first, to see that the work of genuine conversion be perfected in his own heart; that he is truly born again of the incorruptible seed of the word of God, which liveth and abideth for ever; that he is thoroughly cleansed from his old sins; enjoying the remission of sins and justification to life; that the word of God abideth in him, and is fruitful; that he enjoys the spirit of adoption; is sealed with the Holy Spirit of promise; that the Holy Ghost dwelleth in him; that he comes to the light in every thing; is pure in heart, and hath his eye single to the glory of God; that he is sanctified by the truth; purified by obeying it; that he abideth in Christ the true vine; dwelleth in God and God in him; that he hath continual communion with the Father, and with his Son Jesus Christ; that he lives and walks in the Spirit; is led by the Spirit; that he is not proud of these attainments, but simple and of a childlike disposition; that his heart is preserved in a state of transparency, and so free from guile and sin, that he would not be reluctant to have it probed by a truly godly-experienced and judicious Christian of like attainments. Let him see to it that he is meek, lowly, patient, contrite and humble, habituated to self-denial, filled with charity or love which is the bond of perfectness; that his will is entirely submitted and resigned to the will of God; that his meat and drink is to do the will of his Father in heaven; that his attitude is that of a self-devoted, living sacrifice, utterly at the disposal of his God, taking up every cross placed before him; that he meekly and practically regards the saying of Jesus and the precepts of the Christian Scriptures, aiming at a perfect observance of them all; that he may become a finished disciple of Jesus Christ, exercised in all parts of Christian duty and practise, and copying the pattern set by his Lord, devoting soul and body, time and opportunities, money and means, his entire all to the service of Jesus; not wedded to this life, but holding it as loosely as possible, rejoicing in hope of the glory of God, and seeking an increased knowledge of Christ, the fellowship of His sufferings, and the spiritual might of His resurrection. Such a man as this, if called and sent by Christ into His vineyard, is able to make men wise unto salvation; and is the kind of minister whose labours Jesus will deign to bless. Such ministers have adorned and blessed the church in all ages; and such ministers occasionally adorn it still. It is an axiom which holds good in Christianity, as well as in common life, that whatever man has borne, been, or done, man may bear, be, or do; and there is no more impossibility of attaining eminent saintship in the present day, than there was two thousands of years since: with the Scriptures in our hands and the Holy Spirit in our hearts, we possess advantages even beyond those Christians who enjoyed the living ministry of the apostles. He who would be a master in Israel should possess such an experimental knowledge of the Christian religion, as an university cannot bestow, but which is the exclusive endowment of the Holy Ghost. A well-disciplined minister is a father in Christ; an elder in the Christian church; and happy is that flock over which the Holy Ghost hath made him an overseer: who are fed by him, not with college lore, nor with orations such as are emitted by divines not yet out of their teens; but with such instructions as the Holy Ghost teacheth, comparing spiritual things with spiritual. When ministers aim at revivals in their flocks, they must first obtain them in their own souls; for he who has left his first love, is in no condition to communicate the glowing flame to others: he must first remember from whence he has fallen, and repent, and do his first works; strengthen the things that remain; stir up the gift of God in himself; obtain the pure gold of true faith, well tried in the fire, and anoint his mental eyes with the illuminating eye-salve of divine unction; render his body a temple for the Holy Ghost and equip himself with the whole armour of God [1 Cor. 3:16, Eph. 6:11], and then he may efficiently contribute to the health and prosperity of the souls of others; being a discerning, faithful watchman, and a good shepherd to them. I have witnessed such ministers, (who are rightly named 'Great Grace',) lay open the heart, cast down imaginations and every high thing that exalteth itself against the knowledge of God: and with the Spirit's two-edged sword, divide the sinner from his sins, slay the lion, and bring him a lamb-like penitent to the feet of Jesus; then take the new creature by the hand, lead him by the side of still waters [Ps. 23:2], in paths of righteousness; comfort, exhort, warn, instruct, and build him up in our most holy faith, that he may eventually have the joy to present him faultless and perfect in

Christ Jesus [Jude 24]. Oh! that every leader of souls in Britain may speedily become a Joshua, to bring all the Lord's Israel into the promised rest of faith.[32]

In the course of my travels on the Cape, I one day met with a young lady recently married, whose pride and self-consequence were superlatively high; her parents, brothers and sisters were decidedly religious; but her vanity and haughtiness had hitherto resisted the humbling impressions of true godliness. I felt my mind much drawn after this young lady, but she rejected every advance of mine, and contemptuously avoided my conversation. I spent a day at her father's house; during which time she was with us; but she sat as a queen, and maintained all the dignity of haughty reserve to every religious topic; at night, we had family prayer; and I followed the impressions of my mind, in fervently praying for her; and took my leave of the family. In about two years afterwards, I again met with her mother, who informed me that, on that evening, this young lady was brought to repentance towards God: she was afflicted with penitential anguish to an extraordinary degree, ere she was enabled to exercise faith in our Lord Jesus Christ; since that time, she evinced as great anxiety to see and unbosom her mind to me as she had previously to shun and repulse me. Verily, God doeth all things well: all praise to His glorious wisdom and power; His rich and free mercy, and adorable grace.

Having reaped a rich harvest of souls on the Cape, I returned to the city of Boston, where I remained for a few months; the Lord having made my way prosperous, many doors were opened to me, the word of God had free course and was glorified: many who sat in darkness there saw the great and the true light, and turned to the Lord with all their heart; from thence I proceeded to the city of Salem, and laboured amongst the Methodists with much attendant prosperity. The coloured people had a chapel in course of erection, and stood in great need of assistance, the Methodist brethren therefore, in conjunction with several gentlemen in the city, subscribed a considerable sum of money, with which they furnished them with a pulpit and seats for the chapel. When the building was got in readiness, I delivered the first discourse therein, from Zech. ii. 10, "Sing and rejoice, O daughter of Zion; for I come, and I will dwell in the midst of thee, saith the Lord." The Lord graciously manifested and recorded His name there on that occasion; and many considered their ways, and turned from their vanities to serve the living God. The Lord was pleased also to apply a portion of His word with much power to my own soul, as it was delivered by His angel. Zech. iii. 7. "Thus saith the Lord of Hosts, if thou wilt walk in my ways, and if thou wilt keep my charge, then thou shalt also judge my house and shalt also keep my courts, and I will give thee places to walk among these that stand by."

In that city, the ladies who were connected with the several Christian denominations, were in the habit of holding a monthly union prayer-meeting together; and as this brought the different denominations into closer contact with each other, it caused a rich intercourse of sanctified gifts and graces amongst them, for the edification of the general body; it also greatly promoted Christian love, for the pure, genial currents supplied by genuine gospel faith, purified the disciples from party bigotry, and caused them to love one another for the truth's sake. It was delightful indeed to hear Episcopalians, Presbyterians, Baptists, and Methodists, avow the rich enjoyments they had in the spirit of adoption from God, who gave forth the corroborating testimony of His divine witness with their spirits to their heavenly filiations. The Christian church should manifest one fold and one shepherd; one body and spirit; one hope, one Lord, one faith, one baptism; and one God and father of all who is above all, and through all, and in all [Eph. 4:4–6]. O that the Christian community in Great Britain were all of one heart and one soul; only, but earnestly, contending for the faith once delivered to the saints; that there were no divisions among them, but all were speaking the same things, and perfectly joined together in the same mind, and in the same judgment; none being puffed up one against another, knowing that ministerial partizanship, doctrinal divisions, and sectarian prejudices flow from sheer carnality, and savours nothing of the grace of God. Rom. xvi. 17. 1 Cor. iii. 3. During my stay in Salem, a great alteration was effected in the morals of the coloured friends; I hope to be forgiven by my English brethren, in saying, that it is not an uncommon thing for white Christians to reprobate the morals of their sable brethren, without an adequate occasion; the intelligence, the circumstances, and the habits of the two races are widely different: and it is the part of a moted eye and biassed heart to require the same standard tale of bricks from the Ethiopean family! Or, in other words, an observance by them of all the proprieties attached to the refined Christian morals of the more cultivated Saxon stock; the illiterate coloured Christian is competent to, and ought, practically, to carry out the precepts of the Christian religion to the utmost extent his circumstances admit of; but Christian charity will not rashly judge him, for an imperfect conformity to the politer standard of morals and tasteful delicacy, which have been superadded to the Christian precept, by the supererogative pride of high-toned sensibility and civilization; a more perfect exemplification of Christian morals than that which characterized the apostolic era has never been attained by any later age; but its simplicity and want of polish would have presented a very rude and vulgar exhibition in contrast with the whited exterior, the artificial delicacy and current respectability or pride of life of much of the present-day Christianity. The immoralities of the Abyssinian brethren, when they occur, are obvious and glaring, and are easily visited and purged by the discipline of the church; but those of more polished Christians too often flow in a deep and mighty under current: no principles are more vicious, no practices more immoral and debasing, than covetousness and worldly pride; the Scriptures exclude those who are guilty of them from any inheritance in the kingdom of God and Christ; yet it is a fact but too well known, that these vices have an unrestrained course throughout the more civilized Christian communities; and that an attempt to expel these immoralities from those communities, by subjecting all such offenders to the discipline of the church, would fill with confusion, and crumble to ruins every denominational superstructure in Christendom.

The Lord's blessing on my visit to Salem was made apparent by the improvement which followed in the morals and habits of the coloured population; many of whom became truly devout, righteous, holy, godly, spiritual, and heavenly-minded: by devout, I mean, devotional and religious; righteousness consists in being and doing right; holiness is purity internally and practically. Godliness is an assimilation of the human character to that of our heavenly Father; spirituality is such a practical acquaintance with spiritual things, and abiding sense of the existence and agency of spiritual and invisible beings, and converse with them, as gives a complete ascendancy to the moral and mental powers over the animal propensities; but it more especially consists in a discernment of the presence and operations of the Holy Spirit, fellowship with God and his Son Jesus Christ, and the communion of the Holy Spirit, together with an habitual and deep consciousness, and a blooming prospect of the momentous realities of a future life. Heavenly-mindedness consists in having our mind and hope fixed upon the things above; on the mercy-seat and throne of grace, the heavenly Jerusalem; the mansions which Jesus is preparing for us there; the heavenly Mount Zion; the general assembly and church of the first-born; the innumerable company of angels; the blood of sprinkling; the mediator and high-priest of the new covenant; and upon God the judge of all. Many of my sable brethren became eminently spiritual, having ceased to be led by their animal appetites and worldly lusts, they were led by the Holy Spirit of God which dwelt in them, and whose temples they were. In the Methodist connexion, also, I had an extensive circle of young ladies who were constant attendants upon my ministry, and who were in an especial manner my charge in the Lord; these manifested great diligence in their pursuit of the higher attainments of experimental spirituality. The love of God being richly shed abroad in their hearts by the Holy Ghost, many of them attained to considerable eminence in the apprehension of, and conformity to, the love of Christ, which passeth knowledge; abiding in Christ, dwelling in God, and walking in the light as God is in the light, they experienced that perfect love which casteth out fear; the holy vigour and zeal with which they pressed forward after the life of God, the avidity with which they drank until they were filled with the Spirit, and the wonderful revelations God was pleased to manifest to them, provoked me to run forward in the heavenly race with increased earnestness, lest they should overtake, and leave me behind them: but as the Lord set me as their leader, He sustained me as such; and an abundance of grace was given to me as His commissioned servant, to maintain my leadership. I abode in Salem throughout the winter, and a most delightful winter it was.

I also paid a visit to the friends at Lynn; a town to which reference has already been made; the Rev. J. Melvill was the minister stationed there, who invited me to preach in his pulpit, which I did to an overflowing audience: on that occasion, I had the happiness to see many of those dear young men who had attended the camp-meeting as before narrated. On the conclusion of the service, they formed themselves into two ranks down the aisle of the chapel in order to salute me as I passed betwixt them; and we parted in the hope of a joyful meeting on the morning of the resurrection.

From Salem I again returned to Boston, which city I left in May, 1830, in company with a Mrs. Ruby, who had been thither on a visit, and was now returning to Portland, in the State of Maine, in the north-eastern part of America. We had a pleasant passage by water; the night was calm, and we reached Portland about eight o'clock in the morning. It is a beautiful city, situated on the sea coast; built on a considerable elevation, and the houses being white, it presents a very conspicuous and fine appearance from the sea.

On my arrival, I found the friends to be a very benevolent and kind-hearted people: they gave me a very cordial reception; we quickly became well acquainted and at home in each other's company, and it was a blessed visit to my own soul and to their souls also. The Abyssinian chapel, a very neat and pretty erection, was appropriated to my service; and the news of a female being about to preach therein, attracted a great number of persons from all parts of the city; the Lord applied my message to the hearts of many of them, and they cried to Him for mercy, they sought Him with their whole heart, and He was found to them to be a God merciful and gracious, pardoning iniquity, transgression, and sin; and like the eunuch, they went on their way rejoicing [Acts 8:39]. The chapel was constantly filled during my stay, amongst them: many were made happy in the love of God, enjoyed a sense of His approbation and the witness of His Spirit with their spirits that they were the children of God; many strangers were continually attracted to the chapel; and on one Lord's-day, a gentleman was present whose emotion was so strong as to excite much attention: he at length retired to the lobby where he vented his feelings in sobs and tears: he stated to one of the brethren that he was a sea-captain, a stranger to earthly fears, that his heart was attracted and rivetted by the discourse which was in the course of delivery, so that he could not retire from the place; but being unable to repress his feelings, and desirous of evading observation, he preferred standing in the lobby. Another person was there also under similar circumstances, who called upon me the next day, and informed me that he had been a sailor during the last forty years, and had encountered every form of marine danger: that he had belonged to a ship of war, and been accustomed to the roaring of cannons, and all the tragic horrors of naval warfare, but never had felt dismayed by an accumulation of peril; he now wept bitterly, and we both knelt before the Lord in supplication, and the Lord heard and spoke peace to his soul. Many other instances of the Lord's especial favour to me, and blessing upon my ministerial labours in that city I might relate; but the limits I am compelled to assign to the compass of this volume require their omission.

After remaining a few months in Portland, I was moved to travel further into the State of Maine, and I journied in company with Mr. Black, a Baptist minister to the town of Brunswick; a town eminent in the State for its literary institutions. Mr. Black preached there on the Lord's-day, and I was invited to occupy the pulpit of the Baptist chapel on the Monday evening; which I did, and preached to a very crowded auditory, of whom a large number were collegians: at the close of the meeting, I was invited to preach there again. After this, my mind was impressed that I must go to Bath; a town about ten miles distant; though I had received no invitation, possessed no introductory means to any one, neither knew any person there, and had been informed that the town was not inhabited by one person of colour; my mind was therefore somewhat saddened on account of this impression; I knew not how to proceed in it; and committed my way unto God, who in His own way and time brought it to pass.

In a few days I went to preach at a small country village; and, a female from Bath being present at the meeting, I sent a message by her to the religious people of Bath, requesting permission to come and preach to them; this was the first time in my life that I had ever requested as a favour to myself, that which in the nature of things is the communication of a favour. In a few days I received an answer from them, intimating that they neither knew nor had heard of me previously; but that they regularly held a prayer-meeting at certain times at a certain house about a mile from the town, at which I might attend if I thought proper.

Although this reply seemed rather uncourteous and grating to the feelings, yet the matter was from the Lord, and I durst not refuse even an invitation so uncouth. Accordingly a kind sister conveyed me in her chaise to the place on the day of their next prayer meeting: having alighted, we inquired of the housewife if that was the meeting-house; she admitted that it was; 'but,' says she, 'who asked you to come here?' Having given her the name of the friend who had sent to me, she added, 'Oh! then go to him, go to him, he will tell you all about it.' It is to be deplored that some Christians have 'Nabal' so prominently inscribed upon their tempers, that they display an equal moroseness with the canine snarlers:[33] such are unmindful of the authority and disobedient to the laws of their Master, by which they are required to be courteous, gentle and kind; and they greatly disgrace the Christian profession by their churlishness. We departed from that surly abode, and went into the town, but were unable to find one person belonging to the society or who knew anything of our coming; nor could any of them accommodate us with a night's lodging: we therefore rode back to the house where the meeting was to be held, and the time for its commencement was nearly arrived. We again alighted and knocked at the door, and it was opened by the female before mentioned, who, when she saw us, shut it again in our faces and turned away. As she did not lock the door, I opened it and entered into the house. A great many people and the preachers were already assembled; I sat down in the meeting and reflected on the repulsive reception I had met with; and conscious that I had now discharged my duty before God, I resolved, if not requested to preach, to sit in silence and wait before Him.

When the time for service arrived, one of the preachers came to me and said, 'Sister, I suppose you wish to address the meeting,' to which I assented: and as he stated that the assembly were desirous of hearing me, I went into the desk opened the meeting, and preached from Isaiah xlviii. 18, "Oh, that thou hadst hearkened to my commandments! then had thy peace been as a river; and thy righteousness as the waves of the sea." The audience were very numerous and attentive; much feeling was excited and many tears were shed, for the Lord was with me in the work, to give efficacy to the word of His grace. At the conclusion of the service, the society were detained to consult on matters of their own; and I retired to prepare for my departure. When we were ready to enter the chaise, some of the sisters came to us, and informed me that I might be accommodated with a lodging at the residence of a lady in the neighbourhood; but as they did not assign any object for my further stay with them, I declined the offer, and departed. I afterwards learnt that they had been consulting about my preaching in the town on the next Lord's-day, and had arranged for me so to do; though they did not then inform me of it. After the sermon, my soul was filled with an inexpressibly sweet serenity and heavenly peace. On our way home we called at a house on Brunswick plains, which is midway betwixt the two towns, where one of our friends resided; and as they were preparing supper for us, I sat in thoughtful meditation on the varied goodness of God towards me; and looking upwards, the Lord opened my eyes, and I distinctly saw five angels hovering above and engaged in the praises of God: the raptures of my soul were too awful and ecstatic on that occasion for human description: the sensual world are unacquainted with the overwhelming fascinations which thrill through every instinct of the spiritual mind under the complacent manifestation of etherial intelligencies and their enchanting influence. I concluded that this wonderful manifestation was a token for good, and a proof that the Lord was well pleased with the course I had taken; and I was encouraged to hold several meetings throughout the week, and preached on the Lord's-day twice on the plains, and once in Brunswick. I learnt, in the meantime, that a great curiosity had been excited in Bath on account of my visit to that place, and that I was anxiously expected there again. On the Lord's-day morning, immediately after I had commenced the service, one of the Bath preachers came in, and when the service was over, informed me that he was directed to conduct me to Bath to preach there in the evening; but being then engaged to preach in Brunswick in the evening, he was much disappointed at my declining his invitation; however, I promised to call and preach there when on my journey to Bangor, to which town I purposed shortly to go: in a short time, taking leave of the friends at Brunswick, went to Bath, and was very kindly received by Mr. Wilkinson, one of the preachers: in the evening I preached in their spacious chapel to a very large and attentive audience: after service they made a collection, the whole of which they generously presented to me; being a larger sum than I had received from any other congregation in the State of Maine; they then earnestly requested me to remain a few days with them, and preach again ere I proceeded on my journey, to which I was constrained to consent. As the immense concourse retired from the chapel, the noise of so many hundreds of feet unbroken by any human articulation was very remarkable and excited the surprise of some of the friends as being very unusual in that town; but the people obviously had

> "A while forgot their earthly cares,
> And soared above this vale of tears,
> To yon celestial hill."

I attended the different meetings of their classes during my stay there, and enjoyed a very pleasant visit among them; and, having preached to them again, they gave me letters of recommendation to the Methodist ministers who resided along the course of my journey through the State. I could not but gratefully regard the kind dealings of my Heavenly Father towards me in my visits to this people; although my reception was so rude and repulsive at the first, yet my way was enlarged, my messages welcomed, and my subsequent treatment warmly cordial and affectionate: such are frequently the ways in which the Lord conducts His saints—

> "Behind a frowning Providence
> He hides a smiling face."

Having preached to them on the Thursday evening, my departure was arranged for the morrow; the friends having obtained my promise, that, with the Lord's permission, I would come and preach to them again on my return. On the morning, before I left, the superintendent minister of the Circuit came on a visit to Bath from Augusta; and hearing of my preaching there, treated it at first as many other ministers do, with great contempt, and reprobated the ministry of a female; but after hearing somewhat more of the matter, his sentiments became changed, he was introduced to me, and became one of my very kind friends.

It is true, that in the ordinary course of Church arrangement and order, the Apostle Paul laid it down as a rule, that females should not speak in the church, nor be suffered to teach; but the Scriptures make it evident that this rule was not intended to limit the extraordinary directions of the Holy Ghost, in reference to female Evangelists, or oracular sisters; nor to be rigidly observed in peculiar circumstances. St. Paul himself attests that Phoebe was a servant or deaconess of the Church at Cenchrea; and as such was employed by the Church to manage some of their affairs; and it was strange indeed, if she was required to receive the commissions of the Church in mute silence, and not allowed to utter a syllable before them. The Apostle John wrote his second epistle to a Christian lady, as a matron of eminence and authority; exhorting her believing children by her, and bidding her to prove the doctrines of those who visited her in the capacity of Christian teachers: honourable mention is made of many other Christian females who promoted the cause of Jesus; and Paul wished every assistance to be given to those women who laboured with him in the Gospel. Tryphena laboured with Tryphosa in the Lord; mention is made of the services of many of the sisters of Nereus, of the mother of Rufus, many others are also very respectfully referred to by St. Paul. The prophet Joel predicted that God would pour His Spirit on His handmaids, and that they should prophecy as well as His servants; and this prophecy, Peter, on the day of Pentecost, asserted was fulfilled [Acts 2:16–18]; and if so, the Christian dispensation has for its main feature the inspirations of the holy prophetic Spirit, descending on the handmaids as well as on the servants of God; and thus qualifying both for the conversion of men, and spread of the Gospel. Priscilla took upon herself the work of a teacher, when, in conjunction with her husband Aquila, she expounded to Apollos the way of God more perfectly; the four virgin daughters of Philip the Evangelist, were prophetesses or exhorters, probably assisting their father in his evangelic labours: being prophetesses or exhorters, the work in which they were employed was prophecy or exhortation;[34] and those brethren certainly err, who fetter all and every ecclesiastical circumstance, and even the extraordinary inspirations of the Holy Spirit with the regulations given by the apostle to a church, the brethren of which extensively possessed the gift of utterance, and were therefore in no need of female speakers; and a Church, too, which owing to its disorders and excesses, required the most stringent rules for its proper regulation. The superintendent minister desired me to tarry some days in Augusta; furnished me with letters of introduction to the brethren there, and in the event of the preacher, who was appointed to preach on the following Lord's-day in his stead; failing to come, he made the necessary arrangements, and directed me to supply his lack of service. I set off for Augusta in the steam boat at two o'clock, P.M., and arrived there at nine in the evening; and it being dark, I was unable to find the inn to which I had been directed; but the Lord was with me to preserve me. Being alone so late at night, I felt uncomfortable, as a female and a stranger, and wandered about until I came to the principal hotel, into which I entered and received great kindness from the landlord. In the morning he went himself to Mr. Robinson, and informed him I was inquiring for him, whereupon that gentleman came to the hotel for me, conducted me to his house, and very kindly entertained me. From the moment I consented to tarry in Augusta, till the next Lord's-day, I felt a very heavy cloud upon my soul, for I had received no direction from the Lord upon it, but had acted upon my own judgment. I went mourning by day and passed two nights in sleepless sorrow. Mr. Robinson informed me that the committee of the society were about to meet in the evening, that the question of my preaching there must be submitted to them, and he would inform me of their decision, but the time passed by and I heard nothing thereof. On the Lord's-day morning, after breakfast, as I was praying in private to my heavenly Father, and desiring to know why my soul was thus shut up in confusion and obscurity, the Lord was pleased to give me this answer, "Thus saith the Lord, the brethren are divided in their sentiments; nevertheless, though clouds and darkness be with thee, I will deliver thee; my presence shall go with thee, and I will give thee rest." I then went into the parlour, and said to Mrs. Robinson, "My dear madam, since my coming here, I have not enjoyed that rich endowment of the light of the Holy Spirit which I usually experience, nor could I imagine the reason thereof." I further stated, that my heavenly Father and showed me the reason, viz., that I have come amongst a people who are divided in their sentiments; and that the brethren are not perfectly joined together in the same mind, and in the same judgment. She then burst into a flood of tears, and said, "Well, if they will not receive those whom God is pleased to send, we cannot help it." When the time came for morning service, I accompanied Mr. and Mrs. Robinson to the chapel. The congregation assembled, but the minister, who was appointed to preach, did not come: after waiting some time for the preacher, and he not coming,

Mr. R. came and requested me to take the pulpit; but having made no preparation whatever to conduct the public services, I declined, stating that I had no desire to intrude myself upon the attention of the congregation contrary to the feeling of the church; upon this, a gentleman present said he would not bind the rest of the brethren by his peculiar view; that he would go to another meeting, and leave them at liberty to act as they pleased. He then withdrew; and one of the brethren rose and assured me that all the brethren present were of one mind as to my preaching; and hoped that I would consider myself amongst my friends and not feel the least embarrassment.

I then repaired to the desk, and conducted the service, though with but little of my accustomed unction and freedom. In the afternoon, however, it pleased God to grant us a time of refreshing indeed. The chapel, which was large and commodious, was densely crowded; and, at the conclusion, one of the brethren arose and proclaimed that a meeting would be held there in the evening also; and in the evening, so great was the concourse, that crowds remained at the chapel doors unable to gain an entrance; and numbers were forced to retire disappointed of any accommodation. The presence of the Holy One was also manifested, and the glory of God filled the house. Although greatly fatigued with the exertions of this day, at five o'clock on the following morning, I took the stage for Bangor, and rode seventy miles that day over a remarkably uneven ground, sometimes ascending the sides of the mountains, and at other times jolting through the rocky valleys. After a very fatiguing journey we arrived at Bangor at four o'clock, P.M., and I was kindly received by Mr. Brown, a very respectable gentleman of colour, who stood in high repute among the people: this gentleman went and apprised the Methodist preacher of my arrival: who soon came to see me, and gave me invitations to the pulpit, the classes, and the family in which he resided. I attended their quarterly meeting, and also a love feast, with very great enjoyment and profit to my own soul: the meeting was attended with divine power of very perceptible density; the people spoke with great feeling, and fluent utterance; the Spirit of the Lord directed and inspired the meeting, and much good was effected on that occasion. My visit to Bangor was replete with reciprocal benefits to them and myself. I truly saw there the grace of God, and was glad; for the Lord sent the Spirit of His Son into the hearts of many, crying, Abba, Father! and sealed them with His Holy Spirit of promise [Gal. 4:6]. After remaining with them a few days, I took my leave of them and returned by the route by which I came. The day was very rainy; and the coach was closely shut up, that no inside passenger could be seen; nevertheless, I had not been in Augusta an hour, before Mr. Robinson came to the house where I was, to engage me to preach in the chapel that evening. I accordingly, went and preached, during one of the most terrific thunder-storms I ever witnessed; the heavens gathered blackness; the God of glory thundered; He uttered His voice, and that a mighty voice, which divided the flames of fire: the awfulness of the evening gave an increased solemnity to the service; in the night a vessel was lost upon the coast; and all hands except two perished. In the morning I went by the stage coach to Bath; and two young men, the only survivors of the crew of the wrecked vessel were amongst the passengers. I was very kindly received by my dear friends in Bath; and, according to previous engagement, I preached in their Chapel in the evening; and a delightful visitation of the love of God was enjoyed by the congregation. I felt a most spiritual union with this people, which I believe will be renewed with increased delights in the world of bliss; the Lord had enabled me to endure with meekness and patience, the repulsive treatment I met with from them on my first introduction amongst them; and we afterwards became more closely united and endeared to each other, than we perhaps might have been, if my first reception had been more courteous; their subsequent behaviour was full of kindness and tender affection; we enjoyed many happy hours in each other's company, and the time of my departure was painfully affecting. I then returned to Portland, after an absence of about three months; and after an abode there of some few weeks, I journeyed to another part of the Lord's heritage, going from one town to another, the Lord having opened many doors to me, and given me access to every denomination of Christians, my labours greatly abounded. My earthen vessel was continually exhausted, and as continually replenished; my bodily frame was often wearied in the service of my Saviour, Proprietor and Lord; and many an hospitable home was opened by his providential care, to furnish me with refreshment and repose.

> "Here I raise my Ebenezer,
> Hither by thy help I've come,
> And I hope, by thy good pleasure,
> Safely to arrive at home."

At one little town that I visited, it having been announced that I should preach in a large school room usually appropriated for that purpose; when I was proceeding thither, accompanied by some friends, at the time appointed, my mind suddenly became disquieted; and I said, 'what is the matter, for I feel that there is something not right'; the friends who were with me, however, made light of my inquiry; but it soon appeared that some dissolute and ruffianly persons had conspired together to come and break up the meeting; and they had so far intimidated the brethren who should have opened the doors, that they durst not go forward to prepare the place! One of the sisters then procured the key, and opened the room. A great concourse of people assembled; and I commenced the service in entire ignorance of the disturbance which was projected. In a short time afterwards the conspirators entered the room, their leader tarrying at the door; the power of the Lord was visibly present; and the rabble were overawed and restrained from their purpose. Their champion growing impatient, then made his appearance—an unusually stout and ferocious looking man: he came close up to me, making a demonstration as if he intended to seize or strike me, but this producing no impression upon me, he stood over me as if he would take my life; but God was with me, and I felt no fear. He then seated himself beside his companions, pulled their hair, and groaned aloud, in derision of the Methodists! Those groans rested upon my spirit; the thread of my discourse was suspended, and I was directed to rebuke and exhort him personally, telling him that those groans would soon be repeated in reality; and it was not improbable that he might be suddenly cut off from the land of the living, and required to give a woeful account of himself at the bar of God. I thus cleared my soul of his blood, and left him in the hands of God. On the next day, as I was walking in the town, this very man came and civilly accosted me, and invited me to call at his house, which I did, and prayed with him and his family, and departed. Proceeding further, I met with the gang of his confederates; who addressed me, and entreated my forgiveness for their misbehaviour on the previous evening; and while I assured them of my forgiveness, I exhorted them to seek forgiveness from God, whose majesty had been insulted by their disrespectful conduct toward His servants and the ordinance of His worship. I then left the town; and, in a few days afterwards, I learnt that their champion had died suddenly, from the rupture of a blood-vessel in the lungs! having gone from his house but fifteen minutes before in perfect health: this event made a deep impression on the minds of the people in that locality, and caused the fear of God to rest upon many. I then visited another part of that country, where an abundant field of labour was presented before me; and the Lord applied His word as a two-edged sword, to the conviction and awakening of many souls; but lest I should be too much elated with my ministerial prosperity, my course received a check by the oversetting of the chaise in which I was returning one evening from the house of God, by which my ancle was broken, and I was laid by for a time; but after a few months, my hurt was recovered, and I resumed my work in the vineyard of the Lord. I then returned to Portland, and thence proceeded to Boston, which I left for Rhode Island; where I passed some time amongst the Christian brethren. In the town of Providence there was a great shaking among the dry bones; the Spirit of God entered into them, and many began to live.[35] I proceeded from thence to New Bedford, where I was cordially received by the minister of the Freewill Baptist congregation. I preached there many times; and then went to the Island of Nantucket, intending, in a few days, to return to New York and see my daughter, from whom I had been absent more than two years, and whom I had a great desire to see: but God ordered it otherwise; for when about to sail for New York, the wind shifted, and was so contrary, that the vessel could not go out of the harbour, and I returned again on shore to the house of my friend; before the wind became favourable, I was attacked with a very severe fit of illness, by which I was confined for a long time: I therefore sent for my daughter to come to me; and, on her arrival, the interview was very affecting to us both. The physician gave no hopes of my recovery, but prayer was made on my behalf by day and night. Miss Sarah M. Coffin, a young lady in the vicinity, incessantly visited me, and prayed much and fervently for me. One evening, while praying by my bed-side, she used these words, which were written on my heart as with an iron pen, or the point of a diamond—"Lord, of consistent with thy will, spare our sister Elaw, and take my life in her stead; for she is useful to thy cause, and I am but a feeble worm, and but of little worth." Her affection for me was as great as that of Aquila and Priscilla for St. Paul, who would have laid down their own necks upon the block for him [Rom. 16:4]. One day I was so ill, that my attendants were expecting my breath to cease. The medical attendant came in, and informed them, that he was about to fetch the principal physician on the island to see me. The friends were then sitting around me, and an elderly lady, a Baptist, came into the chamber, sat down, and looked at me awhile, and then said, "Mrs. Elaw, I am bidden to tell you, that you will get better; God has a great work for you yet to do, and I think you will travel some thousands of miles yet." On her departure, our second preacher came in, and such was the weakness of my faith in the word of Him who had said, "Thou shalt see London, and declare my name there," that I requested the minister to attend my funeral; gave him a portion of Scripture to preach from, and the hymns I wished to be sung on the occasion. Having promised compliance, if the event so required, he kneeled down and prayed the Lord to grant that I might yet be raised up, to stand forth in the name of God and declare His truth. While he was praying, I felt the evidence of the Holy Spirit, witnessing, that his prayer was heard, and that God had granted the request of his lips. From that very hour I began to amend; and some time after, Miss Coffin came in and asked how I was, saying, that she had requested a lady with whom she was acquainted, a Quakeress, to make special prayer to the Lord for me; for said she, "We cannot have thee die." She further stated that the friendly Quakeress had waited upon God on my behalf, and had received this answer by the Holy Ghost: "She shall get better, and in this Island shall hereafter be her home." As far as my own mind was concerned, I had no anxiety either to live or die, knowing, that for me to live would be for Christ's service, but to die, my gain. I sometimes thought, I shall never see England: yet it was generally met by an internal whisper, "the mouth of the Lord hath spoken it." However after an illness of eight months' duration, my health was re-established, and I was again brought forth to the service of my heavenly master; and the kind friends would not consent for me to leave the island: my daughter also married and settled in it, thus verifying the prediction of the prophetess, that my home should hereafter be on this delightful spot. The Lord thus established my goings here; and, as my strength increased, so also did my labours. I had a numerous class to lead, and much employment in the ministry also. There were two chapels in the occupation of the society; in the one, situated in the upper part of the town, I statedly preached on the Lord's-day afternoon; and, in the evening, I assisted our beloved minister in the large chapel, where we enjoyed a little heaven below. Numerous souls were awakened and converted to God; and inquiry after the way of life and salvation was prevalent in every part of the town. The work of God was our entire pursuit; and we knew nothing among the people, but Jesus Christ, and Him crucified. I was constantly going from house to house, both early and late; and thus I spent two happy years in the pleasant Island of Nantucket, the Lord blessing both my going out and my coming in.

I afterwards took my daughter with me, and went into the land of our nativity to visit our brethren and see how they did: we came to the city of Philadelphia, had a joyful meeting with our brethren, and abode in that city for a little space: while there, I engaged to go to a small town at some distance, whither I had been once before; but my arrangements for this journey were twice frustrated; and on returning from my second disappointment I called upon a friend in Philadelphia, and remarked, that it appeared to be contrary to the mind of God for me to go thither: while thus talking there appeared a young man standing before me, and although conscious that it was a supernatural appearance, I involuntarily exclaimed, "what is this?" The suggestion then took possession of my mind, that if I yet persisted in going thither, the Lord would there convert this young man by my ministry as a token that He had sent me. In a third attempt I was more successful; and when I appeared in the congregation, I looked for him; but saw no young man whose person and apparel I could identify as the man whom I had seen in my vision: however, on the last evening of my stay there, after I had preached, the same young man, habited in the very apparel I had beheld in the vision, came forward and shook hands with me; testifying, that the Lord had sent me to awaken his soul, and separate him from his sins unto the Lord. He corresponded with me several years afterward, and gave evidence that he was standing fast in the faith, and progressing in the knowledge of God, and I was informed that he continually made mention of me in his prayers in the public congregations as well as in private. Having tarried some time with my friends in those parts, we returned back to New York; and having promised to accompany the brethren there to a camp-meeting in the neighbourhood, the time for holding which had not arrived, I left my daughter there, and proceeded on to Albany, which is distant about three hundred miles: the Lord graciously preparing the way by His providential operations. I preached in many chapels throughout that region; and the Methodists opened an extra house purposely for me; a very large and commodious building, but greatly insufficient to contain the masses who flocked thither to hear the word of God: the presence of the Lord accompanied my ministry, and rendered it the power of God to the salvation of many. When it was first announced that a female would preach in that chapel, a gentleman in the vicinity had a strong desire to come and hear me, and proposed for his lady to accompany him; but she objected, that it was unbecoming in a woman to preach; and also, that God never commissioned women to preach: he however, very much urged her, and at length he overcame her objections by persuasions; and they came, and the word was effectually sown in her heart with quickening power from God, her former sentiments became completely reverted; for, as she had never before experienced the searching and converting power of the word under a sermon, she was ready to imagine that none beside myself on earth had received the commission of God to preach the gospel; when she got home, she read of Christ sending the women to inform the disciples and Peter, that he was risen from the dead; she then reprobated the folly of her former objections; for said she, I now perceive that the first preachers of the resurrection were women: thus the Scriptures become as a new volume, when the Lord opens and illuminates the eyes of our mind. The Scriptures ever develop new and surprising truths to the regenerate soul; and in proportion to our measure of grace, and of the Spirit of God, is the illumination which accompanies our perusal of the Scriptures without some perception of their unparalleled glories, the divine lustre of which is so peculiar that the expositions furnished by the wisdom of this world, and all the elucidations of human learning, fail of any imitation of its radiance: it is the high privilege of those who are begotten by the Word of truth to read the Scriptures, not as the word of man, but as they are indeed, the Word of God, a sacred volume, the production of the infinite God; the true key of this heavenly book is the Spirit of truth; under whose guidance and illumination we ascertain and enter into the mind of God; therein beholding as in a mirror, the glory of Jesus, we become increasingly assimilated to the same image, from one degree of glory to another, as by the Spirit of the Lord.

While I was in this district, I had intelligence of my only surviving brother, and took a further journey of three hundred miles to Utica, to see him; I found him there, married and comfortably settled in life. I had not seen him since his departure from our parental roof; at which time I was a child of six years of age. It was an affectingly joyful meeting to us both; and my gratitude to the Lord was heightened by finding in him a fellow-traveller to the kingdom of heaven, and a member of the Baptist church in Utica. I there met with Mrs. Jones, a female preacher, who had come from England, where it appeared her ministry had been popular, though it was otherwise with her in America. Being myself a member of the parent stock, or the old Methodist Society, I possessed an advantage over many other labourers, in having access to many pulpits which they had not. The dear brethren in Utica freely opened their chapels to me; and we enjoyed many very blessed opportunities of edification to our souls. In one of their large chapels in which I preached, a number of young men conspired together, and came to hear me, with their hands filled with stones; intending, if I uttered any sentiments which they disapproved of, to pelt me therewith: my brother had driven me to the place in a carriage and pair; the chapel was amazingly crowded, the presence of the Lord overshadowed the assembly, and the worship suffered no interruption from the young gentlemen, who came, not to be instructed in the way of the truth, but to sit in judgment on and try my discourse by the standard of their petty opinions. After service, my brother went to fetch the horses from some stables adjacent, these tyros were standing there; and he overheard their conversation, discovered their wicked plot and heard them confess that they knew not what ailed them when they entered the chapel; but their arms seemed bound and held down, and were so paralized that they dropped the stones upon the floor, and that their emotions were such during the service as they had never felt before. Having spent a very happy week with my brother, I was compelled to hasten back to New York to fulfil my engagement with the brethren there. On going to the water side to take my passage in the two o'clock steamer, the captain informed me that he had no room for another passenger; though my complexion appeared to be the chief reason of his refusal. I was therefore in a strait, for the performance of my engagement with the brethren in New York depended on my going that day; however, I learnt that there was another steamer about to start at seven in the evening; and on my application, the captain thereof agreed to take me with him. I therefore thanked God and took courage. We had a very pleasant passage, and many of the persons on board belonged to the household of faith; and what with edifying conversation, and the relation of each other's experience, we enjoyed a little Bethel. On the deck in the morning, I noticed several of the gentlemen engaged in very earnest conversation, and perceived that their discourse had reference to me; I therefore withdrew into the cabin, and had been there but a few minutes when one of them came and requested me to preach them a sermon on board. I replied that I felt no desire to preach by the will of man, and to gratify a human curiosity; he then assured me that the gentlemen who concurred in this request, were persons of integrity, whose aim was not novelty and curiosity, but edification. I then objected that the captain might not approve of such an attempt; he said he would ask permission of the captain and withdrew. The captain's consent being obtained, the crew came, and seated themselves in the cabin to the number of sixty. I then read a hymn, prayed, delivered a short address, concluded the service and took my seat. In a short time, I again perceived them in close conversation, and apparently talking about me, and I therefore withdrew; the same gentleman presently called me back, and said, "these gentlemen are greatly gratified by your discourse, and desire your acceptance of your passage money;" upon which he presented me with a sum which more than covered the expense of my passage. I was therefore astonished at the fresh display of the kind providence of my indulgent God; for I was then much straitened in pecuniary matters, and was three hundred miles distant from New York; they then informed me that five of their number were ministers of the gospel, and I saw how remarkably God had overruled matters to prevent my passage in the earliest vessel, to introduce me to so many Christian friends, and arrange for me so convenient a supply of money for my necessities. I arrived in New York safely; and after fulfilling my engagements with the brethren proceeded home to Nantucket, where we found all things well, and the brethren rejoiced at and welcomed our return. We arrived at home on a Saturday, having been a week on our journey from New York, at a very critical point of time. In the evening after our arrival, our dear minister, Mr. Pierce, called to see us, and requested my assistance on the approaching Lord's-day. I therefore resumed my former labours in the congregations. On Tuesday, December 10, 1834, my daughter was safely delivered of her first-born son, and the blessing of the Lord very apparently rested upon the family. Soon after this, our Baptist brethren being destitute of a minister, and the coloured people of that denomination having a chapel on the island, requested me to preach statedly to them; which, with the consent of Mr. Pierce, I did, and the Lord wrought marvellously among them; the holy fire was greatly diffused throughout the town; many of the coloured people were turned to the Lord, and I had the pleasure of seeing them at the sea-side immersed into Christ, they putting on the Lord Jesus in the ordinance of believing baptism. Our Methodist class-meetings also were powerfully attended with the presence and operations of the Holy Spirit; and indeed a wonderful revival of the work of the Lord ensued, which extended to every part of the town, and to every denomination of Christians. On the meeting of the conference, our dear minister, Mr. Pierce, was removed from the island, and the Rev. J. Lovejoy was stationed there in his stead. He manifested himself a faithful minister of the cross of Jesus, and I enjoyed with him the same intimate friendship and unity of faith, of purpose and effort as with Mr. Pierce. My daughter was some time afterwards attacked by a very serious illness, which continued upon her for a long time without any prospect of amendment; but one day, our minister called to see her, and prayed most fervently with her, and during prayer, the Lord vouchsafed a surprising manifestation to her soul, and from that very hour both she and the infant began to recover.

Having laboured for some time at home with very great success, my mind again began to be impressed with the weight of more distant spheres of labour, and my impressions seemed directed to the States of New Hampshire and Vermont. About this time it happened that I was from home a few weeks on a visit; and as I was sitting in the house of God, I was caught up in spirit, away from and far above all sublunary things; and appeared to be standing on a very elevated place in the midst of tens of thousands, who were all seated around, clothed in white; my own complexion and raiment were also white, and I was employed in addressing this immense concourse: it was such a scene as had never before entered into my conceptions; and presently it disappeared and I found myself again in the chapel. I pondered this wonderful vision over in my mind, and concluded that it was given to me as a token that the Lord had destined me for enlarged and more elevated spheres of effort; and the Christian friends to whom I related it, also thought it a prelude to my future ministerial work. After this, I returned home, and in a few weeks afterwards, the same vision, but much nearer and more vivid than before, was presented before me in the chapel, as I was sitting under a sermon; and after a short interval it was presented to me a third time in the class meeting; but more vividly still. I related these visions to Mr. Lovejoy's mother, who concurred in my interpretation of them; adding that she thought it was my duty to go out again on an itinerating ministry; some time after this, the sisters of our society presented me with a quantity of apparel, with some money, which they had secretly prepared and subscribed; bidding me to go in the name of the Lord, and call sinners to repentance. Thus again was that Scripture verified to me, "Seek ye the kingdom of God and His righteousness, and all these things shall be added unto you" [Matt. 6:33].

I left home again in July, 1835; and was absent fifteen months: the Lord graciously prepared the minds of the people everywhere for my ministry; and many received the word with gladness and singleness of heart. I was in Boston when Mr. George Thompson was lecturing there on the abominations of slavery; great crowds were attracted to his lectures, and much light was diffused by his zealous exertions in the cause of emancipation.[36] From Boston I went to Lynn to attend the Conference. I was there introduced to Bishop Hedding, and spent an afternoon in his company. He requested a sight of my testimonials and letters of recommendation, which I handed him; and he expressed his entire satisfaction with them, but inquired if it should be found that my ministry was calculated to excite contention, many persons being strongly averse to the ministry of females, whether I would be willing to relinquish it. To which, I replied, that no ambition of mine, but the special appointment of God, had put me into the ministry; and, therefore, I had no option in the matter; and as to such Christians as take up ignorant and prejudiced objections against my labours; men whose whims are law, who walk after the imagination of their own hearts, and to whom the cause of God is a toy; I could not for a moment study their gratification at the sacrifice of duty. It is an easy matter to adopt a string of notions on religion, and make a great ado about them; but the weight of religious obligation, and the principle of conscientious obedience to God are quite another matter. I enjoyed the good bishop's company, and heard him with pleasure avow that he should be sorry in any way to discourage me.[37]

From Lynn I itinerated from city to city, and from village to village, preaching the gospel of the kingdom in the fear of the Lord; and great was the number of those who believed and were baptised.

On my visit to Flushing, I preached from Isaiah xxxviii. 1, "Set thine house in order; for thou shalt die and not live." Under that sermon many persons were awakened, and among the number was one poor woman who cried to the Lord for mercy, and applied for admission into the church; but her application was rejected, because she was then cohabiting with a man by whom she had borne five children, yet had neglected to comply with the matrimonial form required by the law of the state. Whether her position was that of mere concubinage or marriage de facto; and whether the brethren were in their decision equally justified by Scripture as by the law of the state and the sense of society, are points which may admit of much discussion: the marriage customs and laws set forth by God in the Scriptures, are so widely opposite from those of civilized nations in modern times, that when such cases arise, and the sacred and secular authorities clash upon them, it is not easy to determine what course ought to be pursued by a Christian communion. Happily, however, these parties immediately complied with the requirement of the American marriage law, the usage of society, and the dictum of the church; upon which they were admitted into the Methodist connexion, lived happily in the Lord, and became respected as good members of society.

On leaving Flushing, I took a long and circuitous route, and after an absence of fifteen months, returned home with great peace of mind.

I remained at home this time for the space of three years with the exception of an occasional short journey, and visit of a few weeks; and throughout this period, my mind was often burdened with the weight of a voyage to England. I often argued the matter before the Lord in prayer, pleading my ignorance, my sex, my colour and my inability to minister the gospel in a country so polished and enlightened, so furnished with Bibles, so blessed with ministers, so studded with temples; but the Lord said, "say not, I cannot speak; for thou shalt go to all to whom I send thee, and what I command thee, thou shalt speak" [Jer. 1:7].

In 1837, when on a visit to some religious friends, one morning, I saw a remarkable vision; I appeared to be in a strange place and conversing with a stranger, when three enormous balls of fire came perpendicularly over my head, and each of them exploded and burst at the same moment: I instantly appeared to fall to the ground; but was caught up by an unseen hand, and placed upon an animal, which darted with me through the regions of the air, with the velocity of lightning, and deposited me inside the window of an upper chamber. I there heard the voice of the Almighty, saying, "I have a message for her to go with upon the high seas, and she will go." This occurrence took place just three years prior to my departure from America.

In 1839, the Lord was pleased to send me again into the Southern states; and as I travelled from city to city, I felt the impression that the time was near when I must leave the land of my nativity for a foreign shore. In the town of Providence, Rhode Island, I preached on a Thursday evening in a large room, for Mr. Bedell. On the following Lord's-day, I attended the Wesleyan Chapel, where I heard Mr. Bedell in the morning, and by his invitation, occupied his pulpit in the afternoon, on which occasion the chapel proved much too small for the crowds which assembled; after the service, some leading gentlemen from another denomination came to Mr. Bedell, and offered him the use of their chapel, which was much larger than his, for the evening service. It was thankfully accepted, and I preached there in the evening, to an immense audience. Mr. Bedell and his lady were both of them natives of England; at that time he was stationed in the Providence circuit. I had not been in their company a quarter of an hour when both of them avowed their concurrent impression, that I was destined by the Lord to minister the gospel in a foreign land: such an observation appeared to me very remarkable. From Providence I visited New York, Philadelphia and Baltimore; and wherever I went, the inquiry was continually made, if I was not about shortly to embark for England, accompanied by observations that my ministry was ultimately destined for a different arena than was furnished by America. I went on to the city of Washington, and our meetings there were greatly distinguished by the presence and operations of the Holy Spirit. Lady Hunter, of whom mention is made in my former visit to that city thirteen years before, presented me with a contribution in aid of this purpose; and I could not but remark, how the Lord everywhere moved the minds of my friends to make it a topic of conversation; thereby keeping it always before me, and increasing the stimulus of my mind towards it; and without any solicitation of mine, they presented me their cheerful contributions; yea, both white and coloured brethren, voluntarily came forward with their free-will offerings, to enable me to undertake the voyage, and bade me go and preach to strangers in a strange land, in the name of the Lord. Many were the proofs besides those related in this work, that the Lord gave me of His purpose that I should come to England; and being now many hundreds of miles distant from my daughter, and feeling that the Lord's time had arrived, I wrote to apprise her thereof, and shortly after returned homewards as far as New York, where I attended the anniversary of the abolition society:[38] many of the speakers on that occasion came over to England to attend the great anti-slavery meeting in Exeter Hall. I then returned home; and was very affectionately received by my dear daughter; and made all possible dispatch in preparations for my departure.

The parting moment was painful in the extreme; for my daughter, and her two dear little boys, were entwined in the strongest affections of my heart; but I durst not disobey Him who had said unto me, as He had said unto Abraham, "Get thee out from thy country, and from thy kindred, and from thy father's house, unto a land that I will show thee" [Gen. 12:1]. On the 10th of June 1840, I rose from the bed on which I had laid for the last time; the recollection of that bitter morning even now suffuses my eyes with tears, and interrupts the delineations of my pen: the morning was calm, our minds resigned and peaceful, and we took, and held each other's hand, in silence; which was at length broken by my daughter, who said, "Mother, we part now, but I think we shall yet meet again; the will of the Lord be done, and God be with thee." At nine o'clock A.M., I bade farewell to those dear ties, and started for New York, where I tarried until the 1st July; and then I took the steam-boat to go to the ship Philadelphia,

Captain Morgan, which vessel was lying in quarantine. Soon after our arrival on board, she got under weigh, and set sail for the port of London. My feelings on leaving the land of my nativity, and all that was dear to me on earth, were acutely indescribable; but God commanded, and I obeyed; bidding farewell to my country, and, committing my dear friends to the grace of God. The wind was fair, the passengers agreeable, and we were soon carried beyond the view of land. On the following morning, I awoke and presented my thanksgivings to my heavenly Father for His preserving care of me throughout the night. I then went upon deck, and surveyed the broad canopy above, and the rolling ocean beneath, gently moving wave after wave, as we glided over its tremulous surface. I observed the birds of the air flying over our heads, and wondered, at such a distance from land, that they were able to take such excursions without resting. I beheld the finny tribes pouring forth by thousands. I was now floating on the great and wide sea, wherein are things creeping innumerable, both small and great beasts. There go the ships! there is that great leviathan whom thou hast made to play therein. These wait all upon thee, that thou mayest give them their meat in due season. Oh Lord, how manifold are thy works! in wisdom hast thou made them all! the earth is full of thy riches. Psalm civ. 24, 27.

On the 23rd day of July, we were cheered with the sight of land; and on the 24th, we came to anchor off Falmouth, where most of the cabin passengers left us. On the evening of the 25th, we came safely into the London Docks: this was on a Saturday; and on the morning of the Lord's-day, I first set my foot on British ground. As I proceeded along Ratcliff Highway, I was much surprised to see the shops open, and many kinds of business in the course of transaction, women crying fruits for sale, and the people intent on traffic and marketing. I was indeed astonished, that in the metropolis of the most Christian country in the world, such a want of respect should be indicated towards the day which Jesus signalised by His resurrection, and His apostles practically set apart for the commemoration of His eucharistic sacrament, and the ordinances of His religion. Whether the literal and exact requirements of the fourth commandment be, in the case of Christians, transferred from the Jewish Sabbath to the "Lord's-day," is a point upon which all the disciples of Christ are not agreed; but if Christians are not bound to observe an absolute quietude and rest thereon, they certainly are bound to pay it that respect which is due to the day on which our redemption was assured by the Lord's resurrection—a day which was made sacred by the practice of His apostles, and by their inspired authority, called the "Lord's-day." Having taken apartments in Well-close-square, in the evening I attended at the Countess of Huntingdon's chapel,[39] in Pell-street, and heard a discourse which afforded some encouragement to the heart of a female stranger in a foreign land. Some days elapsed ere I met with any of the Methodist family; but, going on the Wednesday evening again to Pell-street chapel, as I was passing a window, I caught sight of a lady, whose appearance powerfully arrested my attention; and it appeared that the feeling of surprise and interest was mutual. I turned back, and spoke to her, and inquired if she was acquainted with any section of the Methodist body? She said that her daughter should on the following evening conduct me to the Wesleyan chapel of St. George, which she did accordingly; and I found that several class meetings were held on that evening; on that occasion, I met with Mr. A—— who introduced me to Mr. C—— one of the local preachers; and I was admitted into the class led by him, and enjoyed a very sweet time of refreshing from the presence of the Lord. I became acquainted also with Mrs. T.—a true sister in the Lord, who has since fallen asleep in Jesus: and was introduced to a gentleman who interested himself greatly on my behalf, very considerably enlarged the circle of my acquaintance, and even ushered me before the committees of the peace and anti-slavery societies. I found my situation rather awkward in reference to the latter body. I was first received by a deputation of three gentlemen, and afterwards admitted before the board. It was really an august assembly; their dignity appeared so redundant, that they scarcely knew what to do with it all. Had I attended there on a matter of life and death, I think I could scarcely have been more closely interrogated or more rigidly examined; from the reception I met with, my impression was, that they imagined I wanted some pecuniary or other help from them; for they treated me as the proud do the needy. In this, however, they were mistaken. Among many other questions, they demanded to be informed, whether I had any new doctrine to advance, that the English Christians are not in possession of? To which I replied, no; but I was sent to preach Christ, and Him crucified: unto the Jews a stumbling-block, and unto the Greeks foolishness [1 Cor. 1:23]: they also wished to be informed, how it came about that God should send me? to which I replied, that I could not tell; but I knew that God required me to come hither, and that I came in obedience to His sovereign will; but that the

Almighty's design therein was best known to Himself; but behold! said I, "I am here." Pride and arrogancy are among the master sins of rational beings; an high look, a stately bearing, and a proud heart, are abominations in the sight of God, and insure a woeful reverse in a future life. Infidels will indulge in pomposity and arrogance; but Christians are and must be humble and lowly. As a servant of Jesus, I am required to bear testimony in his name, who was meek and lowly, against the lofty looks of man, and the assumptions of such lordly authority and self-importance. Ere this work meets the eye of the public, I shall have sojourned in England five years: and I am justified in saying, that my God hath made my ministry a blessing to hundreds of persons; and many who were living in sin and darkness before they saw my coloured face, have risen up to praise the Lord, for having sent me to preach His Gospel on the shores of Britain; numbers who had been reared to maturity, and were resident in localities plentifully furnished with places of worship and ministers of the gospel, and had scarcely heard a sermon in their lives, were attracted to hear the coloured female preacher, were inclosed in the gospel net, and are now walking in the commandments and ordinances of the Lord. I have travelled in several parts of England, and I thank God He has given me some spiritual children in every place wherein I have laboured.

Soon after my arrival, I met with a gentleman, who advised my immediate return to my own country; adding that if he had been in America before my departure and had known my intention, he would have advised me better: I replied, that I had no will of my own in the matter; but my heavenly Father commanded, and I durst not confer with flesh and blood, but obeyed and came: but like other men destitute of faith in God, he did not comprehend this kind of argument; and persisted in his worldly reasonings, saying that people did not give away their gold here, and I had much better return. It is to be deplored that there are so many Christians of this person's cast: who are of the world; speak in accordance with its principles and sentiments, and walk according to its course. Instead of having little faith, they discover none at all: ignorant of the Scriptures and of the power of God, the love of the Father is not in them. Having parted with this Laodicean gentleman, I called upon Mrs. H., in Princes-square: and my mind being somewhat damped, I sat a few minutes in silence, which Mrs. H. broke by an affectionate inquiry into my circumstances; at the same time, presenting me with a handsome donation;

telling me not to be discouraged, for the Lord would open my way and sustain me: my mind was cheered and my faith strengthened by this opportune proof of the power of God to furnish succours and raise up friends for His people even in a land of strangers.

In a few days after, Mrs. T. introduced me to some of the Bible Christians, or Bryanites, as they are called; who are, I believe, a secession from the Wesleyan Methodists: our reception from them was very cool; but one of the brethren was about to preach in the street; and he invited me to preach in his stead. Accordingly at the time appointed, we repaired to the street and commenced the meeting; a very great crowd assembled, and I preached to them; but the meeting was broken up by two policemen, who came and tapped me on the shoulder, and desired me to desist; they demanded what authority I had for preaching? a gentleman present said, "she has her authority in her hand," that is, "the Word of God:" we then departed.

On the following Lord's-day morning, I attended with Mrs. T., at Salem chapel; and, in the afternoon, I preached in Stepney-fields, to a very numerous auditory. A very heavy thunder shower fell during the service, yet very few persons retired in consequence of it. When the service was terminated, a gentleman and lady came, and inquired of me where I resided? and desired me to call and visit them; which, in the course of a few days, I did, and was very affectionately received: the lady, Mrs. T., then invited me to spend a day with them, to which I consented, and enjoyed a heavenly day in their company. She then engaged me to spend a week with them; I did so, and a delightful week it was. The house was a little Bethel to us, and in the stated morning and evening worship of the family, the Lord manifested Himself in very rich displays of grace. Before my week expired, Mrs. T. sent to my apartments for my trunk, and bade me account her house my home during my sojourn in England. Their second daughter, who has since fallen asleep in Jesus, a most interesting and excellent young lady, was then greatly afflicted with a disease of the heart: our communion in the Spirit was exceedingly choice and precious; I richly enjoyed and highly prized her society.

I visited a number of small chapels in this vast metropolis, and endeavored to advance my heavenly Father's cause by attending many religious tea meetings; some of which I found very edifying and profitable to the soul. I also partook of a breakfast with a number of ministers and friends at Mr. B. T—rs., by his special invitation; and after this, I was sent for to Ramsgate, and travelled through the county of Kent, preaching the word in many of the towns and villages as I passed through them. When in Canterbury, my mind was much struck with the mutations of time upon the works of man. I beheld there some stately edifices which were venerable with age; I ascended the eminence of the Dane John, from which I had a full view of the town; the spot where some of the martyrs of Jesus sealed the truth with their blood, was pointed out to me; and as I gazed upon the memorable place, I thought of those faithful servants of God with much sympathy and yearning of heart.

Having received an invitation from some of the Primitive Methodists in Yorkshire, to go down and labour among them, I went thither by railway, and reached Pontefract about eight o'clock on the evening of the 30th of December, 1840; the distance was great, being about 170 miles; and I was very much fatigued with the journey. The hireling will make the best bargain he can; but they who bear the commissions of Jesus will find no sinecures involved in them, but frequently hard labour and harder fare. On my arrival, I was very kindly received by Mrs. Clift; and after a good night's repose, I was on the next morning much invigorated. On the following day, December 31, Mr. Colson the superintendent minister, and Mr. Crompton his assistant, called to see me, and explained the objects they had in view in sending for me. In the evening we attended a tea meeting of the Sunday School; on which occasion the children sang some beautiful anthems, and repeated some pieces with much correctness; the meeting was afterwards addressed by some of the brethren, and also by myself. At the conclusion of the meeting, we observed a watch night, as is customary with the Methodist societies, which was attended with much of the presence of God, the gracious manifestation of His Spirit, and with spiritual benefit to the souls of many. The weather was very inclement and rigorous; and an abundance of labour was presented before me, which I entered into with much delight and vigour, though with considerable weariness and distress to the body.

> "My shrinking flesh complains,
> And murmurs to contend so long;
> My mind superior is to pains:
> When I am weak, then am I strong."

On the 3rd of January, 1841, I went to Brotherton, and preached in the chapel belonging to the brethren; it was completely crowded, and the Lord was in the midst of us to bless His people with the manifestations of His grace and love. After service, I returned the same evening to Pontefract, very much exhausted with fatigue. On the following day

Mr. T— came to conduct me to Thorp, where I preached in the evening, from "Enter ye at the strait gate," Matt. vii. 13, with considerable energy of spirit; but, throughout my labours in England, I have found a far less favourable soil for the seed of the kingdom in the British mind than in the American. Human nature must be in every country radically the same; God is the same; yet the word preached is generally attended in America with far more powerful and converting results than in Britain. The population of the United States have not been so extensively vitiated by the infidelity and sedition of the press; and being more thinly spread over an immense territorial space, there is less of contamination than in the more condensed masses of English society; and they perhaps possess more honest simplicity of character, and less of the self-sufficiency of a licentious intellectuality and worldly wisdom. It is not for me, however, to account for the cause; the fact is but too apparent. I had many seals to my ministry in Yorkshire, notwithstanding the general barrenness of the mental soil; and found, in many of its towns, and especially in Leeds, a very loving, lively and benevolent Christian people; not only in the Methodist, but in other denominations also; and amongst the society of Friends. I attended one of the meetings of the Friends there, and whilst sitting among them, was moved by the Spirit to address them, and the dear friends received the message which came through the medium of their coloured sister with patience and delight.

I went to Leeds on the 4th of February; a place rendered memorable to the Methodist societies by the labours of Mrs. Fletcher, whose ministry the Lord so signally blest with the communications of His Spirit: the first place I preached at in Leeds was a chapel in Leylands, which had been in the occupation of the late Anne Carr, who had recently departed this life in the faith of Jesus; the place was then in the occupation of her companion in labours, Miss Martha Williams, and the Lord graciously gave me some seals to my ministry in that chapel. From thence, I went, on the 7th, to Mr. R—ds, and laboured with the Primitive Methodists on Quarry Hill. I attended several missionary meetings in their connexion, which were held in various circuits; taking up my abode chiefly at Miss P—s, and Mrs. A—s; under the hospitable roof of the latter friend, I spent many weeks, in peace and happiness, blessed with abundance of blessings spiritual and temporal. I also preached in Stanningley, for the primitive brethren; and for the Wesleyans, in their chapel; on which occasion, a very remarkable solemnity pervaded the assembly; and the Lord was pleased to direct my utterance, and give it such a pointedness, as made it apparent that it was a message from Himself. While I abode in that town, I lodged at Mr. G. W—s, with whose lady I went, by invitation, to breakfast with the minister, Mr. H. who was stationed there; we enjoyed a sweet and refreshing season in the family devotions of the morning; and I felt a strong attachment in the Spirit to Mrs. H—, who, though young in life, was blessed with the possession of deep piety or devotion; and a very sweet unction of the Holy Ghost abode on her spirit. From Stanningly I departed to Pontefract; and, in a few days afterwards, received a letter from a brother at the former place, informing me that one of the brethren there had died suddenly, on the day of my departure; but they sorrowed, at the loss of a dear brother on whose behalf they possessed a well grounded hope. Among others of the towns I visited in Yorkshire, was Bradford. I also preached an anniversary sermon at Shelf; being, while I sojourned there, the guest of Mr. B—y. On my return to Leeds, I met with a gentleman from Hull, who came to conduct me to that place. I accordingly went thither; and abode a few days preaching in different parts of the town. On one evening there were ten persons who professed to find peace with God through our Lord Jesus Christ. On another occasion a female who had left her first love, and lost the vitality as well as the name of spiritual life, was recovered from her lapsed condition and obtained peace to her soul. On my departure I engaged to come to them again, and preach to them on the opening of their new chapel; and this poor woman had desired to open her mind to me, and relate what great things God had done for her by my ministry; but ere that day came, her spirit had taken flight from this region of sin and grief; but she left a message for me on her deathbed, to assure me that she died in the faith of Christ, confiding in the God of her salvation.

From Hull I returned to Leeds; and, during my temporary abode there, the church sustained a loss in the sudden death of our dear brother, William Dawson, who had been a zealous champion in the work of the Lord. Several thousands of persons were congregated together on the day of his interment, to witness the procession, and manifest their respect to the memory of our departed brother. The corpse was brought out into the open air, and one of the ministers offered prayer to God; after which, Mr. Garland delivered an address, the local preachers and leaders then formed in order of procession, six abreast in the front of the hearse, and the cavalcade solemnly proceeded to the place of interment, which was several miles distant from Leeds; the whole distance being thronged by multitudes who anxiously witnessed the scene. From Leeds I took a tour of that part of the country, travelling from town to town, and village to village, preaching the gospel of the kingdom, and testifying to thousands of persons, repentance towards God, and faith in our Lord Jesus Christ. At the appointed time, I fulfilled my engagement at Hull, leaving on the 3rd of July; and on the day following, I preached at Brewery Fields, and had the pleasure to witness the conversion of four souls from darkness to light: at Keithly, I met with a gentleman and his wife, who were from Liverpool on a visit, and who gave me a very pressing invitation to come over to Liverpool and see them, which I promised to do. I preached on an anniversary occasion at Leylands, when seven souls entered into the liberty of the gospel. On the 23rd, I went to Wirksworth, accompanied by sister W—ms, and we were kindly received by Mr. S. E. and the friends there; I preached on the afternoon and evening of the day following in the chapel; when four persons received very manifest spiritual benefit. I also preached in the Wesleyan chapel in that town, and much enjoyed the interviews with its minister with which I was privileged.

Having written to the family in Liverpool who had so pressingly invited me to visit them, to apprise them of my coming, on the 2nd of August, I took leave of sister W. and the kind friends at Wirksworth, and travelled thither by way of Manchester, and arrived in Liverpool about six o'clock in the evening. On going to the residence of the parties who had invited me, I found that the lady and her daughter were absent from home; and the gentleman's memory was so reluctant, that he very distantly recognised me. I was greatly fatigued with my journey, and somewhat disappointed after such a journey, to find my reception so different from the invitation. I soon took my leave of one whom I found not at all careful to entertain strangers, or practice the Christian duty of hospitality, and went in search of lodgings, which I had great difficulty in procuring: but after wandering from place to place, and making many fruitless applications, I at length succeeded. It was of the Lord's goodness that I was at that inauspicious time possessed of sufficient money for my exigencies. My visit to this town was replete with discouragements. I attended several meetings of the association, who were holding their annual conference there at that time. I also made inquiries for the Wesleyans, and attended at Brunswick Chapel; and afterwards called upon the Rev. Mr. H., who received me with kindness, and referred me to Mr. D. the Wesleyan superintendent minister at that station. On my visit to Mr. D., he left directly on my introduction, to attend a funeral; but Mrs. D. entered into conversation with me, and assuming the theologian, reprobated female preaching as unscriptural; adding, that Mr. D. was greatly opposed to it, and always put it down if possible: she further said, that Paul ordained that a woman should not be suffered to speak in the church: but to sit in silence, and ask information of her husband at home. I was, however, too blind to discern, that for a female to warn sinners to flee from the wrath to come; to preach Christ to them, invite them to come to Him, and exhort them to be saved, was equally disorderly and improper with the interruptions of a church in its meetings and services, by the inquisitive questions of the females present; nor could I possibly understand how my ministry, which is directed to bring sinners to repentance, and employed in humble and affectionate attempts to stir up the pure minds of the saints, by way of remembrance and exhortation, involved any dictation or assumption of authority over the male sex. The apostle directed that a woman, when praying or prophecying, should have her head covered [1 Cor. 11:5]; from which it may be inferred, that the praying and prophecying of a woman is allowable; but Mrs. D. was differently minded, and thought that a preaching female ought to depart from the Methodist body, and unite with the Quakers; but the Lord, who raised up Deborah to be a prophetess, and to judge His people, and inspired Hulda[h] to deliver the counsels of God,[40] sent me forth not as a Quakeress but as a Methodist, and chiefly employed me to labour amongst the Methodists. I mentioned to her, some of the methods, by which the Lord made known to me His will, that I should go and preach the gospel; and these she met, by supposing, that it was possible I might have been misled. By this time, Mr. D. returned and his Christian charity seemed put to some little expense on finding that I had not decamped; I presented him my testimonials and certificates; as he returned them, he said, "But do you not know that we do not allow women to preach; and that there is nothing in the Scriptures that will allow of it at all?" Addressing me with much assumed authority and severity. "We do not allow," sounded very uncouthly in my ears in a matter in which the commission of the Almighty is assumed. I again related some of the manifestations made to me by the Holy Ghost in reference to this matter; to which he replied, that he could not see how God could, consistently with Himself, give me such directions. Doubtless he said the truth; for the line of worldly wisdom, self-sufficient reason and opinionated faith, can never gauge the operations of the Spirit of God; and always either rejects them at once, or meets them with, "How can these things be?" He then complimented me by adducing some instances, in which female preachers had misconducted themselves; and wound up his vituperations by saying, that the success of my labours in the ministry proved nothing in my favour; for that God would ever bless his word by whomsoever preached. Perhaps, had I taken upon myself to have investigated this gentleman's call to the ministry, I might have written Tekel upon it,[41] for his spiritual condition falls far short of the standard I have received: but Paul says, "Who art thou that judgeth another man's servant: to his own master he standeth or falleth," and, "Why dost thou judge thy brother" [Rom. 14:4, 10]. I then departed from this iron-hearted abode, somewhat distressed and wounded in spirit and at a loss what step I should take next.

But thanks be unto God; He knoweth how to deliver the godly out of temptations, and will not suffer us to be tempted above what we are able to bear. On the following morning I awoke, with these words passing through my mind,

"Angels are now hovering round us;
Unperceived, they mix the throng;
Wondering at the love which crowned us
Glad to join the holy song.
Hallelujah!
Love and praise to Christ belong."

I then felt the assurance of the Holy Spirit that the dark cloud which had so thickly and heavily pressed upon me was breaking; and a way soon after opened for me to visit Manchester, which in a few days after I did; and took lodgings on Chetham-hill, of Mrs. H— who conducted me to Mr. R—'s, a local preacher, at whose house I was invited to spend the day: in the evening the class met there, and I assisted to lead it; the people were in a healthy, spiritual condition; and we enjoyed a sweet fellowship of the Spirit and communion with each other. On the 28th, I preached in Stanly Street; and on the 31st, in the association chapel in Stork Street, to a numerous audience. In a few days afterwards, I was sent for to visit a lady who was in great distress of mind. On entering the apartment where she was sitting, I shall never forget the expression of despair which sat on her countenance: she informed me that on the previous Lord's-day, she came in the afternoon from motives of curiosity to hear me, and that the discourse had cut her to the heart, and portrayed her character as one self-destroyed by suicidal sin: the Bible was lying by her side; I took it up, opened at, and read from Isaiah lxi. 1–3, "The Spirit of the Lord

God is upon me, because the Lord hath anointed me to preach good tidings unto the meek; he hath sent me to bind up the broken hearted, to proclaim liberty to the captives, and the opening of the prison unto them that are bound; to proclaim the acceptable year of the Lord, and the day of vengeance of our God; to comfort all that mourn; to appoint unto them that mourn in Zion; to give unto them beauty for ashes, the oil of joy for mourning, the garments of praise for the spirit of heaviness, &c." She then broke out in rapturous exclamations, praising God for sending me as a messenger of salvation to her; declaring herself filled with joy, and wondering at the change which had taken place within her soul; she confessed her unworthiness to receive such unexampled mercy and grace; having gone to hear me as she acknowledged, without any thought of good, but of mere curiosity; and she glorified God in me. This dear lady was one of many of the earliest seals to my ministry in Manchester. On one occasion, I accompanied my friend, Mrs. H— to visit a family of her acquaintance; they made no pretensions whatever to religion; but our visit proved a blessing indeed to them; several of their neighbours were present; and among them, a private in the police force and his wife; and, as I inquired of their prospect, relative to a future state of existence, his wife informed me that he had been a religious man, but had fallen from grace; and with much earnestness intreated me to discourse with him in particular. I did so; and the Lord gave me a message to him, which went to his heart; he burst into tears; lamented that his calling was of such a description, that the class of persons to whom he belonged were regarded as the offscouring of the human race, and that few cared for their souls; adding, that the hardships of their situation were peculiarly distressing; and expressed great gratitude to God and acknowledgments to me for the sympathy I had evinced for him. We then bowed down before the Lord in fervent prayer, and all present were greatly moved, and deeply affected. A great door and effectual was opened to me of the Lord, in Manchester; and many there became the crown of my rejoicing in Christ Jesus. I again became fully occupied in the service of my heavenly master, going from chapel to chapel, and from town to town.

I preached one day at the house of Mr. W—, under the bank, from Luke xiii. 7. "Cut it down; why cumbereth it the ground." Many persons were deeply affected under that sermon; and among them, one poor man who came in a few days afterwards to Mrs. W—, and asked permission to meet in the class, stating that he had been wholly deprived of sleep ever since he heard that sermon. On the class-night, I preached a short discourse, which was followed by a prayer-meeting, and this man and four others experienced the pardoning love of God.

On the 15th of September I went by appointment to preach at the house of Mr. L. under the bank; and just before the meeting commenced, the powers of darkness suddenly assailed my spirit, and so burdened and obscured me, that in a short time I had no light or spirit within me; and I commenced the service with a weight upon my mind as if all the people were hanging upon me. A hungry people exhausts a spiritual ministry, a carnal people paralyses it, an unbelieving people drags it down, a rebellious and resisting people grieves it, an erroneous people inflames it—the cause of my darkness, however, was not in the people; nor was I able to ascertain the reason, which has hitherto been hidden from me. In my first prayer the cloud was dispelled, and I proceeded with my work in the light of the Lord; but as I returned home to my lodging, the darkness returned upon my soul. In the morning the Lord smiled upon my soul again; and I arose with a light and cheerful heart, rejoicing in God with joy unspeakable and full of glory.

On the 23rd of October, I preached in the afternoon and evening to numerous audiences at Hayfield, with much freedom; and the people were very attentive and much edified.

On the 27th, Mr. Ellery, the superintendent of the Tonnon Street circuit, with his wife, called and took me home with them; I preached for him in the evening; and seven persons were under the sermon brought into the liberty of the children of God. On the 1st of November, I attended a Wesleyan Missionary meeting at Chetham; and enjoyed it as a time of refreshing from the Lord. On the 7th, I preached morning and afternoon at Tonnon Street Chapel; and preached a charity sermon in the evening, in Berry Street Chapel Salford. While in Manchester, I took an opportunity of going with several of the brethren and sisters to visit the deaf, dumb, and blind school, where we witnessed the substitutes for tongues, ears and eyes in successful operation. Truly marvellous is the immense variety of resources, which the bountiful God of nature has placed within the reach of, and at the service of man.

On the 27th, I went to Glossop to preach three anniversary sermons; on my arrival in the town, Mr. H. came to the coach to meet me, conducted me to his house, and very kindly entertained me: the anniversary was a delightful day; and numbers found it good to be in attendance. I preached again on the following evening, and the place was excessively crowded: on the day after, I returned to Manchester. On the 5th of December I went to Stockport to preach some charity sermons; and the crowd was so great, that it was with great difficulty I reached the pulpit; many hundreds of persons were forced to retire who could not gain admittance. I preached again on the 8th, and spent a very happy week there in visiting the brethren and sisters, and returned again to Manchester. On the 10th, I went to Hollingsworth; on the Lord's-day morning I led the class, and preached in the afternoon and evening in the chapel. On the Monday a great many of the friends brought their provisions together and spent the afternoon in singing, prayer and spiritual conversation: in the evening they all repaired to the chapel, and I preached again to a great congregation. Two gentlemen were present who were utter strangers to all the friends; and, as they placed themselves just before me, laughing and tapping each other, their design was apparently not the edification of their souls. I preached on that evening from Proverbs iii. 5, 6, and, under the sermons, their laughter was checked, and they hung down their heads and strove to conceal their dejection. After service the congregation was detained some time by a very heavy shower of rain; and I sang one of the American hymns; many shed a profusion of tears: and these gentlemen seemed rivetted to the spot, and were the last to retire from the chapel. On the next day, I was about to return to Manchester; and on my way to the coach office, I called at Mr. H—'s, to bid him and his family farewell, when Mrs. H. exclaimed, "Oh! are you going? I am very much disappointed; for I wished you and some other friends to spend the afternoon with us, and I have been making preparations for it; and I was in hopes it would do me good: for I feel that I am a poor and lost sinner; I am very much burdened["]; her tears and sobs suppressed her further utterance; and I needed no further persuasive to stay that day at their house; and on that evening, she obtained peace with God through faith in our Lord Jesus Christ; and on the next Lord's day, she came forth and gave evidence of having become a new creature in Christ Jesus. On the 11th, I returned to Manchester, and removed my lodgings to St. James' street; in the evening, I attended a tea meeting in Beetle-street, at which Mr. F. presided. On the 25th I went to Stalybridge, where I received a message from the friends of Hollingsworth, desiring me to attend a tea meeting there that evening. I accordingly went thither, and found Mrs. H. still rejoicing in the love of God: we had a very comfortable tea meeting. On the Lord's day I preached in the afternoon and evening at Stalybridge; and also on the Monday evening. On the 31th.

Mrs. F—d. of Salford, the lady of the superintendent sent for me to come and spend the day with them; which I did, and it being the last of the year, at nine o'clock in the evening we went to the chapel to commence the watch meeting: several of us were speakers on the occasion, and it was a season of much solemnity and godly comfort. Thus we witnessed the expiration of the year, with thanksgivings for the divine kindness which had been vouchsafed to us therein; and hailed the new year with prayer for and earnests of sustaining grace and prospective mercies. I tarried in Manchester about nine months; visiting and preaching in very many towns and villages in its vicinity and within ten or twenty miles around it; the Lord being with me to direct and sustain my willing exertions in His holy cause. I preached about two hundred times during my continuance here; and ultimately by His direction, took my leave of the dear friends to see them no more in the flesh, till the trumpet of God shall sound the muster of the blood-bought congregation to the throne of Jesus.

On the 13th of June, 1843, I travelled by railway to Huddersfield; met with a very kind reception from Mr. S. Routledge; and, in the afternoon, Mrs. R. accompanied me on a visit to Mr. Keys, a class leader in the Wesleyan connexion. I attended, and led his class in the evening, and enjoyed a happy season with the people. Several of Mr. R.'s work-people were members of his class; and they went and informed Mrs. R. that they had enjoyed a most blessed opportunity with me; the information sunk with great weight into her mind, for she was at the time in great concern about the salvation of her soul, and very much distressed on account of her sins. On my return to her house, she said to me, "I have earnestly endeavoured to find rest for my soul; but there is no rest for me, Mrs. Elaw." We then kneeled down before the Lord in prayer for her, and He removed her burden and manifested His comforts to her spirit through faith in Christ Jesus. On the 17th, I went to Shelf, and visited my kind friends, Mr. and Mrs. B. I assisted in the anniversary sermons of the Primitive Methodists, visited a number of the friends, led several of their classes, and preached also in the Wesleyan chapel, where we enjoyed a very rich manifestation of the presence of God, and a delightful opportunity to our souls. I staid here a fortnight, passing the time very pleasantly in the family of Mr. B. I also visited frequently at Mr. G—ys; his wife is a very godly woman, whose adorning is not of the outward person, but of the hidden man of the heart, in that which is not corruptible; a meek and quiet spirit, which is in the sight of God of great price. This lady is one of the genuine daughters of Sarah;[42] chaste in conversation, subdued in temper and reverent to her husband. Oh, that many flighty, petulant, high-minded and insubordinate wives, who profess the religion of Jesus, would pay more attention to the duties of Christian wives, and like this pious lady, adorn the doctrine of God their Saviour. Little Miss G., a child of ten years of age, had already savingly experienced that the Lord is gracious, and rejoiced in the God of her salvation, she manifested as grave and steady a deportment, as might have been expected from the years of a Christian matron.

I returned to Huddersfield on the 11th of July, where I remained a few weeks; it is delightfully situated; being entirely surrounded with majestic hills, with several streams of water running through it, which conduces much to the prosperity of its manufacturing enterprise. There are in this town four places of worship belonging to the Episcopalians; two very large Wesleyan chapels, and two others occupied by the Primitive Methodists. The houses are neat, and chiefly built of stone; there are several bridges, watering places and baths. It has a large market; and appears to be situated in a fruitful soil, abounding with fruit trees; the gardens are extensive and many of them tastefully laid out; and the approaches to it are by railway and good high roads. On the 29th, I again visited Hull, when I preached morning and evening to immense congregations; and afterwards we held a prayer-meeting; and the Lord blessed the word that day; many were comforted, and many others inquired "what must we do to be saved."

On the 2nd of August, I embarked on board a steamer for London; there were a great many passengers on board; several of whom were from widely distant parts of the earth. Some of the passengers requested me to preach to them, and the captain having given permission, we ascended the poop, and there held our meeting, which many persons seemed much interested. One gentleman afterwards came and inquired my name, saying that he was about to write to his wife, and wished to give her an account of a meeting so interesting and so novel to the crew of a steam-ship. I arrived in London about six o'clock in the evening very much fatigued. On going to my friend's, Mr. T., I found Mrs. T. was absent from home. I lodged that night at Mrs. F—'s; and the day following, I went to my former lodgings in Princes-square. My mind was somewhat cast down by these matters; for, notwithstanding the extensive exercises my faith has experienced, I am often too much a mere creature of circumstances.

On the 7th I went to Great Queen-street chapel to hear Bishop Soul[e] from America,[43] and was very much fatigued with the length of the walk. My mind was at this time very cloudy and dark; and I formed the resolution to call upon and have an interview with the Bishop; but as I began to get myself ready for the visit, I was seized with a fearful tremour and loss of strength. I sunk down upon a chair, and pondered within myself the reason of this visitation, and it occurred to me, that my design of going to the Bishop was taken without the permission of God being first obtained. I therefore abandoned this project, and the cloud on my spirit soon disappeared, and my peace was restored. Shortly afterwards, Mr. D—y came and engaged me to preach in Crosby Row chapel, Borough; Mr. G. engaged me to preach in his chapel, I also made an engagement to preach for Mr. P. and another to preach for Mr. O. in Whites-row chapel. I also preached in Timothy chapel, Ratcliff Highway, for Mr. B. and for many other ministers and congregations in other chapels, after fulfilling a host of engagements and a variety of labour, I receiving an invitation from the north of England; and on the 27th of November I went on board a vessel for Berwick-upon-Tweed. We had a very boisterous passage; and, in the night, a gale of wind laid the vessel completely on her side. The passengers all concluded that we should soon be overwhelmed in a watery grave; but the Lord held our lives in His preserving care, and the vessel was got upright again. At eleven o'clock on the night of the 30th, we came to anchor in the port of Berwick. I went ashore, the same night, to Mr. J. R—'s, the superintendent, who very kindly received me; and thence retired to Mr. G—'s. Many persons were converted to God under my ministry in this town; among the number of whom, was Miss A. G.; she had been to chapel with me, and, on our return, several of the preachers accompanied us; before we parted, we kneeled down in prayer together, and the Lord then and there gave her the knowledge of salvation by the remission of sins. The town of Berwick is one of great antiquity: the people pointed out the remains of an old castle, which is said to have priority over the Christian era; also, the ruins of an old abbey of remote antiquity. The streets of Berwick, I was informed, have been drenched with human blood. There are several places of worship in the town belonging to different denominations; and the pasture fields in the vicinity are very beautiful and green. There is also an elegant pier, which is a convenient promenade for the townspeople, and an extensive fishery. From this place, I went over to Holy Island, and preached to the fishermen, and enjoyed some very blessed meetings among them. This is a place of great antiquity, and was formerly inhabited by a great number of monks. On my return to Berwick, Mr.

R. conducted me to Newcastle-upon-Tyne. I went from thence to Shields on the 25th of December, and reached there late in the evening; but my Heavenly Father had been there before me, and prepared the way. A comfortable home was provided, and generous open hearts to receive the stranger at Mrs. T—'s. When I arrived at her house, I was not aware that it had been arranged for me to lodge there. I therefore sat waiting to go I knew not whither. Mrs. T. bade me take off my out-doors apparel, at which I inquired if I was to stay there? and she replied, "Yes, this is your house as long as you stay in these parts; and we shall receive our reward in heaven." She then related how her mind had been exercised, until she came to the resolution to receive me under her roof. The Lord grant to this dear lady an hundred-fold more in this present time, and in the world to come, everlasting life. My labours here commenced on the 25th, in the new chapel. Mr. R. of Berwick, preached in the morning and evening, and myself in the afternoon: it was an auspicious commencement. On Monday, I attended a tea-meeting, which proved a very interesting time; and many excellent addresses were delivered by the speakers. After this, I went and preached at Newcastle, and returned again to South Shields. The sphere of effort was enlarged before me, and in labours I became more abundant. In heat and cold, through wet and dry weather, by night and day, I laboured in that part of God's vineyard, preaching the gospel of Christ incessantly, wherever opportunity was afforded me. One of the seals to my ministry here, was a descendant of Abraham, according to the flesh—a Jew outwardly, who, believing in the Lord with the heart unto righteousness, became a Jew inwardly also.

The success of my ministry, in Shields, was very gratifying; but here as in many other places, I endured a considerable share of persecution from opponents of female preaching; some opposing my ministry of mere caprice, and others from mistaken convictions. Satan never fails to find a pretext by which to inspire his agents with opposition against that ministry which is of God. While in this neighbourhood, I was sent for to visit a young man confined to his bed with mortal disease: though favoured with Christian parents, it appeared that when in health, he had indulged in sentiments very inimical to revealed religion: subdued however by a sickness which exhausted his spirits and secluded him from the accustomed gaieties of life, he became susceptible of more serious impressions and of juster views. On my first visit to him, he was not only very weak in body, but very dark as to his perceptions of spiritual things. As I read the Scriptures, conversed with and opened to him the way of salvation, he was led to a discernment of the great atonement for sin in the cross of Jesus, and cried to the Lord for mercy: the Lord heard our united prayers, and spoke peace to his soul. He took refuge in the propitiation set forth by the Most High, became justified by faith, and believing, found peace with God through our Lord Jesus Christ. His surviving days were employed in the praise of Him who had called him out of darkness into His marvellous light; and he rejoiced in hope of the glory of God: the love of God was richly shed abroad in his heart by the Holy Ghost; and after languishing a few weeks more in the flesh, he found the rest which he sought; departing to be with Jesus, which is far better than a protracted abode among the ills of mortality.

On the 28th of January, 1843, I preached again at Newcastle, on the opening of a chapel that had been long closed: but was now taken by the Ebenezer society for the cause of the Lord: the meetings were well attended; and I had the pleasure of knowing that some persons were converted to God therein. I generally found Newcastle a very barren and rocky soil to work upon; for the wickedness of the people is very great; and the cry of it, like the cry of Sodom, must ere long reach unto heaven;[44] but nevertheless God hath a chosen remnant even there, whom He delights to bless; and I might enumerate many names here dear to me, whom I love for truth's sake which dwelleth in them.

On the 8th of September, I went to Rainton Hall; and preached on the following Lord's day to a numerous congregation in Middle Rainton; the place was filled with the glory of the Lord, and the people with the Holy Ghost; the next day we had a delightful tea meeting. On the 12th, I visited Colliery-road; passed the day at Mrs. L—'s, took breakfast at Mr. R—'s, and returned to preach at Rainton. Just before I went into the meeting, I was called in to see a sick woman, who related to me a remarkable vision which she had seen. On the 14th, I preached at Pittenton to a very large audience; and the meeting was attended with much power and spiritual assurance; after the service the friends presented me with a small sum of money for which I was thankful to my Heavenly Father. On the 15th, I went to New Lampton, and was cordially received by Mr. J. H—n; on the 15th, I preached to a large assembly, and on the next Lord's-day I preached again to a dense mass of people, and held a prayer meeting after preaching. On retiring from that meeting, I was filled with the love of God too full to conceal my emotion, and I seemed to hear a concert of angelic voices singing the hymns of God in the air over my head.

On the 19th, I went to Lumley, and preached in the new connexion chapel to a large and listening audience. It was a very solemn season; there being a very fatal distemper raging in the town at the time, which had prostrated many persons in death, and rendered their surviving relatives and friends so many bereaved mourners: the next day I returned to New Lampton, greatly exhausted by much travelling and preaching. On the 23rd, I went to Hettingly hole, and visited a young woman then dying, whose death occured a few hours after. On the 24th, I preached in the Seceders Chapel to an immense throng of people; the vapours which arose from so compacted a concourse, as it condensed, ran down the walls in streams of water; and I caught a severe cold on this occasion. On the 27th, I preached there again to another multitude: the day following I spent the afternoon at Mr. W—'s, whose daughter, a widow, was dying: we bowed the knee in prayer to God for her; and I received the assurance that our petitions were granted: she spoke not, but when I arose, she took my hand, and looked at me with an affectionately languishing smile. On the 30th, I went to Colliery row, being in very bad health. I preached three sermons there, and likewise held a love feast; and taking a last farewell of my dear friends, I returned on the 4th of October to New Lampton, and on the 5th, preached at Newbottle, in the Wesleyan chapel; the friends connected with which expressed themselves greatly edified, invited me to preach there again on the following Lord's-day, and gave me a ticket for their tea meeting of Monday. One of the brethren engaged early to inform me by note on what part of the Lord's-day I should occupy their pulpit; however, I received no note from him, and therefore I went not. On the Monday, having a ticket for their tea meeting; I went with several of my friends; but could not obtain admittance; for the interval from Saturday was too great for their memories; they had all forgotten me; nor was there one who was able to recognise the preacher who had so delighted them the previous week, they had probably received a philippic from some petty Authority against female preachers, which had blotted me out altogether from their thought and feeling. On my return in the evening, I was attacked with a very severe fit of illness, which confined me to my bed for five months; but my Heavenly Father was graciously pleased to make my consolations abound throughout this period of affliction; that dear lady Elizabeth Gardiner, was unremitting in her kind attentions to me, and with great benevolence administered to my necessities. Mr. A. gave proof of the constancy of his kindness, and sustained the burden of my sickness without prospect or desire of remuneration; the kind friends loved not in word only, but in deed and in truth; my medical attendant also was very assiduous and kind.

I have felt much gratitude to the Lord for enkindling so great a friendship for me in the bosoms of many persons in England; many of my English acquaintance possess a large share of my affections; and an imperishable image in my memory; but I know by experience the heart of a stranger; many and deep and raging have been the billows of affliction which have rolled over my soul since I crossed the Atlantic Ocean. My reader may perceive that I have not been an idle spectator in my Heavenly Master's cause. During my sojourn in England, I have preached considerably more than a thousand sermons. I have expended all my means in travels of no little extent and duration; devoted my time, employed the energies of my spirit, spent my strength and exhausted my constitution in the cause of Jesus; and received of pecuniary supplies and temporal remunerations in comparison with my time and labours a mere pittance, altogether inadequate to shield me from a thousand privations, hardships, targetfires, vexatious anxieties and deep afflictions, to which my previous life was an utter stranger.

After an absence of six months, on my recovery, I returned to my kind friends in Shields, and the next day went to fulfil an engagement I had entered into when I was last there. As I proceeded to the place, I did not expect to return again alive, my exhaustion and debility was so extreme; but the Lord sustained me; and my strength was equal to my day. I preached four sermons in the space of three days, and returned more convalescent than I went. In a few months' time, I became fully occupied again in the work of the Lord, and continued my labours in Shields, Newcastle and Sunderland until the month of July, 1844, when I bade my kind friends a final farewell, to see them no more until we meet in the kingdom of God. My last address to the dear friends in Shields was attended with a great sensation among the people, and was a very affecting season. On the 31st of July I left Shields, embarking at seven o'clock that evening on board a steam vessel for London. On my arrival in the port of London, I was met at the water side by my very kind friends, Mr. and Mrs. B. T. My soul truly rejoiced to meet my dear brethren and sisters in Christ of this metropolis once more in this vale of tears; and the Lord soon made my way clear on this my third visit to this great city. I have enjoyed much of the divine life in my soul since I have been here; my first residence was in Solomon's terrace, Back Road, St. George in the East; but I was obliged to leave it on account of the intemperate habits of one of its inmates. Drunkenness is an awful vice, and though debasing to both sexes, seems yet more unbecoming in a woman; it is a prolific parent of crime, being the origin of a thousand other evils. The Most High has strikingly reprobated this sin, by attaching to it the capital punishment of banishment from the kingdom of heaven [1 Cor. 6:10]. About the commencement of the present year, 1845, I removed to the residence of Mr. T. Dudley, 19, Charter-house-lane, where I enjoy a comfortable home. I soon after visited Jewin-street chapel; and have cause for thanksgivings to God for directing me to that place of worship. My first visit to this chapel was on the watch night of the evening of December 31, 1844: I also attended at another meeting, commonly known among the Wesleyans as a covenant meeting, the object of which is a renewed dedication of our entire selves to the kingdom, service and glory of Christ. In a few evenings afterwards I joined Mr. Self's class; he is an able and experienced leader; I much enjoy and highly prize his judicious Christian counsel as a class leader: and feel a great attachment to each member of the class; I think the friends are growing in grace, in the knowledge of the truth, and increasing with the increase of the life of God. I esteem class meetings as a most wise and benevolent provision for the spiritual necessities of the saints; they appear somewhat to resemble the ancient church meetings of the primitive Christians which were instituted by the apostles; and might easily be vested with yet closer approximation to them, and increased powers of edification: such meetings greatly tend to preserve the purity and transparency of the renewed heart; there the weary soul is invigorated, the doubting mind confirmed, the dismayed heart encouraged: the tempted are instructed, the heedless are admonished, and the lukewarm stimulated; the classmeeting is the place where the saints compare notes; and behold in each other's experience their own lineaments and image.

Let me exhort my dear Christian friends of every name and denomination, by no means to omit any possible attendance on the means of grace, which are intended for their growth in the divine life and image; that they may not only hold fast where to they have attained, but become filled with the life and power, and display the perfection of the Christian religion; being the children of the resurrection, the sons of God, and receive an abundant entrance into the everlasting kingdom of our Lord and Saviour Jesus Christ. Slumbering virgins, the Bridegroom cometh! Rouse, timely to the midnight cry.[45] I exhort all Christians, believing that there is but one church of Jesus Christ in this wilderness; and I trust she will soon come forth as the morning, leaning on her beloved, fair as the moon, clear as the sun, and terrible as a bannered army. May all who are of the household of faith stand fast in the liberty wherewith Christ has made them free. Dear brethren, the time is short, it is ominous, and it is perilous: be steadfast, unmoveable, always abounding in the work of the Lord. Be not carried about with every wind of doctrine; at the same time, reject not, nor fight against any statement of the Scriptures of truth, but with all confidence, aptitude and simplicity, as little children, receive and adopt all their inspired instructions. Mark, I beseech you, the signs of the times; they are awfully portentous: Christ's words are every where fulfilling, "Because iniquity shall abound the love of many shall wax cold [Matt. 24:12]. Perilous times are verging upon us: He has asked the question, when the Son of man cometh will He find faith on the earth?" Alas, of outward profession there is abundance; but of true faith, a melancholy dearth. May we be prepared to answer this question for ourselves, by keeping our faith in continual exercise.

I have now furnished my readers with an outline of my religious experience, ministerial labours and travels, together with some of the attendant results, both on the continent of America and in England: these humble memoirs will doubtless continue to be read long after I shall have ceased from my earthly labours and existence. I submit them, dear Christian reader, to thy attentive consideration, and commend this little volume and each of its readers to the blessing of the adorable God, the Father, Son and Holy Spirit. Amen.

A BRAND PLUCKED FROM THE FIRE
An Autobiographical Sketch
by
Mrs. Julia A. J. Foote

"Is not this a brand plucked out of the fire?"—Zech. III. 2.

Cleveland, Ohio:
Printed for the Author by W. F. Schneider.
1879.

PREFACE

I have written this little book after many prayers to ascertain the will of God—having long had an impression to do it. I have a consciousness of obedience to the will of my dear Lord and Master.

My object has been to testify more extensively to the sufficiency of the blood of Jesus Christ to save from all sin. Many have not the means of purchasing large and expensive works on this important Bible theme.

Those who are fully in the truth cannot possess a prejudiced or sectarian spirit. As they hold fellowship with Christ, they cannot reject those whom he has received, nor receive those whom he rejects, but all are brought into a blessed harmony with God and each other.

The Christian who does not believe in salvation from all sin in this life, cannot have a constant, complete peace. The evil of the heart will rise up and give trouble. But let all such remember the words of Paul: "I am crucified with Christ; nevertheless, I live; yet not I, but Christ liveth in me; and the life which I now live in the flesh, I live by faith of the Son of God, who loved me, and gave himself for me" [Gal. 2:20]. "Ask, and ye shall receive" [Luke 11:9]. The blood of Jesus will not only purge your conscience from the guilt of sin, and from dead works, but it will destroy the very root of sin that is in the heart, by faith, so that you may serve the living God in the beauty of holiness.

My earnest desire is that many—especially of my own race—may be led to believe and enter into rest; "For we which have believed do enter into rest" [Heb. 4:3]—sweet soul rest.

INTRODUCTION

The author of this sketch is well known in many parts of Ohio, and in other days was known in several States, as an Evangelist. The purity of her life and the success of her labors are acknowledged. After severe mental and spiritual conflicts, she obeyed God, in public labor for his cause, and still continues in this, although, with many, she is thereby guilty of three great crimes.

1. The first is, that of Color. For, though not now the slaves of individual men, our brethren continue to be under the bondage of society. But if there be crime in color, it lies at the door of Him who "hath made of one blood all nations of men for to dwell on all the face of the earth" [Acts 17:26], and who declares himself to be "no respecter of persons" [Acts 10:34]. Holiness takes the prejudice of color out of both the white and the black, and declares that "The [heart's] the standard of the man."

2. In the next place, we see the crime of Womanhood. As though any one, with heart and lips of love, may not speak forth the praises of Him who hath called us out of darkness into light! The "anointing which abideth" unseals all lips, so that in Christ "there is neither male nor female" [1 John 2:27; Gal. 3:28]. Praise God forever!

3. In the last place, our sister, as stated, is an Evangelist. We respect the pastoral office highly, for we know the heart of a pastor; but while the regular field-hands are reaping, pray, let Ruth glean, even if "her hap is to light on a part of the field belonging to Boaz" —Ruth 2:3].

"If you cannot, in the harvest,
  Garner up the richest sheaves,
Many a grain, both ripe and golden,
  Will the careless reapers leave;
Go and glean among the briers,
  Growing rank against the wall;
For it may be that their shadow
  Hides the heaviest wheat of all."

Our dear sister is not a genius. She is simply strong in common sense, and strong in the Lord. Those of us who heard her preach, last year, at Lodi, where she held the almost breathless attention of five thousand people, by the eloquence of the Holy Ghost, know well where is the hiding of her power.

This is a simple narrative of a life of incidents, many of them stirring and strange. We commend it to all; and with it, the soundness of the doctrine and exhortation with which Sister Foote enforces the sublime cause of Holiness.

THOS. K. DOTY

Christian Harvester Office[1]
Cleveland, June, 1879

I

BIRTH AND PARENTAGE.

I was born in 1823, in Schenectady, N.Y. I was my mother's fourth child. My father was born free, but was stolen, when a child, and enslaved. My mother was born a slave, in the State of New York. She had one very cruel master and mistress. This man, whom she was obliged to call master, tied her up and whipped her because she refused to submit herself to him, and reported his conduct to her mistress. After the whipping, he himself washed her quivering back with strong salt water. At the expiration of a week she was sent to change her clothing, which stuck fast to her back. Her mistress, seeing that she could not remove it, took hold of the rough tow-linen under-garment and pulled it off over her head with a jerk, which took the skin with it, leaving her back all raw and sore.

This cruel master soon sold my mother, and she passed from one person's hands to another's, until she found a comparatively kind master and mistress in Mr. and Mrs. Cheeseman, who kept a public house.

My father endured many hardships in slavery, the worst of which was his constant exposure to all sorts of weather. There being no railroads at that time, all goods and merchandise were moved from place to place with teams, one of which my father drove.

My father bought himself, and then his wife and their first child, at that time an infant. That infant is now a woman, more than seventy years old, and an invalid, dependent upon the bounty of her poor relatives.

I remember hearing my parents tell what first led them to think seriously of their sinful course. One night, as they were on their way home from a dance, they came to a stream of water, which, owing to rain the night previous, had risen and carried away the log crossing. In their endeavor to ford the stream, my mother made a misstep, and came very nearly being drowned, with her babe in her arms. This nearly fatal accident made such an impression upon their minds that they said, "We'll go to no more dances;" and they kept their word. Soon after, they made a public profession of religion and united with the M[ethodist] E[piscopal] Church. They were not treated as Christian believers, but as poor lepers. They were obliged to occupy certain seats in one corner of the gallery, and dared not come down to partake of the Holy Communion until the last white communicant had left the table.

One day my mother and another colored sister waited until all the white people had, as they thought, been served, when they started for the communion table. Just as they reached the lower door, two of the poorer class of white folks arose to go to the table. At this, a mother in Israel caught hold of my mother's dress and said to her, "Don't you know better than to go to the table when white folks are there?" Ah! she did know better than to do such a thing purposely. This was one of the fruits of slavery. Although professing to love the same God, members of the same church, and expecting to find the same heaven at last, they could not partake of the Lord's Supper until the lowest of the whites had been served. Were they led by the Holy Spirit? Who shall say? The Spirit of Truth can never be mistaken, nor can he inspire anything unholy. How many at the present day profess great spirituality, and even holiness, and yet are deluded by a spirit of error, which leads them to say to the poor and the colored ones among them, "Stand back a little—I am holier than thou."

My parents continued to attend to the ordinances of God as instructed, but knew little of the power of Christ to save; for their spiritual guides were as blind as those they led.

It was the custom, at that time, for all to drink freely of wine, brandy and gin. I can remember when it was customary at funerals, as well as at weddings, to pass around the decanter and glasses, and sometimes it happened that the pall-bearers could scarcely move out with the coffin. When not handed round, one after another would go to the closet and drink as much as they chose of the liquors they were sure to find there. The officiating clergyman would imbibe as freely as any one. My parents kept liquor in the house constantly, and every morning sling was made, and the children were given the bottom of the cup, where the sugar and a little of the liquor was left, on purpose for them. It is no wonder, isn't it, that every one of my mother's children loved the taste of liquor?

One day, when I was but five years of age, I found the blue chest, where the black bottle was kept, unlocked—an unusual thing. Raising the lid, I took the bottle, put it to my mouth, and drained to the bottom. Soon after, the rest of the children becoming frightened at my actions, ran and told aunt Giney—an old colored lady living in a part of our house—who sent at once for my mother, who was away working. She came in great haste, and at once pronounced me DRUNK. And so I was—stupidly drunk. They walked with me, and blew tobacco smoke into my face, to bring me to. Sickness almost unto death followed, but my life was spared. I was like a "brand plucked from the burning" [Zech. 3:2].

Dear reader, have you innocent children, given you from the hand of God? Children, whose purity rouses all that is holy and good in your nature? Do not, I pray, give to these little ones of God the accursed cup which will send them down to misery and death. Listen to the voice of conscience, the woes of the drunkard, the wailing of poverty-stricken women and children, and touch not the accursed cup. From Sinai come the awful words of Jehovah, "No drunkard shall inherit the kingdom of heaven" [1 Cor. 6:10].

II

RELIGIOUS IMPRESSION—LEARNING THE ALPHABET.

I do not remember having any distinct religious impression until I was about eight years old. At this time there was a "big meeting," as it was called, held in the church to which my parents belonged. Two of the ministers called at our house: one had long gray hair and beard, such as I had never seen before. He came to me, placed his hand on my head, and asked me if I prayed. I said, "Yes, sir," but was so frightened that I fell down on my knees before him and began to say the only prayer I knew, "Now I lay me down to sleep." He lifted me up, saying, "You must be a good girl and pray." He prayed for me long and loud. I trembled with fear, and cried as though my heart would break, for I thought he was the Lord, and I must die. After they had gone, my mother talked with me about my soul more than she ever had before, and told me that this preacher was a good man, but not the Lord; and that, if I were a good girl, and said my prayers, I would go to heaven. This gave me great comfort. I stopped crying, but continued to say, "Now I lay me." A white woman, who came to our house to sew, taught me the Lord's prayer. No tongue can tell the joy that filled my poor heart when I could repeat, "Our Father, which art in heaven." It has always seemed to me that I was converted at this time.

When my father had family worship, which was every Sunday morning, he used to sing,

> "Lord, in the morning thou shalt hear
> My voice ascending high."[2]

I took great delight in this worship, and began to have a desire to learn to read the Bible. There were none of our family able to read except my father, who had picked up a little here and there, and who could, by carefully spelling out the words, read a little in the New Testament, which was a great pleasure to him. My father would very gladly have educated his children, but there were no schools where colored children were allowed. One day, when he was reading, I asked him to teach me the letters. He replied, "Child, I hardly know them myself." Nevertheless, he commenced with "A," and taught me the alphabet. Imagine, if you can, my childish glee over this, my first lesson. The children of the present time, taught at five years of age, can not realize my joy at being able to say the entire alphabet when I was nine years old.

I still continued to repeat the Lord's prayer and "Now I lay me," &c., but not so often as I had done months before. Perhaps I had begun to backslide, for I was but a child, surrounded by children, and deprived of the proper kind of teaching. This is my only excuse for not proving as faithful to God as I should have done.

Dear children, with enlightened Christian parents to teach you, how thankful you should be that "from a child you are able to say that you have known the Holy Scriptures, which are able to make you wise unto salvation, through faith which is in Christ Jesus" [2 Tim. 3:15]. I hope all my young readers will heed the admonition, "Remember now thy Creator in the days of thy youth" [Eccles. 12:1] etc. It will save you from a thousand snares to mind religion young. God says: "I love those that love me, and those that seek me early shall find me" [Prov. 8:17]. Oh! I am glad that we are never too young to pray, or too ignorant or too sinful. The younger, the more welcome. You have nothing to fear, dear children; come right to Jesus.

Why was Adam afraid of the voice of God in the garden? It was not a strange voice; it was a voice he had always loved. Why did he flee away, and hide himself among the trees? It was because he had disobeyed God. Sin makes us afraid of God, who is holy; nothing but sin makes us fear One so good and so kind. It is a sin for children to disobey their parents. The Bible says: "Honor thy father and thy mother" [Exod. 20:12]. Dear children, honor your parents by loving and obeying them. If Jesus, the Lord of glory, was subject and obedient to his earthly parents, will you not try to follow his example? Lift up your hearts to the dear, loving Jesus, who, when on earth, took little children in his arms, and blessed them. He will help you, if you pray, "Our Father, which art in heaven, thy dear Son, Jesus Christ, my Saviour, did say, 'Suffer little children to come unto me' [Matt. 19:14]. I am a little child, and I come to thee. Draw near to me, I pray thee. Hear me, and forgive the many wicked things I have done, and accept my thanks for the many good gifts thou hast given me. Most of all, I thank thee, dear Father, for the gift of thy dear Son, Jesus Christ, who died for me, and for whose sake I pray thee hear my prayer. Amen."

III

THE PRIMES—GOING TO SCHOOL.

When I was ten years of age I was sent to live in the country with a family by the name of Prime. They had no children, and soon became quite fond of me. I really think Mrs. Prime loved me. She had a brother who was dying with consumption, and she herself was a cripple. For some time after I went there, Mr. John, the brother, was able to walk from his father's house, which was quite near, to ours, and I used to stand, with tears in my eyes, and watch him as he slowly moved across the fields, leaning against the fence to rest himself by the way. I heard them say he could not live much longer, and that worried me dreadfully; and then I used to wonder if he said his prayers. He always treated me kindly, and often stopped to talk with me.

One day, as he started for home, I stepped up to him and said, "Mr. John, do you say your prayers?" and then I began to cry. He looked at me for a moment, then took my hand in his and said: "Sometimes I pray; do you?" I answered, "Yes sir." Then said he, "You must pray for me"—and turned and left me. I ran to the barn, fell down on my knees, and said: "Our Father, who art in heaven, send that good man to put his hand on Mr. John's head." I repeated this many times a day as long as he lived. After his death I heard them say he died very happy, and had gone to heaven. Oh, how my little heart leaped for joy when I heard that Mr. John had gone to heaven; I was sure the good man had been there and laid his hand on his head. "Bless the Lord, O my soul, and all that is within me praise his holy name" [Ps. 103:1], for good men and good women, who are not afraid to teach dear children to pray.

The Primes being an old and influential family, they were able to send me to a country school, where I was well treated by both teacher and scholars.

Children were trained very differently in those days from what they are now. We were taught to treat those older than ourselves with great respect. Boys were required to make a bow, and girls to drop a courtesy, to any person whom they might chance to meet in the street. Now, many of us dread to meet children almost as much as we do the half-drunken men coming out of the saloons. Who is to blame for this? Parents, are you training your children in the way they should go? Are you teaching them obedience and respect? Are you bringing your little ones to Jesus? Are they found at your side in the house of God, on Sunday, or are they roving the streets or fields? Or, what is worse, are they at home reading books or newspapers that corrupt the heart, bewilder the mind, and lead down to the bottomless pit? Father, mother, look on this picture, and then on the dear children God has given you to train up for lives of usefulness that will fit them for heaven. May the dear Father reign in and rule over you, is the prayer of one who desires to meet you all in heaven.

IV

MY TEACHER HUNG FOR CRIME.

My great anxiety to read the Testament caused me to learn to spell quite rapidly, and I was just commencing to read when a great calamity came upon us. Our teacher's name was John Van Paten. He was keeping company with a young lady, who repeated to him a remark made by a lady friend of hers, to the effect that John Van Paten was not very smart, and she didn't see why this young lady should wish to marry him. He became very angry, and, armed with a shotgun, proceeded to the lady's house, and shot her dead. She fell, surrounded by her five weeping children. He then started for town, to give himself up to the authorities. On the way he met the woman's husband and told him what he had done. The poor husband found, on reaching home, that John's words were but too true; his wife had died almost instantly.

After the funeral, the bereaved man went to prison and talked with John and prayed for his conversion until his prayers were answered, and John Van Paten, the murderer, professed faith in Christ.

Finally the day came for the condemned to be publicly hung (they did not plead emotional insanity in those days). Everybody went to the execution, and I with the rest. Such a sight! Never shall I forget the execution of my first school-teacher. On the scaffold he made a speech, which I cannot remember, only that he said he was happy, and ready to die. He sang a hymn, the chorus of which was,

> "I am bound for the kingdom;
> Will you go to glory with me?"

clasping his hands, and rejoicing all the while.

The remembrance of this scene left such an impression upon my mind that I could not sleep for many a night. As soon as I fell into a doze, I could see my teacher's head tumbling about the room as fast as it could go; I would waken with a scream, and could not be quieted until some one came and staid with me.

Never since that day have I heard of a person being hung, but a shudder runs through my whole frame, and a trembling seizes me. Oh, what a barbarous thing is the taking of human life, even though it be "a life for a life," as many believe God commands [Exod. 21:23]. That was the old dispensation. Jesus said: "A new commandment I give unto you, that ye love one another" [John 13:34]. Again: "Resist not evil; but whosoever shall smite thee on they right cheek, turn to him the other also" [Matt. 5:39]. Living as we do in the Gospel dispensation, may God help us to follow the precepts and example of Him, who, when he was reviled, reviled not again, and in the agony of death prayed: "Father, forgive them, for they know not what they do" [Luke 23:34]. Christian men, vote as you pray, that the legalized traffic in ardent spirits may be abolished, and God grant that capital punishment may be banished from our land.

V

AN UNDESERVED WHIPPING.

All this time the Primes had treated me as though I were their own child. Now my feelings underwent a great change toward them; my dislike for them was greater than my love had been, and this was the reason. One day, Mrs. Prime, having company, sent me to the cellar to bring up some little pound cakes, which she had made a few days previously. There were but two or three left; these I brought to her. She asked me where the rest were. I told her "I didn't know." At this she grew very angry, and said, "I'll make you know, when the company is gone." She, who had always been so kind and motherly, frightened me so by her looks and action that I trembled so violently I could not speak. This was taken as an evidence of my guilt. The dear Lord alone knows how my little heart ached, for I was entirely innocent of the crime laid to my charge. I had no need to steal anything, for I had a plenty of everything there was.

There was a boy working for Mr. Prime that I always thought took the cakes, for I had seen him put his hand into his pocket hastily, and wipe his mouth carefully, if he met any one on his way from the cellar. But what could I do? I could not prove it, and his stout denial was believed as against my unsupported word.

That night I wished over and over again that I could be hung as John Van Paten had been. In the darkness and silence, Satan came to me and told me to go to the barn and hang myself. In the morning I was fully determined to do so. I went to the barn for that purpose, but that boy, whom I disliked very much, was there, and he laughed at me as hard as he could. All at once my weak feelings left me, and I sprang at him in a great rage, such as I had never known before; but he eluded my grasp, and ran away, laughing. Thus was I a second time saved from a dreadful sin.

That day, Mr. and Mrs. Prime, on their return from town, brought a rawhide. This Mrs. Prime applied to my back until she was tired, all the time insisting that I should confess that I took the cakes. This, of course, I could not do. She then put the rawhide up, saying, "I'll use it again to-morrow; I am determined to make you tell the truth."

That afternoon Mrs. Prime went away, leaving me alone in the house. I carried the rawhide out to the wood pile, took the axe, and cut it up into small pieces, which I threw away, determined not to be whipped with that thing again. The next morning I rose very early, before any one else was up in the house, and started for home. It was a long, lonely road, through the woods; every sound frightened me, and made me run for fear some one was after me. When I reached home, I told my mother all that had happened, but she did not say very much about it. In the afternoon Mr. and Mrs. Prime came to the house, and had a long talk with us about the affair. My mother did not believe I had told a falsehood, though she did not say much before me. She told me in after years that she talked very sharply to the Primes when I was not by. They promised not to whip me again, and my mother sent me back with them, very much against my will.

They were as kind to me as ever, after my return, though I did not think so at the time. I was not contented to stay there, and left when I was about twelve years old. The experience of that last year made me quite a hardened sinner. I did not pray very often, and, when I did, something seemed to say to me, "That good man, with the white hair, don't like you any more."

VI

VARIED EXPERIENCES—FIRST AND LAST DANCING.

I had grown to be quite a large girl by this time, so that my mother arranged for me to stay at home, do the work, and attend the younger children while she went out to days' work. My older sister went to service, and the entire care of four youngsters devolved upon me—a thing which I did not at all relish.

About this time my parents moved to Albany, where there was an African Methodist Church. My father and mother both joined the church, and went regularly to all the services, taking all the children with them. This was the first time in my life that I was able to understand, with any degree of intelligence, what religion was. The minister frequently visited our house, singing, praying, and talking with us all. I was very much wrought upon by these visits, and began to see such a beauty in religion that I resolved to serve God whatever might happen. But this resolution was soon broken, having been made in my own strength.

The pomps and vanities of this world began to engross my attention as they never had before. I was at just the right age to be led away by improper acquaintances. I would gain my mother's consent to visit some of the girls, and then would go off to a party, and once went to the theater, the only time I ever went in my life. My mother found this out, and punished me so severely that I never had any desire to go again. Thus I bartered the things of the kingdom for the fooleries of the world.

All this time conviction followed me, and there were times when I felt a faint desire to serve the Lord; but I had had a taste of the world, and thought I could not part with its idle pleasures. The Holy Spirit seemed not to strive with me; I was apparently left to take my fill of the world and its pleasures. Yet I did not entirely forget God. I went to church, and said my prayers, though not so often as I had done. I thank my heavenly Father that he did not quite leave me to my own self-destruction, but followed me, sometimes embittering my pleasures and thwarting my schemes of worldly happiness, and most graciously preserving me from following the full bent of my inclination.

My parents had at this time a great deal of trouble with my eldest sister, who would run away from home and go to dances—a place forbidden to us all. The first time I ever attempted to dance was at a quilting, where the boys came in the evening, and brought with them an old man to fiddle. I refused several invitations, fearing my mother might come or send for me; but as she did not, I yielded to the persuasions of the old fiddler, and went on to the floor with him, to dance.

The last time I made a public effort at dancing I seemed to feel a heavy hand upon my arm pulling me from the floor. I was so frightened that I fell; the people all crowded around me, asking what was the matter, thinking I was ill. I told them I was not sick, but that it was wrong for me to dance. Such loud, mocking laughter as greeted my answer, methinks is not often heard this side the gates of torment, and only then when they are opened to admit a false-hearted professor of Christianity. They called me a "little Methodist fool," and urged me to try it again. Being shamed into it, I did try it again, but I had taken only a few steps, when I was seized with a smothering sensation, and felt the same heavy grasp upon my arm, and in my ears a voice kept saying, "Repent! repent!" I immediately left the floor and sank into a seat. The company gathered around me, but not with mocking laughter as before; an invisible presence seemed to fill the place. The dance broke up—all leaving very quietly. Thus was I again "plucked as a brand from the burning."

Had I persisted in dancing, I believe God would have smitten me dead on the spot. Dear reader, do you engage in the ensnaring folly of dancing? Reflect a moment; ask yourself, What good is all this dissipation of body and mind? You are ruining your health, squandering your money, and losing all relish for spiritual things. What good does it do you? Does dancing help to make you a better Christian? Does it brighten your hopes of happiness beyond the grave? The Holy Spirit whispers to your inmost soul, to come out from among the wicked and be separate.

I am often told that the Bible does not condemn dancing—that David danced. Yes, David did dance, but he danced to express his pious joy to the Lord [2 Sam. 6:14]. So Miriam danced, but it was an act of worship, accompanied by a hymn of praise [Exod. 15:20]. Herod's daughter, who was a heathen, danced, and her dancing caused the beheading of one of God's servants [Matt. 14:6–10]. Do you find anything in these examples to countenance dancing? No, no; a thousand times, no. Put away your idols, and give God the whole heart.

After the dance to which I have alluded, I spent several days and nights in an agony of prayer, asking God to have mercy on me; but the veil was still upon my heart. Soon after this, there was a large party given, to which our whole family were invited. I did not care to go, but my mother insisted that I should, saying that it would do me good, for I had been moping for several days. So I went to the party. There I laughed and sang, and engaged in all the sports of the evening, and soon my conviction for sin wore away, and foolish amusements took its place.

Mothers, you know not what you do when you urge your daughter to go to parties to make her more cheerful. You may even be causing the eternal destruction of that daughter. God help you, mothers, to do right.

VII

MY CONVERSION.

I was converted when fifteen years old. It was on a Sunday evening at a quarterly meeting. The minister preached from the text: "And they sung as it were a new song before the throne, and before the four beasts and the elders, and no man could learn that song but the hundred and forty and four thousand which were redeemed from earth." Rev. xiv. 3.

As the minister dwelt with great force and power on the first clause of the text, I beheld my lost condition as I never had done before. Something within me kept saying, "Such a sinner as you are can never sing that new song." No tongue can tell the agony I suffered. I fell to the floor, unconscious, and was carried home. Several remained with me all night, singing and praying. I did not recognize any one, but seemed to be walking in the dark, followed by some one who kept saying, "Such a sinner as you are can never sing that new song." Every converted man and woman can imagine what my feelings were. I thought God was driving me on to hell. In great terror I cried: "Lord, have mercy on me, a poor sinner!" The voice which had been crying in my ears ceased at once, and a ray of light flashed across my eyes, accompanied by a sound of far distant singing; the light grew brighter and brighter, and the singing more distinct, and soon I caught the words: "This is the new song—redeemed, redeemed!" I at once sprang from the bed where I had been lying for twenty hours, without meat or drink, and commenced singing: "Redeemed! redeemed! glory! glory!" Such joy and peace as filled my heart, when I felt that I was redeemed and could sing the new song. Thus was I wonderfully saved from eternal burning.

I hastened to take down the Bible, that I might read of the new song, and the first words that caught my eye were: "But now, thus saith the Lord that created thee, O Jacob, and he that formed thee, O Israel, fear not, for I have redeemed thee; I have called thee by thy name; thou art mine. When thou passest through the waters, I will be with thee, and through the rivers they shall not overflow thee; when thou walkest through the fire, thou shalt not be burned, neither shall the flame kindle upon thee." Isaiah xliii. 1, 2.

My soul cried, "Glory! glory!" and I was filled with rapture too deep for words. Was I not indeed a brand plucked from the burning? I went from house to house, telling my young friends what a dear Saviour I had found, and that he had taught me the new song. Oh! how memory goes back to those childish days of innocence and joy.

Some of my friends laughed at me, and said: "We have seen you serious before, but it didn't last long." I said: "Yes, I have been serious before, but I could never sing the new song until now."

One week from the time of my conversion, Satan tempted me dreadfully, telling me I was deceived; people didn't get religion in that way, but went to the altar, and were prayed for by the minister. This seemed so very reasonable that I began to doubt if I had religion. But, in the first hour of this doubting, God sent our minister in to talk with me. I told him how I was feeling, and that I feared I was not converted. He replied: "My child, it is not the altar nor the minister that saves souls, but faith in the Lord Jesus Christ, who died for all men." Taking down the Bible, he read: "By grace are ye saved, through faith, and that not of yourselves; it is the gift of God" [Eph. 2:8]. He asked me then if I believed my sins had all been forgiven, and that the Saviour loved me. I replied that I believed it with all my heart. No tongue can express the joy that came to me at that moment. There is great peace in believing. Glory to the Lamb!

VIII

A DESIRE FOR KNOWLEDGE—INWARD FOES.

I studied the Bible at every spare moment, that I might be able to read it with a better understanding. I used to read at night by the light of the dying fire, after the rest of the family had gone to bed. One night I dropped the tongs, which made such a noise that my mother came to see what was the matter. When she found that I had been in the habit of reading at night, she was very much displeased, and took the Bible away from me, and would not allow me to have it at such times any more.

Soon after this, my minister made me a present of a new Bible and Testament. Had he given me a thousand dollars, I should not have cared for it as I did for this Bible. I cherished it tenderly, but did not read in it at night, for I dared not disobey my mother.

I now felt the need of an education more than ever. I was a poor reader and a poor writer; but the dear Holy Spirit helped me by quickening my mental faculties. O Lord, I will praise thee, for great is thy goodness! Oh, that everything that hath a being would praise the Lord! From this time, Satan never had power to make me doubt my conversion. Bless God! I knew in whom I believed.

For six months I had uninterrupted peace and joy in Jesus, my love. At the end of that time an accident befell me, which aroused a spirit within me such as I had not known that I possessed. One day, as I was sitting at work, my younger brother, who was playing with the other small children, accidentally hit me in the eye, causing the most intense suffering. The eye was so impaired that I lost the sight of it. I was very angry; and soon pride, impatience, and other signs of carnality, gave me a great deal of trouble. Satan said: "There! you see you never were converted." But he could not make me believe that, though I did not know the cause of these repinings within.

I went to God with my troubles, and felt relieved for a while; but they returned again and again. Again I went to the Lord, earnestly striving to find what was the matter. I knew what was right, and tried to do right, but when I would do good, evil was present with me. Like Gad, I was weak and feeble, having neither might, wisdom nor ability to overcome my enemies or maintain my ground without many a foil.[3] Yet, never being entirely defeated, disabled or vanquished, I would gather fresh courage, and renew the fight. Oh, that I had then had some one to lead me into the light of full salvation!

But instead of getting light, my preacher, class-leader, and parents, told me that all Christians had these inward troubles to contend with, and were never free from them until death; that this was my work here, and I must keep fighting and that, when I died, God would give me a bright crown. What delusion! However, I believed my minister was too good and too wise not to know what was right; so I kept on struggling and fighting with this inbeing monster, hoping all the time I should soon die and be at rest—never for a moment supposing I could be cleansed from all sin, and live.

I had heard of the doctrine of Holiness, but in such a way as to give me no light, nor to beget a power in me to strive after the experience. How frivolous and fruitless is that preaching which describes the mere history of the work and has not the power of the Holy Ghost. My observation has shown me that there are many, ah! too many shepherds now, who live under the dreadful woe pronounced by the Lord upon the shepherds of Israel (Ezek. xxxiv.).

IX

VARIOUS HOPES BLASTED.

The more my besetting sin troubled me, the more anxious I became for an education. I believed that, if I were educated, God could make me understand what I needed; for, in spite of what others said, it would come to me, now and then, that I needed something more than what I had, but what that something was I could not tell.

About this time Mrs. Phileos and Miss Crandall met with great indignity from a pro-slavery mob in Canterbury, Conn., because they dared to teach colored children to read.[4] If they went out to walk, they were followed by a rabble of men and boys, who hooted at them, and threw rotten eggs and other missiles at them, endangering their lives and frightening them terribly.

One scholar, with whom I was acquainted, was so frightened that she went into spasms, which resulted in a derangement from which she never recovered. We were a despised and oppressed people; we had no refuge but God. He heard our cries, saw our tears, and wonderfully delivered us.

Bless the Lord that he is "a man of war!" [Exod. 15:3]. "I am that I am" is his name [Exod. 3:14]. Mr. and Mrs. Phileos and their daughter opened a school in Albany for colored children of both sexes. This was joyful news to me. I had saved a little money from my earnings, and my father promised to help me; so I started with hopes, expecting in a short time to be able to understand the Bible, and read and write well. Again was I doomed to disappointment: for some inexplicable reason, the family left the place in a few weeks after beginning the school. My poor heart sank within me. I could scarcely speak for constant weeping. That was my last schooling. Being quite a young woman, I was obliged to work, and study the Bible as best I could. The dear Holy Spirit helped me wonderfully to understand the precious Word.

Through temptation I was brought into great distress of mind; the enemy of souls thrust sore at me; but I was saved from falling into his snares—saved in the hour of trial from my impetuous spirit, by the angel of the Lord standing in the gap, staying me in my course.

> "Oh, bless the name of Jesus! he maketh the rebel a
> priest and king;
> He hath bought me and taught me the new song to sing."

I continued to live in an up-and-down way for more than a year, when there came to our church an old man and his wife, who, when speaking in meeting, told of the trouble they once had had in trying to overcome their temper, subdue their pride, etc. But they took all to Jesus, believing his blood could wash them clean and sanctify them wholly to himself; and, oh! the peace, the sweet peace, they had enjoyed ever since. Their words thrilled me through and through.

I at once understood what I needed. Though I had read in my Bible many things they told me, I had never understood what I read. I needed a Philip to teach me.[5]

I told my parents, my minister, and my leader that I wanted to be sanctified. They told me sanctification was for the aged and persons about to die, and not for one like me. All they said did me no good. I had wandered in the wilderness a long time, and now that I could see a ray of the light for which I had so long sought, I could not rest day nor night until I was free.

I wanted to go and visit these old people who had been sanctified, but my mother said: "No, you can't go; you are half crazy now, and these people don't know what they are talking about." To have my mother refuse my request so peremptorily made me very sorrowful for many days. Darkness came upon me, and my distress was greater than before, for, instead of following the true light, I was turned away from it.

X

DISOBEDIENCE, BUT HAPPY RESULTS.

Finally, I did something I never had done before: I deliberately disobeyed my mother. I visited these old saints, weeping as though my heart would break. When I grew calm, I told them all my troubles, and asked what I must do to get rid of them. They told me that sanctification was for the young believer, as well as the old. These words were a portion in due season. After talking a long time, and they had prayed with me, I returned home, though not yet satisfied.

I remained in this condition more than a week, going many times to my secret place of prayer, which was behind the chimney in the garret of our house. None but those who have passed up this way know how wretched every moment of my life was. I thought I must die. But truly, God does make his little ones ministering angels—sending them forth on missions of love and mercy. So he sent that dear old mother in Israel to me one fine morning in May. At the sight of her my heart seemed to melt within me, so unexpected, and yet so much desired was her visit. Oh, bless the Lord for sanctified men and women!

There was no one at home except the younger children, so our coming together was uninterrupted. She read and explained many passages of Scripture to me, such as, John xvii; 1 Thess. iv. 3; v. 23; 1 Cor. vi. 9–12; Heb. ii. 11; and many others—carefully marking them in my Bible. All this had been as a sealed book to me until now. Glory to Jesus! the seals were broken and light began to shine upon the blessed Word of God as I had never seen it before.

The second day after that pilgrim's visit, while waiting on the Lord, my large desire was granted, through faith in my precious Saviour. The glory of God seemed almost to prostrate me to the floor. There was, indeed, a weight of glory resting upon me. I sang with all my heart,

"This is the way I long have sought,
And mourned because I found it not."

Glory to the Father! glory to the Son! and glory to the Holy Ghost! who hath plucked me as a brand from the burning, and sealed me unto eternal life. I no longer hoped for glory, but I had the full assurance of it. Praise the Lord for Paul-like faith! "I am crucified with Christ: nevertheless, I live; yet not I, but Christ liveth in me" [Gal. 2:20]. This, my constant prayer, was answered, that I might be strengthened with might by his Spirit in the inner man; that being rooted and grounded in love, I might be able to comprehend with all saints what is the length, and breadth, and heighth, and depth, and to know the love of Christ which passeth knowledge, and be filled with all the fullness of God.

I had been afraid to tell my mother I was praying for sanctification, but when the "old man" [Rom. 6:6] was cast out of my heart, and perfect love took possession, I lost all fear. I went straight to my mother and told her I was sanctified. She was astonished, and called my father and told him what I had said. He was amazed as well, but said not a word. I at once began to read to them out of my Bible, and to many others, thinking, in my simplicity, that they would believe and receive the same blessing at once. To the glory of God, some did believe and were saved, but many were too wise to be taught by a child—too good to be made better.

From this time, many, who had been my warmest friends, and seemed to think me a Christian, turned against me, saying I did not know what I was talking about—that there was no such thing as sanctification and holiness in this life—and that the devil had deluded me into self-righteousness. Many of them fought holiness with more zeal and vigor than they did sin. Amid all this, I had that sweet peace that passeth all understanding springing up within my soul like a perennial fountain—glory to the precious blood of Jesus!

"The King of heaven and earth
Deigns to dwell with mortals here."

XI

A RELIGION AS OLD AS THE BIBLE.

The pastor of our church visited me one day, to talk about my "new religion," as he called it. I took my Bible and read many of my choice passages to him, such as—"Come and hear, all ye that fear God, and I will declare what he hath done for my soul." (Psa. lxvi. 16.) "Blessed is he whose transgression is forgiven, whose sin is covered." (Psa. xxxii. 1.) While reading this verse, my whole being was so filled with the glory of God that I exclaimed: "Glory to Jesus! he has freed me from the guilt of sin, and sin hath no longer dominion over me [Rom. 6:14]; Christ makes me holy as well as happy."

I also read these words from Ezekiel xxxvi.: "Then will I sprinkle clean water upon you, and ye shall be clean; from all your filthiness and from all your idols will I cleanse you; a new heart also will I give you, and a new spirit will I put within you, and I will take away the stony heart out of your flesh, and I will give you a heart of flesh. And I will put my Spirit within you, and cause you to walk in my statutes, and ye shall keep my judgments, and do them."

I stopped reading, and asked the preacher to explain these last verses to me. He replied: "They are all well enough; but you must remember that you are too young to read and dictate to persons older than yourself, and many in the church are dissatisfied with the way you are talking and acting." As he answered me, the Lord spoke to my heart and glory filled my soul. I said: "My dear minister, I wish they would all go to Jesus, in prayer and faith, and he will teach them as he has taught me." As the minister left me, I involuntarily burst forth into praises:

> "My soul is full of glory inspiring my tongue,
> Could I meet with angels I would sing them a song."

Though my gifts were but small, I could not be shaken by what man might think or say.

I continued day by day, month after month, to walk in the light as He is in the light, having fellowship with the Trinity and those aged saints. The blood of Jesus Christ cleansed me from all sin, and enabled me to rejoice in persecution.

Bless the Lord, O my soul, for this wonderful salvation, that snatched me as a brand from the burning, even me, a poor, ignorant girl!

And will he not do for all what he did for me? Yes, yes; God is no respecter of persons. Jesus' blood will wash away all your sin and make you whiter than snow.

XII

MY MARRIAGE.

Soon after my conversion, a young man, who had accompanied me to places of amusement, and for whom I had formed quite an attachment, professed faith in Christ and united with the same church to which I belonged. A few months after, he made me an offer of marriage. I struggled not a little to banish the thought from my mind, chiefly because he was not sanctified. But my feelings were so strongly enlisted that I felt sure he would some day be my husband. I read to him and talked to him on the subject of a cleansed heart. He assented to all my arguments, saying he believed and would seek for it.

The few weeks that he remained with us I labored hard with him for his deliverance, but he left us to go to Boston, Mass. We corresponded regularly, he telling me of his religious enjoyment, but that he did not hear anything about sanctification. Great was my anxiety lest the devil should steal away the good seed out of his heart. The Lord, and he only, knows how many times I besought him to let the clear light of holiness shine into that man's heart. Through all this my mind was stayed upon God; I rested in the will of the Lord.

One night, about a month after his departure, I could not sleep, the tempter being unusually busy with me. Rising, I prostrated myself before the Lord. While thus upon my face, these words of God came to me: "For we have not an high priest which cannot be touched with the feeling of our infirmities; but was in all points tempted like as we are, yet without sin." (Heb. iv. 15.) I at once rose up, thanking God for his precious words: I took my Bible and read them over and over again; also the eighteenth verse of the second chapter of Hebrews. I was not conscious of having committed sin, and I cried out: "Leave me, Satan; I am the Lord's." At that the tempter left, and I surrendered myself and all my interests into the hands of God. Glory to his holy name! "For it pleased the Father that in him should all fullness dwell" [Col. 1:19], and of his fullness have I received, and grace for grace.

"Praise God from whom all blessings flow,
Praise him all creatures here below."

The day following this night of temptation was one of great peace—peace flowing as a river, even to overflowing its banks, and such glory of the Lord appeared as to almost deprive me of bodily powers. I forgot all toil and care.

This was just a year after my heart was emptied of sin. Through faith I received the Saviour, and in the same have continued ever since and proved him able to keep from sin. Bless God! all my desires are satisfied in him. He is indeed my reconciled God, the Christ Jesus whose precious blood is all my righteousness.

"Nought of good that I have done
Nothing but the blood of Jesus."

Glory to the blood that hath bought me! glory to the blood that hath cleansed me! glory to the blood that keeps me clean!—me, a brand plucked from the fire.

George returned in about a year to claim me as his bride. He still gave evidence of being a Christian, but had not been cleansed from the carnal mind. I still continued to pray for his sanctification, and desired that it should take place before our union but I was so much attached to him that I could not resist his pleadings; so, at the appointed time, we were married, in the church, in the presence of a large number of people, many of whom followed us to my father's house to offer their congratulations.

We staid at home but one day after the ceremony. This day I spent in preparing for our departure and in taking leave of my friends. Tenderly as I loved my parents, much as I loved the church, yet I found myself quite willing to leave them all in the divine appointment.

The day following, accompanied by several friends, we started for Boston, in an old-fashioned stage-coach, there being no railroads at that time. As I rode along I admired the goodness of God, and my heart overflowed with gratitude to him, who had blessed me with power to choose his will and make me able to say with truth, "I gladly forsake all to follow thee."

Once, the thought of leaving my father's house, to go among strangers, would have been terrible, but now I rejoiced in being so favored as to be called to make this little sacrifice, and evince my love to him who saith: "He that loveth father or mother more than me is not worthy of me" [Matt. 10:37].

XIII

REMOVAL TO BOSTON—THE WORK OF FULL SALVATION.

On our arrival in Boston, after a long, wearisome journey, we went at once to the house of Mrs. Burrows, where my husband had made arrangements for me to board while he was away at work during the week. He worked in Chelsea, and could not come to look after my welfare but once a week. The boarders in this house were mostly gentlemen, nearly all of whom were out of Christ. Mrs. Burrows was a church-member, but knew nothing of the full joys of salvation.

I went to church the first Sabbath I was there, remained at class-meeting, gave my letter of membership to the minister, and was received into the church. In giving my first testimony, I told of my thorough and happy conversion, and of my sanctification as a second, distinct work of the Holy Ghost.

After class-meeting, a good many came to me, asking questions about sanctification; others stood off in groups, talking, while a few followed me to my boarding-house. They all seemed very much excited over what I had told them. I began to see that it was not the voice of man that had bidden me go out from the land of my nativity and from my kindred, but the voice of my dear Lord. I was completely prepared for all that followed, knowing that "All things work together for good to them that love God" [Rom. 8:28]. Change of people, places and circumstances, weighed nothing with me, for I had a safe abiding place with my Father. Some people had been to me in such an unchristianlike spirit that I had spoken to and about them in rather an incautious manner. I now more and more saw the great need of ordering all my words as in the immediate presence of God, that I might be able to maintain that purity of lips and life which the Gospel required. God is holy, and if I would enjoy constant communion with him I must guard every avenue of my soul, and watch every thought of my heart and word of my tongue, that I may be blameless before him in love. The Lord help me evermore to be upon my guard, and having done all, to stand. Amen and amen.

In a few months my husband rented a house just across the road from my boarding-house, and I went to housekeeping. "Mam" Riley, a most excellent Christian, became as a mother to me in this strange land, far from my own dear mother. Bless the Lord! He supplied all my needs. "Mam" Riley had two grown daughters, one about my own age, married, who had two children. They were dear Christian women, and like sisters to me. The mother thought she once enjoyed the blessing of heart purity, but the girls had not heard of such a thing as being sanctified and permitted to live. The elder girl, who was a consumptive and in delicate health, soon became deeply interested in the subject. She began to hunger and thirst after righteousness, and did not rest until she was washed and made clean in the blood of Jesus. Her clear, definite testimony had a great effect upon the church, as her family was one of the first in point of wealth and standing in the community.

God wonderfully honored the faith of this young saint in her ceaseless labor for others. We attended meetings and visited from house to house, together, almost constantly, when she was able to go out. Glory to God! the church became much aroused; some plunged into the ocean of perfect love, and came forth testifying to the power of the blood. Others disbelieved and ridiculed this "foolish doctrine," as they called it, saying it was just as impossible to live without committing sin as it was to live without eating, and brought disjointed passages of Scripture to bear them out.

XIV

EARLY FRUIT GATHERED HOME.

After I went to Boston I was much drawn out in prayer for the sanctification of believers. Notwithstanding the enemy labored by various means to hinder the work of grace, yet the Lord wrought a wonderful change in many.

The mother of my friend received a fresh baptism, and came back into the light, praising the Lord. That the Holy Spirit might keep my dear "Mam" Riley pure until death, was my prayer.

The health of my dear friend, Mrs. Simpson, began rapidly to fail. One morning, in reply to my question as to her health, she said: "Dear sister, I have been in great pain through the night, but you know Jesus said, 'I will never leave thee nor forsake thee' [Heb. 13:5]. Praise God, who has been with me in great mercy through the darkness of the night." I remained with her the following night, and such calmness, patience and resignation through suffering, I never had witnessed. Toward morning she was more easy, and asked for her husband. When he came, she embraced him, repeated passages of Scripture to him, and exhorted him, as she had many times before, to receive God in all his fullness.

There, in that death-chamber, in the stillness of night, we prayed for that pious and exemplary man, that he might present his body a living sacrifice. He was deeply moved upon by the Holy Spirit, so that he cried aloud for deliverance; but almost on the instant began to doubt, and left the room. His wife requested me to read and talk to her about Jesus, which I did, and she was filled with heavenly joy and shouted aloud: "Oh, the blood, the precious blood of Jesus cleanses me now!"

Her mother, who was sleeping in an adjoining room, was awakened by the noise and came in, saying, as she did so: "This room is filled with the glory of God. Hallelujah! Amen."

As the morning dawned, Mrs. Simpson sank into a quiet slumber, which lasted several hours. She awoke singing:

> "How happy are they who their Saviour obey,
> And have laid up their treasure above."

She was comparatively free from pain for several days, though very weak. She talked to all who came to see her of salvation free and full. Her last morning on earth came. She was peaceful and serene, with a heavenly smile upon her countenance. She asked me to pray, which I did with streaming eyes and quivering voice. She then asked us to sing the hymn,

> "Oh, for a thousand tongues to sing
> My great Redeemer's praise."

She sang with us in a much stronger voice than she had used for many days. As we sang the last verse, she raised herself up in bed, clapped her hands and cried: "He sets the prisoner free! Glory! glory! I am free! They have come for me!" She pointed toward the east. Her mother asked her who had come.

She said: "Don't you see the chariot and horses? Glory! glory to the blood!"

She dropped back upon her pillow, and was gone. She had stepped aboard the chariot, which we could not see, but we felt the fire.

While many in the room were weeping, her mother shed not a tear, but shouted, "Glory to God!" Then, with her own hands, she assisted in arranging and preparing the remains for burial. Thus did another sanctified saint enter into eternal life. Though her period of sanctification was short, it was full of precious fruit.

XV

NEW AND UNPLEASANT REVELATIONS.

My husband had always treated the subject of heart purity with favor, but now he began to speak against it. He said I was getting more crazy every day, and getting others in the same way, and that if I did not stop he would send me back home or to the crazy-house. I questioned him closely respecting the state of his mind, feeling that he had been prejudiced. I did not attempt to contend with him on the danger and fallacy of his notions, but simply asked what his state of grace was, if God should require his soul of him then. He gave me no answer until I insisted upon one. Then he said: "Julia, I don't think I can ever believe myself as holy as you think you are."

I then urged him to believe in Christ's holiness, if he had no faith in the power of the blood of Christ to cleanse from all sin. He that hath his hope purifies himself as God is pure. We knelt in prayer together, my husband leading, and he seemed much affected while praying. To me it was a precious season, though there was an indescribable something between us—something dark and high. As I looked at it, these words of the poet came to me:

"God moves in a mysterious way,
His wonders to perform."

From that time I never beheld my husband's face clear and distinct, as before, the dark shadow being ever present. This caused me not a little anxiety and many prayers. Soon after, he accepted an offer to go to sea for six months, leaving me to draw half of his wages. To this arrangement I reluctantly consented, fully realizing how lonely I should be among strangers. Had it not been for dear "Mam" Riley, I could hardly have endured it. Her precept and example taught me to lean more heavily on Christ for support. God gave me these precious words: "Be careful for nothing, but in everything, by prayer and supplication, with thanksgiving, let your requests be made known unto God" [Phil. 4:6]. Truly, God is the great Arbiter of all events, and "because he lives, I shall live also."[6]

The day my husband went on ship-board was one of close trial and great inward temptation. It was difficult for me to mark the exact line between disapprobation and Christian forbearance and patient love. How I longed for wisdom to meet everything in a spirit of meekness and fear, that I might not be surprised into evil or hindered from improving all things to the glory of God.

While under this apparent cloud, I took the Bible to my closet, asking Divine aid. As I opened the book, my eyes fell on these words: "For thy Maker is thine husband" [Isa. 54:5]. I then read the fifty-fourth chapter of Isaiah over and over again. It seemed to me that I had never seen it before. I went forth glorifying God.

XVI

A LONG-LOST BROTHER FOUND.

Having no children, I had a good deal of leisure after my husband's departure, so I visited many of the poor and forsaken ones, reading and talking to them of Jesus, the Saviour. One day I was directed by the Spirit to visit the Marine Hospital. In passing through one of the wards I heard myself called by my maiden name. Going to the cot from whence the voice came, I beheld what seemed to me a human skeleton. As I looked I began to see our family likeness, and recognized my eldest brother, who left home many years before, when I was quite young. Not hearing from him, we had mourned him as dead. With a feeble voice, he told me of his roving and seafaring life; "and now sister," he said, "I am dying."

I asked him if he was willing to die—if he was ready to stand before God. "No, oh, no!" he said. I entreated him to pray. He shook his head, saying, "I can't pray; my heart is too hard, and my mind dark and bewildered," and then cried out, in the agony of his soul, "Oh, that dreadful, burning hell! how can I escape it?"

I urged him to pray, and to believe that Jesus died for all. I prayed for him, and staid with him as much as possible. One morning, when I went to see him, I was shown his lifeless remains in the dead-house. This was, indeed, a solemn time for me.

I had very little hope in my brother's death. But there is an High Priest who ever liveth to make intercession for all [Heb. 7:25], and I trust that he prevailed. The Lord is the Judge of all the earth, and all souls are in his hands, and he will in no wise clear the guilty, though merciful and wise. Willful unbelief is a crying sin, and will not be passed by without punishment. God judges righteously, and is the avenger of all sin. Justice is meted out to all, either here or in eternity. Praise the Lord! My whole soul joins in saying, "Praise the Lord!

God, in great mercy, returned my husband to me in safety, for which I bowed in great thankfulness. George told me that the ship was a poor place to serve the Lord, and that the most he heard was oaths. He said that sometimes he would slip away and pray, and that, upon one occasion, the captain came upon him unawares, and called him "a fool," and told him to get up and go to work. Notwithstanding all this, my husband shipped for a second voyage. Praise the Lord! he saved me from a painful feeling at parting. With joy could I say, "Thou everywhere-present God! thy will be done."

During the year I had been from home, letters from my parents and friends had come to me quite often, filling me with gladness and thanksgiving for the many blessings and cheering words they contained. But now a letter came bringing the intelligence that my family were about to move to Silver Lake, which was much farther from me. I tremblingly went to my heavenly Father, who gave me grace and strength at once.

XVII

MY CALL TO PREACH THE GOSPEL.

For months I had been moved upon to exhort and pray with the people, in my visits from house to house; and in meetings my whole soul seemed drawn out for the salvation of souls. The love of Christ in me was not limited. Some of my mistaken friends said I was too forward, but a desire to work for the Master, and to promote the glory of his kingdom in the salvation of souls, was food to my poor soul.

When called of God, on a particular occasion, to a definite work, I said, "No, Lord, not me." Day by day I was more impressed that God would have me work in his vineyard. I thought it could not be that I was called to preach—I, so weak and ignorant. Still, I knew all things were possible with God, even to confounding the wise by the foolish things of this earth. Yet in me there was a shrinking.

I took all my doubts and fears to the Lord in prayer, when, what seemed to be an angel, made his appearance. In his hand was a scroll, on which were these words: "Thee have I chosen to preach my Gospel without delay." The moment my eyes saw it, it appeared to be printed on my heart. The angel was gone in an instant, and I, in agony, cried out, "Lord, I cannot do it!" It was eleven o'clock in the morning, yet everything grew dark as night. The darkness was so great that I feared to stir.

At last "Mam" Riley entered. As she did so, the room grew lighter, and I arose from my knees. My heart was so heavy I scarce could speak. Dear "Mam" Riley saw my distress, and soon left me.

From that day my appetite failed me and sleep fled from my eyes. I seemed as one tormented. I prayed, but felt no better. I belonged to a band of sisters whom I loved dearly, and to them I partially opened my mind. One of them seemed to understand my case at once, and advised me to do as God had bid me, or I would never be happy here or hereafter. But it seemed too hard—I could not give up and obey.

One night as I lay weeping and beseeching the dear Lord to remove this burden from me, there appeared the same angel that came to me before, and on his breast were these words: "You are lost unless you obey God's righteous commands." I saw the writing, and that was enough. I covered my head and awoke my husband, who had returned a few days before. He asked me why I trembled so, but I had not power to answer him. I remained in that condition until morning, when I tried to arise and go about my usual duties, but was too ill. Then my husband called a physician, who prescribed medicine, but it did me no good.

I had always been opposed to the preaching of women, and had spoken against it, though, I acknowledge, without foundation. This rose before me like a mountain, and when I thought of the difficulties they had to encounter, both from professors and non-professors, I shrank back and cried, "Lord, I cannot go!"

The trouble my heavenly Father has had to keep me out of the fire that is never quenched, he alone knoweth. My husband and friends said I would die or go crazy if something favorable did not take place soon. I expected to die and be lost, knowing I had been enlightened and had tasted the heavenly gift. I read again and again the sixth chapter of Hebrews.

XVIII

HEAVENLY VISITATIONS AGAIN.

Nearly two months from the time I first saw the angel, I said that I would do anything or go anywhere for God, if it were made plain to me. He took me at my word, and sent the angel again with this message: "You have I chosen to go in my name and warn the people of their sins." I bowed my head and said, "I will go, Lord."

That moment I felt a joy and peace I had not known for months. But strange as it may appear, it is not the less true, that, ere one hour had passed, I began to reason thus: "I am elected to preach the Gospel without the requisite qualifications, and, besides, my parents and friends will forsake me and turn against me; and I regret that I made a promise." At that instant all the joy and peace I had felt left me, and I thought I was standing on the brink of hell, and heard the devil say: "Let her go! let her go! I will catch her." Reader, can you imagine how I felt? If you were ever snatched from the mouth of hell, you can, in part, realize my feelings.

I continued in this state for some time, when, on a Sabbath evening—ah! that memorable Sabbath evening—while engaged in fervent prayer, the same supernatural presence came to me once more and took me by the hand. At that moment I became lost to everything in this world. The angel led me to a place where there was a large tree, the branches of which seemed to extend either way beyond sight. Beneath it sat, as I thought, God the Father, the Son, and the Holy Spirit, besides many others, whom I thought were angels. I was led before them: they looked me over from head to foot, but said nothing. Finally, the Father said to me: "Before these people make your choice, whether you will obey me or go from this place to eternal misery and pain." I answered not a word. He then took me by the hand to lead me, as I thought, to hell, when I cried out, "I will obey thee, Lord!" He then pointed my hand in different directions, and asked if I would go there. I replied, "Yes, Lord." He then lead me, all the others following, till we came to a place where there was a great quantity of water, which looked like silver, where we made a halt. My hand was given to Christ, who led me into the water and stripped me of my clothing, which at once vanished from sight. Christ then appeared to wash me, the water feeling quite warm.

During this operation, all the others stood on the bank, looking on in profound silence. When the washing was ended, the sweetest music I had ever heard greeted my ears. We walked to the shore, where an angel stood with a clean, white robe, which the Father at once put on me. In an instant I appeared to be changed into an angel. The whole company looked at me with delight, and began to make a noise which I called shouting. We all marched back with music. When we reached the tree to which the angel first led me, it hung full of fruit, which I had not seen before. The Holy Ghost plucked some and gave me, and the rest helped themselves. We sat down and ate of the fruit, which had a taste like nothing I had ever tasted before. When we had finished, we all arose and gave another shout. Then God the Father said to me: "You are now prepared, and must go where I have commanded you." I replied, "If I go, they will not believe me." Christ then appeared to write something with a golden pen and golden ink, upon golden paper. Then he rolled it up, and said to me: "Put this in your bosom, and, wherever you go, show it, and they will know that I have sent you to proclaim salvation to all." He then put it into my bosom, and they all went with me to a bright, shining gate, singing and shouting. Here they embraced me, and I found myself once more on earth.

When I came to myself, I found that several friends had been with me all night, and my husband had called a physician, but he had not been able to do anything for me. He ordered those around me to keep very quiet, or to go home. He returned in the morning, when I told him, in part, my story. He seemed amazed, but made no answer, and left me.

Several friends were in, during the day. While talking to them, I would, without thinking, put my hand into my bosom, to show them my letter of authority. But I soon found, as my friends told me, it was in my heart, and was to be shown in my life, instead of in my hand. Among others, my minister, Jehial [Jehiel] C. Beman, came to see me.[7] He looked very coldly upon me and said: "I guess you will find out your mistake before you are many months older." He was a scholar, and a fine speaker; and the sneering, indifferent way in which he addressed me, said most plainly: "You don't know anything." I replied: "My gifts are very small, I know, but I can no longer be shaken by what you or any one else may think or say."

XIX

PUBLIC EFFORT— EXCOMMUNICATION.

From this time the opposition to my lifework commenced, instigated by the minister, Mr. Beman. Many in the church were anxious to have me preach in the hall, where our meetings were held at that time, and were not a little astonished at the minister's cool treatment of me. At length two of the trustees got some of the elder sisters to call on the minister and ask him to let me preach. His answer was: "No; she can't preach her holiness stuff here, and I am astonished that you should ask it of me." The sisters said he seemed to be in quite a rage, although he said he was not angry.

There being no meeting of the society on Monday evening, a brother in the church opened his house to me, that I might preach, which displeased Mr. Beman very much. He appointed a committee to wait upon the brother and sister who had opened their doors to me, to tell them they must not allow any more meetings of that kind, and that they must abide by the rules of the church, making them believe they would be excommunicated if they disobeyed him. I happened to be present at this interview, and the committee remonstrated with me for the course I had taken. I told them my business was with the Lord, and wherever I found a door opened I intended to go in and work for my Master.

There was another meeting appointed at the same place, which I, of course, attended; after which the meetings were stopped for that time, though I held many more there after these people had withdrawn from Mr. Beman's church.

I then held meetings in my own house; whereat the minister told the members that if they attended them he would deal with them, for they were breaking the rules of the church. When he found that I continued the meetings, and that the Lord was blessing my feeble efforts, he sent a committee of two to ask me if I considered myself a member of his church. I told them I did, and should continue to do so until I had done something worthy of dismembership.

At this, Mr. Beman sent another committee with a note, asking me to meet him with the committee, which I did. He asked me a number of questions, nearly all of which I have forgotten. One, however, I do remember: he asked if I was willing to comply with the rules of the discipline. To this I answered: "Not if the discipline prohibits me from doing what God has bidden me to do; I fear God more than man." Similar questions were asked and answered in the same manner. The committee said what they wished to say, and then told me I could go home. When I reached the door, I turned and said: "I now shake off the dust of my feet as a witness against you [Mark 6:11; Luke 9:5]. See to it that this meeting does not rise in judgment against you."

The next evening, one of the committee came to me and told me that I was no longer a member of the church, because I had violated the rules of the discipline by preaching.

When this action became known, the people wondered how any one could be excommunicated for trying to do good. I did not say much, and my friends simply said I had done nothing but hold meetings. Others, anxious to know the particulars, asked the minister what the trouble was. He told them he had given me the privilege of speaking or preaching as long as I chose, but that he could not give me the right to use the pulpit, and that I was not satisfied with any other place. Also, that I had appointed meeting on the evening of his meetings, which was a thing no member had a right to do. For these reasons he said he had turned me out of the church.

Now, if the people who repeated this to me told the truth—and I have no doubt but they did—Mr. Beman told an actual falsehood. I had never asked for his pulpit, but had told him and others, repeatedly, that I did not care where I stood—any corner of the hall would do. To which Mr. Beman had answered: "You cannot have any place in the hall." Then I said: "I'll preach in a private house." He answered me: "No, not in this place; I am stationed over all Boston." He was determined I should not preach in the city of Boston. To cover up his deceptive, unrighteous course toward me, he told the above falsehoods.

From his statements, many erroneous stories concerning me gained credence with a large number of people. At that time, I thought it my duty as well as privilege to address a letter to the Conference, which I took to them in person, stating all the facts. At the same time I told them it was not in the power of Mr. Beman, or any one else, to truthfully bring anything against my moral or religious character—that my only offence was in trying to preach the Gospel of Christ—and that I cherished no ill feelings toward Mr. Beman or any one else, but that I desired the Conference to give the case an impartial hearing, and then give me a written statement expressive of their opinion. I also said I considered myself a member of the Conference, and should do so until they said I was not, and gave me their reasons, that I might let the world know what my offence had been.

My letter was slightingly noticed, and then thrown under the table. Why should they notice it? It was only the grievance of a woman, and there was no justice meted out to women in those days. Even ministers of Christ did not feel that women had any rights which they were bound to respect.

XX

WOMEN IN THE GOSPEL.

Thirty years ago there could scarcely a person be found, in the churches, to sympathize with any one who talked of Holiness. But, in my simplicity, I did think that a body of Christian ministers would understand my case and judge righteously. I was, however, disappointed.

It is no little thing to feel that every man's hand is against us, and ours against every man, as seemed to be the case with me at this time; yet how precious, if Jesus but be with us. In this severe trial I had constant access to God, and a clear consciousness that he heard me; yet I did not seem to have that plenitude of the Spirit that I had before. I realized most keenly that the closer the communion that may have existed, the keener the suffering of the slightest departure from God. Unbroken communion can only be retained by a constant application of the blood which cleanseth.

Though I did not wish to pain any one, neither could I please any one only as I was led by the Holy Spirit. I saw, as never before, that the best men were liable to err, and that the only safe way was to fall on Christ, even though censure and reproach fell upon me for obeying his voice. Man's opinion weighed nothing with me, for my commission was from heaven, and my reward was with the Most High.

I could not believe that it was a short-lived impulse or spasmodic influence that impelled me to preach. I read that on the day of Pentecost[8] was the Scripture fulfilled as found in Joel ii. 28, 29; and it certainly will not be denied that women as well as men were at that time filled with the Holy Ghost, because it is expressly stated that women were among those who continued in prayer and supplication, waiting for the fulfillment of the promise. Women and men are classed together, and if the power to preach the Gospel is short-lived and spasmodic in the case of women, it must be equally so in that of men; and if women have lost the gift of prophecy, so have men.

We are sometimes told that if a woman pretends to a Divine call, and thereon grounds the right to plead the cause of a crucified Redeemer in public, she will be believed when she shows credentials from heaven; that is, when she works a miracle. If it be necessary to prove one's right to preach the Gospel, I ask of my brethren to show me their credentials, or I can not believe in the propriety of their ministry.

But the Bible puts an end to this strife when it says: "There is neither male nor female in Christ Jesus" [Gal. 3:28]. Philip had four daughters that prophesied, or preached. Paul called Priscilla, as well as Aquila, his "helper," or, as in the Greek, his "fellow-laborer." Rom. xv. 3; 2 Cor. viii. 23; Phil. ii. 5; 1 Thess. iii. 2. The same word, which, in our common translation, is now rendered a "servant of the church," in speaking of Phebe (Rom. xix. 1.), is rendered "minister" when applied to Tychicus. Eph. vi. 21. When Paul said, "Help those women who labor with me in the Gospel," he certainly meant that they did more than to pour out tea.[9] In the eleventh chapter of First Corinthians Paul gives directions, to men and women, how they should appear when they prophesy or pray in public assemblies; and he defines prophesying to be speaking to edification, exhortation and comfort.

I may further remark that the conduct of holy women is recorded in Scripture as an example to others of their sex. And in the early ages of Christianity many women were happy and glorious in martyrdom. How nobly, how heroically, too, in later ages, have women suffered persecution and death for the name of the Lord Jesus.

In looking over these facts, I could see no miracle wrought for those women more than in myself.

Though opposed, I went forth laboring for God, and he owned and blessed my labors, and has done so wherever I have been until this day. And while I walk obediently, I know he will, though hell may rage and vent its spite.

XXI

THE LORD LEADETH—LABOR IN PHILADELPHIA.

As I left the Conference, God wonderfully filled my heart with his love, so that, as I passed from place to place, meeting one and another of the ministers, my heart went out in love to each of them as though he had been my father; and the language of 1 Pet. i. 7, came forcibly to my mind: "The trial of our faith is much more precious than of gold that perisheth, though it be tried by fire." Fiery trials are not strange things to the Lord's annointed. The rejoicing in them is born only of the Holy Spirit. Oh, praise his holy name for a circumcised heart, teaching us that each trial of our faith hath its commission from the Father of spirits. Each wave of trial bears the Galilean Pilot on its crest. Listen: his voice is in the storm, and winds and waves obey that voice: "It is I; be not afraid" [John 6:20]. He has promised us help and safety in the fires, and not escape from them.

"And hereby we know that he abideth in us, by the Spirit which he hath given us." 1 John iii. 24. Glory to the Lamb for the witness of the Holy Spirit! He knoweth that every step I have taken has been for the glory of God and the good of souls. However much I may have erred in judgment, it has been the fault of my head and not of my heart. I sleep, but my heart waketh; bless the Lord.

Had this opposition come from the world, it would have seemed as nothing. But coming, as it did, from those who had been much blessed—blessed with me—and who had once been friends of mine, it touched a tender spot; and had it not been for the precious blood of Jesus, I should have been lost.

While in Philadelphia, attending the Conference, I became acquainted with three sisters who believed they were called to public labors in their Master's vineyard. But they had been so opposed, they were very much distressed and shrank from their duty. One of them professed sanctification. They had met with more opposition from ministers than from any one else.

After the Conference had adjourned, I proposed to these sisters to procure a place and hold a series of meetings. They were pleased with the idea, and were willing to help if I would take charge of the meetings. They apprehended some difficulty, as there had never been a meeting there under the sole charge of women. The language of my heart was:

> "Only Thou my Leader be
> And I still will follow Thee."

Trusting in my Leader, I went on with the work. I hired a large place in Canal street, and there we opened our meetings, which continued eleven nights, and over one Sabbath. The room was crowded every night—some coming to receive good, others to criticise, sneer, and say hard things against us.

One of the sisters left us after a day or two, fearing that the Church to which she belonged would disown her if she continued to assist us. We regretted this very much, but could only say, "An enemy hath done this" [Matt. 13:28]

These meetings were a time of refreshing from the presence of the Lord. Many were converted, and a few stepped into the fountain of cleansing.

Some of the ministers, who remained in the city after the Conference, attended our meetings, and occasionally asked us if we were organizing a new Conference, with a view of drawing out from the churches. This was simply to ridicule our meeting.

We closed with a love-feast, which caused such a stir among the ministers and many of the church-members, that we could not imagine what the end would be. They seemed to think we had well nigh committed the unpardonable sin.

XXII

A VISIT TO MY PARENTS—FURTHER LABORS.

Some of the dear sisters accompanied me to Flatbush, where I assisted in a bush meeting.[10] The Lord met the people in great power, and I doubt not there are many souls in glory to-day praising God for that meeting.

From that place I went home to my father's house in Binghamton, N.Y. They were filled with joy to have me with them once more, after an absence of six years. As my mother embraced me, she exclaimed: "So you are a preacher, are you?" I replied: "So they say." "Well, Julia," said she, "when I first heard that you were a preacher, I said that I would rather hear you were dead." These words, coming so unexpectedly from my mother, filled me with anguish. Was I to meet opposition here, too? But my mother, with streaming eyes, continued: "My dear daughter, it is all past now. I have heard from those who have attended your meetings what the Lord has done for you, and I am satisfied."

My stay in Binghamton was protracted several months. I held meetings in and around the town, to the acceptance of the people, and, I trust, to the glory of God. I felt perfectly satisfied, when the time came for me to leave, that my work was all for the Lord, and my soul was filled with joy and thankfulness for salvation. Before leaving, my parents decided to move to Boston, which they did soon after.

I left Binghamton the first of February, 1855,[11] in company with the Rev. Henry Johnson and his wife, for Ithaca, N.Y., where I labored a short time. I met with some opposition from one of the A.M.E. Church trustees. He said a woman should not preach in the church.[12] Beloved, the God we serve fights all our battles, and before I left the place that trustee was one of the most faithful at my meetings, and was very kind to assist me on my journey when I left Ithaca. I stopped one night at Oswego, at Brother Loyd's, and I also stopped for a short time at Onondaga, returned to Ithaca on the 14th of February, and staid until the 7th of March, during which time the work of grace was greatly revived. Some believed and entered into the rest of full salvation, many were converted, and a number of backsliders were reclaimed. I held prayer-meetings from house to house. The sisters formed a woman's prayer-meeting, and the whole church seemed to be working in unison for Christ.

March 7th I took the stage for Geneva, and, arriving late at night, went to a hotel. In the morning Brother Rosel Jeffrey took me to his house and left me with his wife. He was a zealous Christian, but she scoffed at religion, and laughed and made sport during family worship. I do not know, but hope that long ere this she has ceased to ridicule the cause or the followers of Christ. In the latter part of the day Brother Condell came and invited me to his house. I found his wife a pleasant Christian woman. Sabbath afternoon I held a meeting in Brother Condell's house. The colored people had a church which the whites had given them. It was a union church, to be occupied on alternate Sundays by the Methodists and Baptists.

According to arrangement, this Sunday evening was the time for the Methodists to occupy the church. The Rev. Dawsey, of Canandaigua, came to fill his appointment, but, when we arrived at the church, the Baptist minister, William Monroe, objected to our holding a meeting in the house that evening, and his members joined with him in his unchristian course. Rather than have any trouble, we returned to Brother Condell's house. The minister preached and I followed with a short exhortation. The Lord was present to bless. They made an appointment for me to preach at the union meeting-house on the following Tuesday evening.

Monday evening I went with some of the sisters to the church, where there was a meeting for the purpose of forming a moral reform society.

After the meeting, Brother Condell asked the trustees if they had any objection to having me speak in the church the next evening. To this, Minister Monroe and another man—I had almost said a fiend in human shape—answered that they did not believe in women's preaching, and would not admit one in the church, striving hard to justify themselves from the Bible, which one of them held in his unholy hands.

I arose to speak, when Mr. Monroe interrupted me. After a few words I left the house. The next afternoon, while taking tea at the house of one of the sisters, Minister Monroe came in to tell me he heard that our brethren had said they would have the church for me if they had to "shed blood." He asked me if I wanted to have anything to do with a fight of that kind. I replied: "The weapons with which I fight are not carnal, and, if I go to a place and am invited to use the weapons God has given me, I must use them to his glory."

"Well," said he, "I shall be in the pulpit at an early hour, and will not leave it though they break my head."

"Mr. Monroe," said I, "God can take you from the pulpit without breaking your head." At this he became very much excited, and raved as if he were a madman. For two hours he walked the floor, talking and reading all the time. I made him no reply and tried not to notice him, and finally he left me.

At the proper time we went to the church. It was full, but everything was in confusion. Mr. Monroe was in the pulpit. I saw at once that God could not be glorified in the midst of such a pandemonium; so I withdrew at once. I was told they kept up the contention until after ten o'clock. Mr. Monroe tried hard to get our trustees to say I should not preach in the place, but they would give him no such promise.

As I was obliged to leave in a few days, to meet other appointments, our men procured a large house, where I held a meeting the next evening. All that attended were quiet and orderly; one man arose for prayers.

Dear sisters, who are in the evangelistic work now, you may think you have hard times; but let me tell you, I feel that the lion and lamb are lying down together, as compared with the state of things twenty-five or thirty years ago. Yes, yes; our God is marching on. Glory to his name!

XXIII

INDIGNITIES ON ACCOUNT OF COLOR—GENERAL CONFERENCE.

I reached Rochester on the 16th of March, where I remained three weeks, laboring constantly for my Master, who rewarded me in the salvation of souls. Here God visited me after the same manner he did Elijah, when Elijah prayed to die [1 Kings 19:4]. He strengthened me and bid me go forward with the promises recorded in the first chapter of Joshua.

April 21st I bade good-bye to Brother John H. Bishop's people, who had entertained me while in Rochester, and went to Binghamton to visit my parents again. I found them all well, and labored constantly for the Lord while I was there. I remained at home until the 8th of May, when I once more started out on my travels for the Lord. There was but one passenger in the stage besides myself. He gave his name as White, seemed very uneasy, and, at each stopping place, he would say: "I am afraid the public will take me for an abolitionist to-day;" thus showing his dark, slave-holding principles.

I staid one night in Oxford, at Mr. Jackson's. At six o'clock the next morning I took passage on the canal packet "Governor Seward," with Captain George Keeler. That night, at a late hour, I made my way into the ladies' cabin, and, finding an empty berth, retired. In a short time a man came into the cabin, saying that the berths in the gentlemen's cabin were all occupied, and he was going to sleep in the ladies' cabin. Then he pointed to me and said: "That nigger has no business here. My family are coming on board the boat at Utica, and they shall not come where a nigger is." They called the captain, and he ordered me to get up; but I did not stir, thinking it best not to leave the bed except by force. Finally they left me, and the man found lodging among the seamen, swearing vengeance on the "niggers."

The next night the boat stopped at a village, and the captain procured lodging for me at an inn. Thus I escaped further abuse from that ungodly man.

The second night we reached Utica, where I staid over Sunday. Then I went to Schenectady, where I remained for a few days, working for my Master. Then I went to Albany, my old home. Sunday afternoon I preached in Troy, and that Sunday evening in Albany, to a crowded house. There were many of my old friends and acquaintances in the audience. This was the most solemn and interesting meeting I ever held. The entire audience seemed moved to prayer and tears by the power of the Holy Ghost.

On May 21st I went to New York. During the year that followed I visited too large a number of places to mention in this little work.

I went from Philadelphia in company with thirty ministers and Bishop Brown,[13] to attend the General Conference, which was held in Pittsburgh, Pa. The ministers chartered the conveyance, and we had a very pleasant and interesting journey. The discussions during the day and meetings at night, on the canal boat, were instructive and entertaining. A very dear sister, Ann M. Johnson, accompanied me. The grand, romantic scenery, which I beheld while crossing the Alleghany mountains, filled me with adoration and praise to the great Creator of all things. We reached Pittsburgh on the 4th of June, and the General Conference of the A.M.E. Church convened on the 6th of June. The Conference lasted two weeks, and was held with open doors.

The business common to such meetings was transacted with spirit and harmony, with few exceptions. One was, a motion to prevent Free Masons from ministering in the churches. Another, to allow all the women preachers to become members of the conferences. This caused quite a sensation, bringing many members to their feet at once. They all talked and screamed to the bishop, who could scarcely keep order. The Conference was so incensed at the brother who offered the petition that they threatened to take action against him.[14]

I remained several weeks, laboring among the people, much to the comfort of my own soul, and, I humbly trust, to the upbuilding of my dear Master's kingdom. I found the people very kind and benevolent.

XXIV

CONTINUED LABORS—DEATH OF MY HUSBAND AND FATHER.

From Pittsburgh I went to Cincinnati, where I found a large number of colored people of different denominations. The Methodists had a very good meeting-house on Sixth street, below Broad street. The members appeared to enjoy religion, but were very much like the world in their external appearance and cold indifference toward each other.

The station and circuit joined in holding a camp-meeting. The minister urged me very strongly to attend, which I did. Several souls professed faith in Christ at this meeting, but only one was willing to receive him in all his fullness.

After this meeting I labored in quite a number of places in Ohio. At some places I was kindly received, at others I was not allowed to labor publicly.

While thus laboring far from home, the sad intelligence of my husband's death came to me so suddenly as to almost cause me to sink beneath the blow. But the arm of my dear, loving, heavenly Father sustained me, and I was enabled to say: "Though he slay me, yet will I trust in him" [Job 13:15]. I immediately hastened home to Boston, where I learned the particulars of my husband's death, which occurred on ship-board several months before. None but the dear Lord knew what my feelings were. I dared not complain, and thus cast contempt on my blessed Saviour, for I knew he would not lay more upon me than I could bear. He knows how to deliver the godly out of temptation and affliction; all events belong to him. All we have to be careful for is, to know of a truth that Christ is formed in our hearts the hope of glory, and hath set up his kingdom there, to reign over every affection and desire. Glory to the Lamb, who giveth me power thus to live!

After arranging my affairs at home, I went to Albany, where my sister lived, staid a short time with her, and held some meetings there. Then I went to Bethlehem, where I held several meetings, one in the M.E. Church, which was arranged only after there had been considerable controversy about letting a woman preach in their house. From there I went to Troy, where I also held meetings. In each of these places this "brand plucked from the burning" was used of God to his glory in saving precious souls. To his name be all the glory!

I spent one Sunday in Poughkeepsie, working for Jesus. I then went to New York, where I took the boat for Boston. We were detained some hours by one of the shafts breaking. I took a very severe cold by being compelled to sit on deck all night, in the cold, damp air—prejudice not permitting one of my color to enter the cabin except in the capacity of a servant. O Prejudice! thou cruel monster! wilt thou ever cease to exist? Not until all shall know the Lord, and holiness shall be written upon the bells of the horses—upon all things in earth as well as in heaven. Glory to the Lamb, whose right it is to reign!

Upon my arrival home I found my father quite ill. He was sick for several months, and I remained at home until after his death, which event took place in May, 1849. He bore his long, painful illness with Christian patience and resignation. Just before leaving us for the better world, he called each of his children that were present to his bedside, exhorting them to live here in such a manner that they might meet him in heaven. To me he said: "My dear daughter, be faithful to your heavenly calling, and fear not to preach full salvation." After some precious words to his weeping wife, my dear father was taken to his eternal rest. Bless the Lord, O my soul, for an earnest, Christian father! Reader, I trust it is your lot to have faithful, believing parents.

XXV

WORK IN VARIOUS PLACES.

June 18th, 1849, I bade my mother and family farewell, and started out on my mission again. I stopped in New York, where I was joined by Sister Ann M. Johnson, who became my traveling companion. We went to Philadelphia, where we were entertained by Brother and Sister Lee. The dear, kind friends welcomed us warmly. Sister Johnson did not feel moved to labor in public, except to sing, pray, and recount her experience. I labored constantly while in this city, going from church to church.

On the 28th we went to Snow Hill, where we spent one Sunday. We visited Fethersville, Bordentown, Westchester and Westtown, all to the glory of God. I must say, the dear Holy Spirit wonderfully visited the people in all these places. Many were converted, and, now and then, one would step into the fountain of cleansing.

July 20th we left for New York, stopping at Burlington, Trenton, Princeton, Rahway, Brunswick and Newark. In each of these places we spent several days, much to our comfort and the apparent good of the churches. We arrived in New York city August 3d, and went to Bridgeport (Conn.) by boat. We found the church there in a very unsettled condition because of unbelief. We next went to New Haven, where we had some precious meetings. In Providence, R.I., we also received God's blessing on our labors.

At this time I received a pressing invitation from Rev. Daniel A. Paine [Payne], who is now bishop of the A.M.E. Church, to visit Baltimore, which I accepted.[15] Upon our arrival there we were closely questioned as to our freedom, and carefully examined for marks on our persons by which to identify us if we should prove to be runaways. While there, a daughter of the lady with whom we boarded ran away from her self-styled master. He came, with others, to her mother's house at midnight, burst in the door without ceremony, and swore the girl was hid in the house, and that he would have her, dead or alive. They repeated this for several nights. They often came to our bed and held their light in our faces, to see if the one for whom they were looking was not with us. The mother was, of course, in great distress. I believe they never recovered the girl. Thank the dear Lord we do not have to suffer such indignities now, though the monster, Slavery, is not yet dead in all its forms.

We remained some time in Baltimore, laboring mostly in Brother Paine's charge. We then went to Washington, D.C., where our Conference was in session. The meetings were excellent, and great good was being done, when an incident occurred which cast a gloom over the whole Conference. One day, when a number of the ministers, Sister Johnson and myself, were dining at the house of one of the brethren, a slaveholder came and searched the house for a runaway. We realized more and more what a terrible thing it was for one human being to have absolute control over another.

We remained in Washington a few weeks, laboring for Christ. Although, at the time, it seemed as though Satan ruled there supreme, God gave us to know that his righteousness was being set up in many hearts. Glory to his excellent name.

The larger portion of the past year had been a time of close trial, yet I do not recollect ever closing a year more fully in Christ than I did that one. On taking a retrospective view of it, I found great cause for humiliation as well as thankfulness. I was satisfied with the Lord's dealings with me; my mind was kept in peace, while many had declined on the right hand and on the left; I was thankful that any were spared to bear the standard of the Redeemer.

Since I first entered the vineyard of my divine Master, I have seen many a star fall, and many a shining light go out and sink into darkness. Many, who have been singularly owned and blessed of God, have deserted his standard in the day of trial; yet, through his abounding grace, have I been kept. Glory be to the keeping power of the blood that cleanseth me, even me, from all sin!

XXVI

FURTHER LABORS—A "THRESHING" SERMON.

In June, 1850, I crossed the Alleghany mountains the second time. I was very sick on the journey, and on arriving in Pittsburgh, was not able to sit up. Finding me in a raging fever, my friends called in a physician, and, as I continued to grow worse, another one. For three weeks my life was despaired of; and finally, on beginning to recover, it was many months before I felt quite well. In this severe affliction grace wonderfully sustained me. Bless the Lord!

I was advised to go down the Ohio river for the benefit of my health. Therefore, as soon as I was able to do so, I started for Cincinnati. I staid there several weeks with some friends by the name of Jones. The Lord so strengthened me, that, in a few months, I was able to resume my labors.

In October we went to Columbus. We labored there and in that vicinity for some time, content that in our protracted effort quite a number were converted. There were three persons there who said they had once enjoyed the blessing of sanctification, but were not then clear in the experience. Oh, how few are advocates for full salvation! Some will hold the whole truth in profession when and where it is not opposed, but, if they must become fools for the truth's sake, they compromise with error. Such have not and will not come to the perfect rest and inheritance of the saints on earth.

In April, 1851, we visited Chillicothe, and had some glorious meetings there. Great crowds attended every night, and the altar was crowded with anxious inquirers. Some of the deacons of the white people's Baptist church invited me to preach in their church, but I declined to do so, on account of the opposition of the pastor, who was very much set against women's preaching. He said so much against it, and against the members who wished me to preach, that they called a church meeting, and I heard that they finally dismissed him.

The white Methodists invited me to speak for them, but did not want the colored people to attend the meeting. I would not agree to any such arrangement, and, therefore, I did not speak for them. Prejudice had closed the door of their sanctuary against the colored people of the place, virtually saying: "The Gospel shall not be free to all." Our benign Master and Saviour said: "Go, preach my Gospel to all" [Mark 16:15].

We visited Zanesville, Ohio, laboring for white and colored people. The white Methodists opened their house for the admission of colored people for the first time. Hundreds were turned away at each meeting, unable to get in; and, although the house was so crowded, perfect order prevailed. We also held meetings on the other side of the river. God the Holy Ghost was powerfully manifest in all these meetings. I was the recipient of many mercies, and passed through various exercises. In all of them I could trace the hand of God and claim divine assistance whenever I most needed it. Whatever I needed, by faith I had. Glory! glory!! While God lives, and Jesus sits on his right hand, nothing shall be impossible unto me, if I hold fast faith with a pure conscience.

On the 27th we went to Detroit, Mich. On the way, Sister Johnson had a very severe attack of ague, which lasted for several weeks. My soul had great liberty for God while laboring in this place.

One day, quite an influential man in the community, though a sinner, called on me and appeared deeply concerned about his soul's welfare. He urged me to speak from Micah iv. 13: "Arise and thresh, O daughter of Zion," etc. I took his desire to the Lord, and was permitted to speak from that passage after this manner: 710 B.C. corn was threshed among the Orientals by means of oxen or horses, which were driven round an area filled with loose sheaves. By their continued tramping the corn was separated from the straw. That this might be done the more effectually, the text promised an addition to the natural horny substance on the feet of these animals, by making the horn iron and the hoof brass.

Corn is not threshed in this manner by us, but by means of flails, so that I feel I am doing no injury to the sentiment of the text by changing a few of the terms into which are the most familiar to us now. The passage portrays the Gospel times, though in a more restricted sense it applies to the preachers of the word. Yet it has a direct reference to all God's people, who were and are commanded to arise and thresh. Glory to Jesus! now is this prophecy fulfilled—Joel ii. 28 and 29. They are also commanded to go to God, who alone is able to qualify them for their labors by making their horns iron and their hoofs brass. The Lord was desirous of imparting stability and perpetuity to his own divine work, by granting supernatural aid to the faithful that they might perform for him those services for which their own feeble and unassisted powers were totally inadequate. More than this, it is encouraging to the saints to know that they are provided with weapons both offensive and defensive.

The threshing instrument is of the former description. It is of the same quality as that which is quick and powerful and sharper than any two-edged sword. "For this purpose the Son of God was manifested, that he might destroy the works of the devil," and this is one of the weapons which he employs in the hands of his people to carry his gracious designs into execution, together with the promise that they shall beat in pieces many people. Isa. xxiii. 18; lx. 6–9.

There are many instances of the successful application of the Gospel flail, by which means the devil is threshed out of sinners. With the help of God, I am resolved, O sinner, to try what effect the smart strokes of this threshing instrument will produce on thy unhumbled soul. This is called the sword of the Spirit, and is in reality the word of God. Such a weapon may seem contemptible in the eyes of the natural man; yet, when it is powerfully wielded, the consequences are invariably potent and salutary. Bless God! the Revelator says: "They overcame by the blood of the Lamb and by the word of their testimony; and they loved not their lives unto the death" [Rev. 12:11]. The atonement is the greatest weapon. In making trial of its efficacy, little children have caused the parent to cry aloud for mercy; but, in every case, much of its heavenly charm and virtue depends upon the mode in which it is applied.

This Gospel flail should be lifted up in a kind and loving spirit. Many shrink at sight of the flail, and some of us know, by blessed experience, that when its smart strokes are applied in the power and demonstration of the Holy Spirit, it causes the very heart to feel sore and painful. Penitent soul, receive the castigation, and you will feel, after it, like saying: "Now let me be crucified, and this work of the devil, inbred sin, put to death, that Christ may live and reign in me without a rival."

To the glory of God I wish to say, that the unconverted man, who gave me the text for the above discourse, gave his heart to God, together with many others, before we left Detroit. In after years I was informed of his happy death. Praise the Lord for full and free salvation! Reader, have you this salvation—an ever-flowing fountain—in your soul? God grant it. Amen!

XXVII

MY CLEVELAND HOME—LATER LABORS.

In June, 1851, we went to Canada, where we were kindly received. We labored in different churches with great success. We found many living Christians there—some holding high the light of full salvation, and others willing to be cleansed. After spending a few weeks there, we crossed to Buffalo, but did not make any stay there at that time.

The places visited during that year are too numerous to mention here. Suffice it to say, the great Head of the Church went before us, clearing the way and giving us unmistakable evidence of his presence in every battle. Hallelujah!

We returned to Columbus to fill an appointment which was awaiting us. After this, we made arrangements to go to Cleveland. One of the brethren engaged our passage and paid the fare, but we were not permitted to leave until four days afterward. At that time a colored person was not allowed to ride in the stage if any white passenger objected to it. There were objections made for three mornings, but, on the fourth, the stage called for us, and we had safe journey to Cleveland. We expected to make a visit only, as in other cities; but the All-Father intended otherwise, and, more than twenty years ago, Cleveland became my home. After settling down, we still continued to visit neighboring cities and labor for Christ.

It was about this time that I became afflicted with the throat difficulty, of which I shall speak later. Beloved, the dear Lord only knows how sorely I was tried and tempted over this affliction.

St. James speaks of temptations as being common to the most holy of men, and also as a matter of joy and rejoicing to such as are exercised thereby, if so be they are not overcome by them [James 1:2–4, 12–15]. I think all temptation has a tendency to sin, but all temptation is not sin. There is a diversity of temptations, and a diversity of causes from which temptations proceed. Some come immediately from our corrupt nature, and are in themselves sinful. Others arise from the infirmity of our nature, and these every Christian has to contend with so long as he sojourns in a tabernacle of clay. There are also temptations which come directly from the enemy of souls. These our blessed Lord severely labored under, and so do the majority of his children. "Blessed is the man that endureth temptation"!

During the years that I rested from my labors and tried to recover my health, God permitted me to pass through the furnace of trial, heated seven times hotter than usual. Had not the three-one God been with me, I surely must have gone beneath the waves. God permits afflictions and persecutions to come upon his chosen people to answer various ends. Sometimes for the trial of their faith, and the exercise of their patience and resignation to his will, and sometimes to draw them off from all human dependence, and to teach them to trust in Him alone. Sometimes he suffers the wicked to go a great way, and the ungodly to triumph over us, that he may prove our steadfastness and make manifest his power in upholding us. Thus it was with me. I had trusted too much in human wisdom, and God suffered all these things to come upon me. He upheld me by his grace, freeing me from all care or concern about my health or what man could do. He taught me to sit patiently, and wait to hear my Shepherd's voice; for I was resolved to follow no stranger, however plausibly he might plead.

I shall praise God through all eternity for sending me to Cleveland, even though I have been called to suffer.

In 1856, Sister Johnson, who had been my companion during all these years of travel, left me for her heavenly home. She bore her short illness without a murmur, resting on Jesus. As she had lived, so she died, in the full assurance of faith, happy and collected to the last, maintaining her standing in the way of holiness without swerving either to the right or to the left. Glory to the blood that keeps us!

My now sainted mother, who was then in feeble health, lived with me in Cleveland for a few years. As the time for her departure drew near, she very much desired to visit her two daughters—one in Albany, the other in Boston. I feared she was not able to endure the journey, but her desire was so strong, and her confidence in God so great that he would spare her to see her girls again, that I finally consented that she should undertake the journey. I put her in charge of friends who were going east, and she reached my sister's house in safety. She had been with them but a few weeks, when she bade them a long farewell and passed peacefully to heaven. I shall see her again where parting is unknown.

The glorious wave of holiness, which has been rolling through Ohio during the past few years, has swept every hindrance out of my way, and sent me to sea once more with chart and compass.

> "The Bible is my chart; it is a chart and compass too,
> Whose needle points forever true."

When I drop anchor again, it will be in heaven's broad bay.

Glory to Jesus for putting into my hand that precious, living light, *"The Christian Harvester."* May it and its self-sacrificing editor live many years, reflecting holy light as they go.

If any one arise from the perusal of this book, scoffing at the word of truth which he has read, I charge him to prepare to answer for the profanation at the peril of his soul.

XXVIII

A WORD TO MY CHRISTIAN SISTERS.

DEAR SISTERS: I would that I could tell you a hundredth part of what God has revealed to me of his glory, especially on that never-to-be-forgotten night when I received my high and holy calling. The songs I heard I think were those which Job, David and Isaiah speak of hearing at night upon their beds, or the one of which the Revelator says "no man could learn."[16] Certain it is, I have not been able to sing it since, though at times I have seemed to hear the distant echo of the music. When I tried to repeat it, it vanished in the dim distance. Glory! glory! glory to the Most High!

Sisters, shall not you and I unite with the heavenly host in the grand chorus? If so, you will not let what man may say or do, keep you from doing the will of the Lord or using the gifts you have for the good of others. How much easier to bear the reproach of men than to live at a distance from God. Be not kept in bondage by those who say, "We suffer not a woman to teach," thus quoting Paul's words [1 Cor. 14:34], but not rightly applying them. What though we are called to pass through deep waters, so our anchor is cast within the veil, both sure and steadfast? Blessed experience! I have had to weep because this was not my constant experience. At times, a cloud of heaviness has covered my mind, and disobedience has caused me to lose the clear witness of perfect love.

One time I allowed my mind to dwell too much on my physical condition. I was suffering severely from throat difficulty, and took the advice of friends, and sought a cure from earthly physicians, instead of applying to the Great Physician. For this reason my joy was checked, and I was obliged to cease my public labors for several years. During all this time I was less spiritual, less zealous, yet I was not willing to accept the suggestion of Satan, that I had forfeited the blessing of holiness. But alas! the witness was not clear, and God suffered me to pass through close trials, tossed by the billows of temptation.

Losing my loving husband just at this time, I had much of the world to struggle with and against.

Those who are wholly sanctified need not fear that God will hide his face, if they continue to walk in the light even as Christ is in the light. Then they have fellowship with the Father and the Son, and become of one spirit with the Lord. I do not believe God ever withdraws himself from a soul which does not first withdraw itself from him, though such may abide under a cloud for a season, and have to cry: "My God! my God! why hast thou forsaken me?" [Matt. 27:46].

Glory to God, who giveth us the victory through our Lord Jesus Christ! His blood meets all the demands of the law against us. It is the blood of Christ that sues for the fulfillment of his last will and testament, and brings down every blessing into the soul.

When I had well nigh despaired of a cure from my bodily infirmities, I cried from the depths of my soul for the blood of Jesus to be applied to my throat. My faith laid hold of the precious promises—John xiv. 14; Mark ii. 23; xi. 24. At once I ceased trying to join the iron and the clay—the truth of God with the sayings and advice of men. I looked to my God for a fresh act of his sanctifying power. Bless his name! deliverance did come, with the balm, and my throat has troubled me but little since. This was ten years ago. Praise the Lord for that holy fire which many waters of trial and temptation cannot quench.

Dear sisters in Christ, are any of you also without understanding and slow of heart to believe, as were the disciples? Although they had seen their Master do many mighty works, yet, with change of place or circumstances, they would go back upon the old ground of carnal reasoning and unbelieving fears. The darkness and ignorance of our natures are such, that, even after we have embraced the Saviour and received his teaching, we are ready to stumble at the plainest truths! Blind unbelief is always sure to err; it can neither trace God nor trust him. Unbelief is ever alive to distrust and fear. So long as this evil root has a place in us, our fears can not be removed nor our hopes confirmed.

Not till the day of Pentecost did Christ's chosen ones see clearly, or have their understandings opened; and nothing short of a full baptism of the Spirit will dispel our unbelief. Without this, we are but babes—all our lives are often carried away by our carnal natures and kept in bondage; whereas, if we are wholly saved and live under the full sanctifying influence of the Holy Ghost, we cannot be tossed about with every wind, but, like an iron pillar or a house built upon a rock, prove immovable. Our minds will then be fully illuminated, our hearts purified, and our souls filled with the pure love of God, bringing forth fruit to his glory.

XXIX

LOVE NOT THE WORLD.

"If any man love the world, the love of the Father is not in him." 1 John ii. 15. The spirit which is in the world is widely different from the Spirit which is of God; yet many vainly imagine they can unite the two. But as we read in Luke x. 26, so it is between the spirit of the world and the Spirit which is of God. There is a great gulf fixed between them—a gulf which cuts off all union and intercourse; and this gulf will eternally prevent the least degree of fellowship in spirit.

If we be of God and have the love of the Father in our hearts, we are not of the world, because whatsoever is of the world is not of God. We must be one or the other. We can not unite heaven and hell—light and darkness. Worldly honor, worldly pleasure, worldly grandeur, worldly designs and worldly pursuits are all incompatible with the love of the Father and with that kingdom of righteousness, peace and joy in the Holy Ghost, which is not of the world, but of God. Therefore, God says: "Be not conformed to the world, but be ye transformed by the renewing of your mind, that ye may prove what is that good, and acceptable and perfect will of God." Rom. xii. 2.

As we look at the professing Christians of to-day, the question arises, Are they not all conformed to the maxims and fashions of this world, even many of those who profess to have been sanctified? But they say the transforming and renewing here spoken of means, as it says, the mind, not the clothing. But, if the mind be renewed, it must affect the clothing. It is by the Word of God we are to be judged, not by our opinion of the Word; hence, to the law and the testimony. In a like manner the Word also says: "That women adorn themselves in modest apparel, with shamefacedness and sobriety, not with broidered hair, or gold, or pearls, or costly array, but which becometh a woman professing godliness, with good works." 1 Tim. ii. 9, 10; 1 Pet. iii. 3–5. I might quote many passages to the same effect, if I had time or room. Will you not hunt them up, and read carefully and prayerfully for yourselves?

Dear Christians, is not the low state of pure religion among all the churches the result of this worldly-mindedness? There is much outward show; and doth not this outward show portend the sore judgments of God to be executed upon the ministers and members? Malachi ii. 7, says: "The priest's lips should keep knowledge," etc. But it is a lamentable fact that too many priests' lips speak vanity. Many profess to teach, but few are able to feed the lambs, while the sheep are dying for lack of nourishment and the true knowledge of salvation.

The priests' office being to stand between God and the people, they ought to know the mind of God toward his people—what the acceptable and perfect will of God is. Under the law, it was required that the priests should be without blemish—having the whole of the inward and outward man as complete, uniform and consistent as it was possible to be under that dispensation; thereby showing the great purity that is required by God in all those who approach near unto him. "Speak unto Aaron and his sons that they separate themselves" [Lev. 22:2], etc. The Lord here gives a charge to the priests, under a severe penalty, that in all their approaches they shall sanctify themselves. Thus God would teach his ministers and people that he is a holy God, and will be worshiped in the beauty of holiness by all those who come into his presence.

Many may fill his office in the church outwardly, and God may in much mercy draw nigh to the people when devoutly assembled to worship him; but, if the minister has not had previous recourse to the fountain which is opened for sin and uncleanness, and felt the sanctifying and renewing influences of the Holy Ghost, he will feel himself shut out from these divine communications. Oh, that God may baptize the ministry and church with the Holy Ghost and with fire.

By the baptism of fire the church must be purged from its dead forms and notions respecting the inbeing of sin in all believers till death. The Master said: "Now ye are clean through the word which I have spoken unto you; abide in me," etc. [John 15:3–4]. Oh! blessed union. Christian, God wants to establish your heart unblamable in holiness. 1 Thess. i. 13; iv. 7; Heb. xii. 14; Rom. vi. 19. Will you let him do it, by putting away all filthiness of the flesh as well as of the spirit? "Know ye not that ye are the temple of God?" etc. 1 Cor. iii. 16, 17; 2 Cor. vi. 16, 17. Thus we will continue to search and find what the will of God is concerning his children. 1 Thess. iv. 3, 4. Bless God! we may all have that inward, instantaneous sanctification, whereby the root, the inbeing of sin, is destroyed.

Do not misunderstand me. I am not teaching absolute perfection, for that belongs to God alone. Nor do I mean a state of angelic or Adamic perfection, but Christian perfection—an extinction of every temper contrary to love.

"Now, the God of peace sanctify you wholly—your whole spirit, soul and body. 2 Thess. v. 23.[17] Glory to the blood!" "Faithful is he that calleth you, who also will do it." Paul says: He is able to do exceeding abundantly, above all that we ask or think. Eph. iii. 20.

Beloved reader, remember that you cannot commit sin and be a Christian, for "He that committeth sin is of the devil" [1 John 3:8]. If you are regenerated, sin does not reign in your mortal body; but if you are sanctified, sin does not exist in you. The sole ground of our perfect peace from all the carnal mind is by the blood of Jesus, for he is our peace, whom God hath set forth to be a propiation [propitiation?], through faith in his blood. "By whom also we have access by faith into this grace wherein we stand" [Rom. 5:2]—having entered into the holiest by the blood of Jesus.

Let the blood be the sentinel, keeping the tempter without, that you may have constant peace within; for Satan cannot swim waters. Isa. xxx. 7.

XXX

HOW TO OBTAIN SANCTIFICATION.

"Mixture of joy and sorrow
  I daily do pass through;
Sometimes I'm in the valley,
  Then sinking down with woe.

Chorus—Holy, holy, holy is the Lamb
    Holy is the Lamb of God,
    Whose blood doth make me clean.

"Sometimes I am exalted,
  On eagle's wings I fly;
Rising above Mount Pisgah,
  I almost reach the sky.—*Chorus.*

"Sometimes I am in doubting,
  And think I have no grace;
Sometimes I am a-shouting,
  And camp-meeting is the place.—*Chorus.*

"Sometimes, when I am praying,
  It almost seems a task;
Sometimes I get a blessing,
  The greatest I can ask.—*Chorus.*

"Sometimes I read my Bible,
  It seems a sealed book;
Sometimes I find a blessing
  Wherever I do look.—*Chorus.*

"Oh, why am I thus tossed—
  Thus tossed to and fro?
Because the blood of Jesus
  Hasn't washed me white as snow.—*Chorus.*

"Oh, come to Jesus now, and drink
  Of that holy, living stream;
Your thirst he'll quench, your soul revive,
  And cleanse you from all sin."—*Chorus.*

How is sanctification to be obtained? An important question. I answer, by faith. Faith is the only condition of sanctification. By this I mean a faith that dies out to the world and every form of sin; that gives up the sin of the heart; and that believes, according to God's promise, he is able to perform, and will do it now—doeth it now.

Why not yield, believe, and be sanctified now—now, while reading? "Now is the day of salvation" [2 Cor. 6:2]. Say: "Here, Lord, I will, I do believe; thou hast said now—now let it be—now apply the blood of Jesus to my waiting, longing soul."

"Hallelujah! 'tis done!
I believe on the Son;
I am saved by the blood
Of the crucified One."

Now, dear reader, I conclude by praying that this little work may be blessed of God to your spiritual and everlasting good. I trust also that it will promote the cause of holiness in the Church.

Now, unto Him who is able to do exceeding abundantly, above all that we ask or think, according to the power that worketh in us; unto Him be glory in the church by Christ Jesus throughout all ages, world without end. Amen.[18]

NOTES

Introduction

1. *A Narrative of the Most Remarkable Particulars in the Life of James Albert Ukawsaw Gronniosaw, An African Prince* (1770; rpt. Newport, R.I.: S. Southwick, 1774); *Narrative of the Lord's Wonderful Dealings with John Marrant, A Black,* ed. William Aldridge (London: Gilbert and Plummer, 1785); George White, *A Brief Account of the Life, Experiences, Travels, and Gospel Labours of George White* (New York: John C. Totten, 1810). Robert B. Stepto discusses the Afro-American "pregeneric myth" in his *From Behind the Veil* (Urbana: University of Illinois Press, 1979), pp. ix, 167–68.

2. David Brion Davis, *The Problem of Slavery in Western Culture* (Ithaca, N.Y.: Cornell University Press, 1966), p. 90.

3. For instance, see the white slaveholding deist whose attempted conversion Jarena Lee records at the end of her autobiography.

4. In *All Loves Excelling: American Protestant Women in World Missions* (Grand Rapids, Michigan: Eerdman, 1968), p. 67, Robert Pierce Beaver notes that "the first single woman, not a widow," to be sent overseas for missionary work was Betsey Stockton, a black woman who served as both a "domestic assistant" to a white missionary family and as a schoolteacher on the mission staff at Lahinah, Hawaii, in 1823. Beaver discusses other antebellum women missionaries on pp. 59–84. For further information, see Barbara Welter, "She Hath Done What She Could: Protestant Women's Missionary Careers in Nineteenth-Century America," *American Quarterly* 30 (Winter 1978): 624–38.

5. Nancy G. Prince, *A Narrative of the Life and Travels of Mrs. Nancy Prince* (Boston: The Author, 1850). This book was reprinted in 1853 and again in 1856.

6. Olive Gilbert's biography, *Narrative of Sojourner Truth, A Northern Slave* (Boston: The Author, 1850), introduced antislavery readers to the story of Isabella, an indomitable New York-born slave who, upon seizing her freedom in 1826, felt increasingly drawn to the life of itinerant evangelism. In 1843 she adopted the name Sojourner Truth and committed herself to a life of pilgrimage proclaiming the truth as she saw it. By the mid-nineteenth century, her mission would lead her into prominent advocacy of abolitionism and women's rights. See Arthur H. Fauset, *Sojourner Truth* (Chapel Hill: University of North Carolina Press, 1938), and Jacqueline Bernard, *Journey Toward Freedom: The Story of Sojourner Truth* (New York: W. W. Norton, 1967).

7. For excerpts from and comments on the work of Keckley, Dubois, and Taylor, see Bert James Loewenberg and Ruth Bogin, eds., *Black Women in Nineteenth-Century American Life* (University Park, Pa.: Pennsylvania State University Press, 1976), pp. 39–47, 70–77, 89–94; and Dorothy Sterling, *We Are Your Sisters: Black Women in the Nineteenth Century* (New York: W. W. Norton, 1984), pp. 248–52, 459–60.

8. An internationally known Holiness evangelist, Amanda Berry Smith recounted her youth, conversion, and ministry in *An Autobiography* (Chicago: Meyer & Bros., 1893). The spiritual evolution of Rebecca Cox Jackson from

African Methodism to leadership as a preaching "eldress" in a Shaker community in Watervliet, New York, is recorded in her antebellum manuscript autobiography, edited by Jean McMahon Humez in *Gifts of Power: The Writings of Rebecca Jackson, Black Visionary, Shaker Eldress* (Amherst: University of Massachusetts Press, 1981). For discussions of less prominent pioneering black female preachers, see Jualynne Dodson, "Nineteenth-Century A. M. E. Preaching Women," in Hilah F. Thomas and Rosemary Skinner Keller, eds., *Women in New Worlds* (Nashville: Abingdon, 1981), pp. 276–89; and Nancy Hardesty, Lucille Sider Dayton, and Donald W. Dayton, "Women in the Holiness Movement: Feminism in the Evangelical Tradition," in Rosemary Ruether and Eleanor McLaughlin, eds., *Women of Spirit* (New York: Simon and Schuster, 1979), pp. 225–54.

9. Further explanation of the doctrine of "sanctification," with respect particularly to John Wesley's influential views of the subject, follows later in this discussion. For a depiction of the religious environment in which Foote grew up, see Whitney R. Cross, *The Burned-over District: The Social and Intellectual History of Enthusiastic Religion in Western New York, 1800–1850* (Ithaca, N.Y.: Cornell University Press, 1950), pp. 56, 75, 104, 240–41. The rise of the Holiness movement in antebellum America is recounted in Melvin Easterday Dieter, *The Holiness Revival of the Nineteenth Century* (Metuchen, N.J.: Scarecrow, 1980). See also Timothy Smith's chapters on "The Holiness Revival at Oberlin" and "Sanctification in American Methodism" in his *Revivalism and Social Reform in Mid-Nineteenth-Century America* (New York: Abingdon, 1957), pp. 103–34. In their essay on "Women in the Holiness Movement," (*Women of Spirit,* pp. 230–31), Hardesty, Dayton, and Dayton show how perfectionism and holiness revivals touched the lives of early feminists like Elizabeth Cady Stanton, Antoinette Brown, and Lucy Stone.

10. Jarena Lee does not mention her family name in her account of her early life. Thus we are compelled to refer to her by her married name throughout this biographical sketch. Because Zilpha Elaw and Julia Foote do not reveal their family names either, subsequent sketches of their lives in this introduction refer to them by their married names.

11. Allen's role in the founding of the independent African Methodist Episcopal Church is discussed in Carol V. R. George, *Segregated Sabbaths* (New York: Oxford University Press, 1973). Both George and Charles H. Wesley discuss Allen's relationships with the Englishwoman Dorothy Ripley and Jarena Lee. See Wesley's *Richard Allen* (Washington, D.C.: Associated Publishers, 1935), pp. 114–15, 196–98, and *Segregated Sabbaths,* pp. 128–29. George's account of Allen's dealings with Lee ignores the former's initial rebuff of Lee's request for his endorsement of her preaching career.

12. Sources for this biographical sketch are: *The Life and Religious Experience of Jarena Lee* (Philadelphia: The Author, 1836); *Religious Experience and Journal of Mrs. Jarena Lee* (Philadelphia: The Author, 1849); Daniel A. Payne, *History of the African Methodist Episcopal Church* (Nashville, Tenn.: A.M.E. Sunday-School Union, 1891), pp. 190, 237, 273; Charles H. Wesley, *Richard Allen,* pp. 197–98; Jualynne Dodson, "Nineteenth-Century A.M.E. Preaching Women," p. 287; and Clarence E. Walker, *A Rock in a Weary Land: The African Methodist Episcopal Church During the Civil War and Reconstruction* (Baton Rouge: Louisiana State University Press, 1982), p. 25. See also David W. Wills, "Womanhood and Domesticity in the A.M.E. Tradition: The Influence of Daniel Alexander Payne," in David W. Wills and Richard Newman, eds., *Black Apostles at Home and Abroad* (Boston: G. K. Hall, 1982), pp. 137–40.

13. All biographical information on Zilpha Elaw is taken from *Memoirs of the Life, Religious Experience, Ministerial Travels and Labours of Mrs. Zilpha Elaw* (London: The Author, 1846). Further information on the American camp meeting appears in Charles A. Johnson, *The Frontier Camp Meeting* (Dallas: Southern Methodist University Press, 1955) and Dickson D. Bruce, Jr., *And They All Sang Hallelujah: Plain-Folk Camp-Meeting Religion 1800–1845* (Knoxville: University of Tennessee Press, 1974).

14. The information used in this biographical sketch is taken from Julia A. J. Foote, *A Brand Plucked from the Fire* (Cleveland, Ohio: The Author, 1879); Melvin Easterday Dieter, *The Holiness Revival of the Nineteenth Century,* pp. 118–27; and William J. Walls, *The African Methodist Episcopal Zion Church* (Charlotte, N.C.: A.M.E. Zion Publishing House, 1974), pp. 111–12.

15. Useful information on black women's visionary experience during conversion appears in Humez, ed., *Gifts of Power,* pp. 42–50, and in Clifton H. Johnson, ed., *God Struck Me Dead: Religious Conversion Experiences and Autobiographies of Ex-Slaves* (Philadelphia: United Church Press, 1969), pp. 65–67, 93–101.

16. See Sacvan Bercovitch, *The Puritan Origins of the American Self* (New Haven: Yale University Press, 1975), pp. 11, 13–15, 17–18; Daniel B. Shea, *Spiritual Autobiography in Early America* (Princeton, N.J.: Princeton University Press, 1968), pp. 249–56; Sidney Mead, "The Rise of the Evangelical Conception of the Ministry in America," in H. Richard Niebuhr and Daniel Williams, eds., *The Ministry in Historical Perspective* (New York: Harpers, 1956), pp. 207–49; Donald M. Scott, "Abolition as a Sacred Vocation," in Lewis Perry and Michael Fellman, eds., *Antislavery Reconsidered* (Baton Rouge: Louisiana State University Press, 1979), pp. 53–60; and Edmund S. Morgan, *Visible Saints: The History of a Puritan Idea* (New York: New York University Press, 1963), pp. 88–91.

17. Barbara Welter, *Dimity Convictions: The American Woman in the Nineteenth Century* (Athens: Ohio University Press, 1976), pp. 21–23, 86; Mary P. Ryan, "The Power of Women's Networks: A Case Study of Female Moral Reform in Antebellum America," *Feminist Studies* 5 (Spring 1979): 66–85. For a detailed study of the feminist significance of the rise of women's benevolent and reform associations in the cities of the antebellum North, see Barbara J. Berg, *The Remembered Gate: Origins of American Feminism* (New York: Oxford University Press, 1978).

18. For the role of the exhorter in the A.M.E. church, see Richard Allen and Jacob Tapisco, *The Doctrines and Discipline of the African Methodist Episcopal Church* (Philadelphia: Allen and Tapisco, 1817), pp. 161–62.

19. Harald Lindström, *Wesley and Sanctification* (London: Epworth, 1950), pp. 92, 113–20, 148.

20. Ibid., pp. 100–101.

21. Foote, *A Brand Plucked from the Fire,* p. 305.

22. Lee, Elaw, and Foote help to exemplify the thesis of Carl N. Degler's *At Odds: Women and the Family in America* (New York: Oxford University Press, 1980), which argues that the subordination of women in the family has long been a major stumbling block to the cause of women's equality in society. See especially his chapter entitled "The World is Only a Large Home," (pp. 298–327), which treats women's activity in evangelical and reform movements in the first half of the nineteenth century.

23. See Barbara Brown Zikmund, "The Feminist Thrust of Sectarian Christianity," in Ruether and McLaughlin, eds., *Women of Spirit,* pp. 205–24.

24. See Hardesty, Dayton, and Dayton, "Women in the Holiness Movement," p. 242, where an 1851 controversy involving an itinerant female preacher's failure to remain by the bedside of a dying child is recorded.

25. See Dred Scott v. Sandford, 19 Howard 393, as quoted in Henry Steele Commager, ed., *Documents of American History* (New York: Appleton-Century-Crofts, 1973), pp. 340–42.

26. Elaw, *Memoirs,* p. 210.

27. See Beecher as quoted in Smith, *Revivalism and Social Reform,* pp. 159–60.

28. Maria W. Stewart, "Religion and the Pure Principles of Morality," first printed in Boston in pamphlet form in 1831 before being included in *Productions of Mrs. Maria W. Stewart* (Boston: n.p., 1835). The quotation is from p. 6 of Stewart's *Productions.*

29. Frances E. W. Harper, "Our Greatest Want," *Anglo-African Magazine* 1 (May 1859): 160.

The Life and Religious Experience of Jarena Lee

1. Joseph Pilmore (1739–1825) accepted John Wesley's call for volunteers to evangelize the American colonies and in 1769 became the first Methodist preacher in Philadelphia. See the sketch of his life in *DANB,* vol. 15, 609–10.

2. Richard Allen (1760–1831), born a slave in Philadelphia, was converted to Christianity and purchased his freedom at the age of seventeen, whereupon he became a wagon driver during the Revolutionary War and began an itinerant preaching career. Discrimination against blacks in the St. George's Methodist Episcopal Church in Philadelphia moved Allen, with the help of Absalom Jones, to organize in protest the Free African Society, on April 12, 1787. Seven years later, the society's first church, the Bethel African Methodist Episcopal Church, was dedicated into service under the preaching leadership of Allen. In 1799 Bishop Francis Asbury ordained Allen a deacon, making him the first black to receive ordination in the Methodist Episcopal church in America. During the next fifteen years other A.M.E. congregations were established in Delaware, Maryland, New York, and neighboring states. On April 9, 1816, Allen and the leaders of these more recent black churches founded the first independent Afro-American denomination in the United States, the African Methodist Episcopal church. Allen was consecrated as the first bishop of the A.M.E. church on April 11, 1816. See Charles H. Wesley's *Richard Allen: Apostle of Freedom,* 2d ed. (Washington, D.C.: Associated Publishers, 1969) and Allen's narrative, *The Life, Experience and Gospel Labors of the Rt. Rev. Richard Allen* (1833).

3. In her narrative, Lee often quotes verses from popular hymns of the day. Her sources include *A Collection of Hymns, for the Use of the Methodist Episcopal Church* (1823) and *The African Methodist Episcopal Church Hymn Book* (1818, rev. 1836).

4. Belshazzar, king of Babylon after Nebuchadnezzar, is the subject of the fifth chapter of the Book of Daniel.

5. Lee alludes to 2 Cor. 12:2–4, although it was not Paul but an unnamed acquaintance of Paul who was "caught up to the third heaven."

6. Lee's commissioning experience echoes that of several biblical prophets and missionaries. See Jer. 1:9; Exod. 4:1, 12; and Luke 21:15.

7. By this time the Free African Society had become the Bethel African Methodist Episcopal Church.

8. Before 1817, when the A.M.E. church adopted its own *Doctrines and Discipline,* the black Methodists under Allen's leadership accepted the rules of church government and the Articles of Faith that John Wesley selected for the Methodist Episcopal church. Wesleyan Methodists did not allow the formal ordination of women as preachers, although Wesley himself was willing to admit unofficially of "exceptions" to this rule of church polity. See Earl Kent Brown, "Women of the Word," in Hilah F. Thomas and Rosemary Skinner Keller, eds., *Women in New Worlds* (Nashville: Abingdon, 1981), pp. 69–87.

9. Lee refers to Mary Magdalene, who was the first to inform Jesus' disciples of his resurrection in John 20:11–18.

10. At the 1818 Annual Conference of the A.M.E. church, the death of "Joseph Lea, a man of God, who has labored for many years in the ministry" was noted for church records, after which time the Snow Hill church's trustee applied to the conference "to take charge of the spiritual concerns of their church." Daniel A. Payne, *History of the African Methodist Episcopal Church* (Nashville: A.M.E. Sunday-School Union, 1891), I, 26.

11. Among the Methodists, both white and black, exhortation was regularly distinguished from true preaching and usually followed it during a worship service. Exhorters were not licensed to speak from or interpret a biblical text. They were expected to limit themselves to pleas for close attention to the message preached, repentance, and acceptance of the present opportunity for salvation.

12. As Roman proconsul of Achaia in Southern Greece, Gallio refused to arbitrate a dispute between a group of Corinthian Jews and Paul the Apostle. Instead he dismissed the Jewish leaders who wanted Paul tried for breaking religious laws. His indifference to religious issues placed before him seems to be the characteristic that Lee alludes to. See Acts 18:12–17.

13. Lee refers to William Cornish, an early A.M.E. minister and deacon, not the more famous Samuel E. Cornish, the black abolitionist, newspaper editor, and Presbyterian minister.

14. Rev. Richard Williams of Baltimore was a delegate to the first General Convention of the A.M.E. church in 1816, when the Ecclesiastic Compact of the new denomination was written. His leadership in the church was rewarded by his ordination as elder in 1824.

15. Paul, formerly Saul, of Tarsus traveled to Jerusalem to preach the evangelization of the gentiles in Acts 15:2–12. He had formerly persecuted Christians in Jerusalem according to Acts 8:1–3.

16. For more information on a later edition of Lee's journal, see the Textual Note.

Zilpha Elaw's *Memoirs*

1. Elaw adopts a salutation and invocation reminiscent of that employed by Paul the Apostle in his letters to early Christian churches. See, for instance, the opening verses of 1 Corinthians or the Letter to the Philippians.

2. From internal evidence in her *Memoirs,* Zilpha Elaw appears to have been born around 1790.

3. If, as it appears from her autobiography, Elaw grew up in the vicinity of Philadelphia, her statement about the "first appearance" of the Methodists in that part of Pennsylvania is probably in error. The earliest Methodist church in America had been founded in Philadelphia in 1770, and, according to the pioneering Bishop Francis Asbury's *Journal and Letters* (1958), there were 180

practicing Methodists in Philadelphia as early as 1773. Elaw became a member of a Methodist Episcopal society in one of the outlying regions around Philadelphia in 1808.

4. The verse that appears in Elaw's *Memoirs,* as in Jarena Lee's narrative, is drawn from Methodist hymnbook sources such as *The Methodist Harmonist* (1833) and *A Collection of Hymns, for the use of the Methodist Episcopal Church, Principally from the Collection of the Rev. John Wesley* (1836).

5. Elaw compares herself to the Ethiopian eunuch, who, after learning of Jesus, was converted to Christianity through the ministry of the Apostle Philip. See Acts 8:26ff. Julia Foote also compares herself to the Ethiopian eunuch early in her autobiography.

6. Although Elaw refers to the Mitchels, as her "master" and "mistress," her relationship to them was that of a servant girl, not a slave. After March 1, 1780, the Pennsylvania state legislature decreed that all children born in the state would be free persons regardless of the status of their parents.

7. Elaw draws this notion from Gen. 2:18, in which God creates the woman Eve as a "help-meet" for Adam, the first man.

8. The citation from Hebrews does not deal with marriage to an unbeliever.

9. "The wise man" is the Preacher in Eccles. 1:14, who condemns pleasure-seeking among the many "vanities" of a worldly life.

10. This is probably a reference to President James Madison's reinvocation of the Non-Intercourse Act on March 2, 1811, which shut off commerce between the United States and Great Britain on the eve of the War of 1812.

11. Elaw's description of the camp meeting provides considerable information about the way in which this peculiarly American form of mass revivalism functioned. Important scholarly studies of the camp meeting phenomenon in antebellum evangelical life are Charles A. Johnson, *The Frontier Camp Meeting* (Dallas: Southern Methodist University Press, 1955), and Dickson D. Bruce, Jr., *And They All Sang Hallelujah: Plain-Folk Camp-Meeting Religion, 1800–1845* (Knoxville: University of Tennessee Press, 1974).

12. In what was apparently her first effort in public religious leadership, Elaw served, quite spontaneously, as one of the "praying persons" whose duty in the camp meeting was to aid and encourage convicted sinners in their "recovery." See Bruce, *And They All Sang Hallelujah,* pp. 76–77.

13. Phoebe, a colleague of Paul the Apostle in the early Christian church, is mentioned in Rom. 16:1–2.

14. Enoch, one of the early descendants of Adam, is praised in Gen. 5:19–24 as a man who "walked with God."

15. Here as elsewhere in her autobiography, Elaw attacks deism as universalism and scepticism and thus a special threat to evangelical Christianity.

16. Segregation of the races and, during preaching services, of the sexes was the general rule in camp meetings. See Bruce, *And They All Sang Hallelujah,* p. 73. For additional insight into the racial mores of Southern Methodist camp meetings, see Frederick Douglass, *My Bondage and My Freedom* (New York and Auburn: Miller, Orton & Mulligan, 1855), pp. 193–94.

17. In her first preaching effort, Elaw played a role similar to that of the convert exhorter in the camp meeting. The structure of camp meeting revivals was flexible enough to allow for spontaneous exhortations from nonprofessional preachers who, like Zilpha Elaw, felt moved by the spirit to address a congregation. Dickson D. Bruce notes that "exhorting as new converts" was one of the few ways in which women could assume a visible leadership role in camp meetings (pp. 74–76).

18. Because of his dreams, Joseph, the favorite son of Jacob, was hated by his eleven jealous brothers in Gen. 37:1–5. Paul recalls the times when "no man stood with me" in 2 Tim. 4:16.

19. In the antebellum South it was customary to jail and auction off any free Negro who could not prove his or her free status through certificates registered and issued by the courts of the state. As the Virginia Supreme Court of Appeals ruled in 1840, "In the case of a person visibly appearing to be a negro, the presumption is that he is a slave," and the burden of proof otherwise lay with the accused. Moreover, since 1832, Virginia prohibited any slave or free Negro from conducting religious meetings in the day or night-time. Elaw's punishment for breaking this law would have been a public whipping of up to thirty-nine lashes. See Benjamin Quarles, *The Negro in the Making of America* (New York: Macmillan, 1969), pp. 86–88, and Luther P. Jackson, *Free Negro Labor and Property Holding in Virginia, 1830–1860* (New York: American Historical Association, 1942), p. 21.

20. Elaw implicitly compares herself among the Virginians to Jesus in Samaria when he told a woman drawing water at a well of the secrets of her heart and "all things that ever [she] did." See John 4:7–30. By linking the Virginians with the Samaritans, Elaw endows the slave state with qualities of alienation and apostasy that helped make the Samaritans a despised people to the Jews of the Bible. At the same time, she identifies herself with Christ on his saving mission among the Samaritans.

21. Since 1683 the Janneys of Pennsylvania had been active and committed members of the Society of Friends. Jacob Janney moved to Loudon County, Virginia, around 1745; his grandson, Abijah, became a successful miller and farmer in that region until his wife died in 1813, whereupon he moved to Alexandria. Antislavery in politics, the antebellum Virginia Janneys produced an important emancipation activist in the person of Samuel M. Janney, from whose *Memoirs* (Philadelphia: Friends Book Association, 1881) this information about Abijah Janney is taken.

22. Elaw probably refers to Major Henry Lee (1787–1837), son of General "Light-Horse Harry" Lee and half-brother of Robert E. Lee, who in 1828 lived in Washington and was employed as a political writer for Andrew Jackson during his campaign for the presidency. The following year, when his wife Anne McCarty Lee supposedly invited Elaw to her home, the Lees passed in Washington awaiting Senate confirmation of the major's nomination as consul-general to Algiers.

23. John Rodgers (1773–1838), one of the most distinguished officers in the early United States Navy, made his home in Washington, D.C., with his wife, Minerva Denison Rodgers, throughout the 1820s, except during a brief tour of duty in the Mediterranean from 1825 to 1827. In 1823 Commodore Rodgers served as Secretary of the Navy. See C. O. Paullin, *Commodore John Rodgers* (1910).

24. The reference is to Paul's letter to Philemon, a Greek slaveowner whose bondman, Onesimus, Paul was returning to his master with the recommendation that Philemon receive his formerly "unprofitable" slave as "a brother beloved" in the Christian faith.

25. Elaw probably refers to the second tables of stone on which God wrote his commandments for the Israelites after Moses broke the first tables in his outrage over the worship of the golden calf. See Exod. 34:1–16.

26. According to Paul the Apostle, Demas forsook him and the Christian ministry because of his love of "the present world." 2 Tim. 4:10.

27. Although there is no scriptural evidence that Moses visited Mount

Tabor, it was the site of a major military victory for the Israelites during the time of Deborah the prophet. See Judges 4:6–15.

28. In the Book of Nehemiah, Sanballat the Horonite is an antagonist of Nehemiah and other exiled Jews who rebuild the city of Jerusalem despite Sanballat's ridicule and opposition.

29. The ark was a holy chest made by divine command according to specifications laid out in Exod. 24:10–22. It housed the two tables of the law of the covenant between God and Israel and contained the Holy of Holies, where God was presumed to dwell. Its care was entrusted only to a particular priestly clan and only the high priest was allowed to look into it. Uzziah (not "Uzzah") was a very successful warrior king of Judah whose career is recounted in 2 Chron. 26:1–23. Because he tried to usurp priestly offices in the temple, he was stricken with leprosy and was ostracized by his people and "cut off from the house of the Lord."

30. Probably this is John N. Maffit, a flamboyant revivalist who was born in Ireland, became an itinerant Methodist preacher in 1822, and became famous enough to serve for a time as chaplain to the United States Congress.

31. The Urim and Thummim ("command and truth") are a sort of divine oracle, which, in Exod. 28:30, is commanded to be carried in the breastplate of the high priest of Israel. The First Epistle General of John 2:20 refers to the "unction from the Holy One," which provides special knowledge to the Christian.

32. Joshua, successor to Moses, led the Israelites into the Promised Land of Canaan; the Book of Joshua recounts the conquest of Canaan under his military leadership.

33. Nabal's rudeness and meanness in response to David's request for aid and succor made his name synonymous with churlishness and bestiality. See 1 Sam. 25:2–42.

34. In the sixteenth chapter of his epistle to the Romans, Paul asks the Christians in Rome to "greet" or "salute" a number of their fellow-believers traveling or living in their midst, including "Tryphaena and Tryphosa, who labor in the Lord," Nereus and his sister, "Rufus chosen in the Lord, and his mother and mine," "Priscilla and Aquila, my helpers in Christ Jesus," and several other female apostles and "saints" whom Elaw does not cite. Priscilla's expounding of the Gospel to Apollos is recounted in Acts 18:24–26. Philip's four virgin daughters who prophesied are mentioned in Acts 21:9.

35. Elaw appropriates from Ezek. 37:1–14, in which the prophet addresses a valley of dry bones and with God's help creates of them an army of living men.

36. George Thompson (1804–78) became well known in his native Britain in the early 1830s as an antislavery activist before coming to America on a lecture tour in 1834. An associate of radical abolitionists like William Lloyd Garrison, he was publicly denounced by President Andrew Jackson, and a few months after Elaw heard him, he fled Boston, where threats had been made on his life, and returned to England to continue his reformist work.

37. Elijah Hedding (1780–1850), one of the most energetic agents of expansion in the Methodist Episcopal Church in the first decades of the nineteenth century, was consecrated bishop in 1824. He strongly opposed abolitionist agitation in the northern conferences of the church and refused to judge slavery as inherently sinful. On the other hand, he was an active supporter of lay evangelists like Zilpha Elaw and advocated holiness revivals throughout American Methodism.

38. The American Anti-Slavery Society was founded in New York City in 1833 by Theodore Dwight Weld and Arthur and Lewis Tappan.

39. Selina, Countess of Huntingdon (1707–91) was an early convert to Methodism and opened her house in London for preaching services in 1746. She used her wealth as a member of the peerage to build sixty-four chapels, which at her death were called the "Countess of Huntingdon Connexion."

40. Deborah, judge, prophet, and savior of Israel from the oppression of Jabin, King of the Canaanites, is extolled in the fourth and fifth chapters of the Book of Judges. Huldah's prophecy to Josiah, the King of Judah, appears in 2 Kings 22:14–20 and 2 Chron. 34:22–28.

41. "Tekel" is translated in Dan. 5:27 as "Thou art weighed in the balances, and art found wanting."

42. Sarah was the half-sister and wife of Abraham, the patriarch honored by Jews, Christians, and Moslems as the founder of the true religion. As mother of Isaac, she preserved Abraham's line and ensured the fulfillment of God's promise to Abraham in Genesis 12:2 that his descendants should make "a great nation."

43. Joshua Soule (1781–1867) was elected bishop of the Methodist Episcopal church in 1824. He journeyed to England in 1842 as a fraternal delegate to the British Wesleyan Conference.

44. The wickedness and annihilation of the city of Sodom is narrated in Gen. 18:16–33 and 19:1–28.

45. See the Parable of the Ten Virgins in Matt. 25:1–13.

Julia Foote's *A Brand Plucked from the Fire*

1. The *Christian Harvester,* founded in 1873 in Canton, Ohio, by Rev. Thomas K. Doty, was an evangelical publication that subscribed to the tenets of the Holiness movement.

2. The verse inserted into Foote's text comes from the same kinds of hymnbook sources that Jarena Lee and Zilpha Elaw had available to them, in particular *The Methodist Harmonist* (1833) and *Hymnal of the Methodist Church, with Tunes* (1878).

3. Gad was one of the original twelve tribes of Israel. See Gen. 30:10 and 49:19.

4. Prudence Crandall opened a female boarding school in Canterbury, Connecticut, in the fall of 1832 but closed it soon thereafter as a result of community resistance to the fact that she had admitted one black pupil. In February 1833 she opened a school for black girls, which was forcibly closed in late May by an act of the state legislature making any such school as hers illegal. Much litigation ensued over the school's right to exist. During this time the school was the target of attempted arson and other destructive assaults which effectively prevented it from opening again. See Alfred T. Child, Jr., "Prudence Crandall and the Canterbury Experiment," *Bulletin of the Friends Historical Association,* 22 (1933): 35–55.

5. Foote compares herself to the Ethiopian eunuch who learned of Jesus and was converted to Christianity as a result of the ministry of the Apostle Philip. Acts 8:26ff.

6. At times in her autobiography Foote incorporates quotations that appear to be taken from the Bible but are not traceable to a specific scriptural source.

7. Rev. Jehiel C. Beman, pastor of the African Methodist Episcopal Zion

Church of Boston since 1838, was a leading antislavery orator in the city and president of the Massachusetts Temperance Society of Colored People.

8. The day of Pentecost is recounted in the second chapter of Acts, where the Apostle Peter quotes from Joel 2:28–32.

9. Philip's daughters who prophesied are mentioned in Acts 21:8–9. Foote's references to Priscilla, Aquila, and Phebe are not exactly scripturally accurate. Priscilla and her husband Aquila, exiled from Italy because of Roman persecution of Jews or Christians of Jewish descent, are called by Paul his "helpers" in Christ in Rom. 16:3. This pair is also mentioned in Acts 18:1–3, 18, 26; 1 Cor. 16:19; and 2 Tim. 4:19. Phebe, "a servant of the church" at Cenchreae, the eastern port of Corinth, is praised by Paul in his letter to the Romans 16:1–2. The Greek word that Paul applied in common to himself (see 1 Cor. 3:5), Phebe, and Tychicus is *diakonos* ("servant"). The servanthood of the Christian ministry *(diakonia)* connotes self-abnegation, not servility. See Letty M. Russell, "Women and Ministry," in Alice L. Hageman, ed., *Sexist Religion and Women in the Church* (New York: Association, 1974), pp. 48, 55. Paul's pleas for help to those women who worked with him in evangelistic missions appears in Phil. 4:3. All quotations are taken from the King James version of the Bible.

10. A bush meeting was a religious service held in a forest or grove.

11. This is a printer's error; read "1845."

12. This trustee was following Paul's injunction against women speaking in church, which appears in 1 Cor. 14:34–35.

13. Morris Brown (1770–1849) founded in Charleston, South Carolina, the first A.M.E. church in the antebellum South. A prosperous freeman and part-time preacher, he fled his native state under suspicion after the Denmark Vesey insurrectionary plot was discovered in 1822. With his family Brown settled in Philadelphia, became an assistant to Richard Allen, and was elected the second bishop of the African Methodist Episcopal church on May 25, 1828.

14. Foote probably refers to the 1844 General Conference of the A.M.E. church, which defeated a motion to make suitable provisions in the church's governance for the authorization of women preachers. Motions to license women to preach were also voted down at the 1848 and 1852 General Conference meetings. Daniel A. Payne's *History of the African Methodist Episcopal Church* (1891) and Charles Spencer Smith's *A History of the African Methodist Episcopal Church* (1922), both published as official histories by the church, discuss these developments, though without much sympathy.

15. Daniel Alexander Payne (1811–93) distinguished himself in a variety of intellectual pursuits while serving as a leader and the sixth bishop of the A.M.E. church. Though an outspoken advocate of a liberal education for all ministers in the church, he took a more conservative line on women's education and was suspicious of untrained, self-appointed evangelists like Jarena Lee. Between 1845 and 1850, he pastored the Bethel A.M.E. Church of Baltimore, where his opposition to various forms of "extravagances in worship" so infuriated one female parishioner that she attacked him with a club. While recording this event in his autobiography, *Recollections of Seventy Years* (1888), he says nothing of a call inviting Julia Foote to visit and work with him in Baltimore. A useful essay on Payne's very influential views of women in the church and home is David W. Wills, "Womanhood and Domesticity in the A.M.E. Tradition: The Influence of Daniel Alexander Payne," in *Black Apostles*

at Home and Abroad, ed. David W. Wills and Richard Newman (Boston: G. K. Hall, 1982), pp. 133–46.

16. Foote may be referring to Job 35:10; Ps. 42:8; Isa. 30:29; and Rev. 14:3.
17. The verse is 1 Thess. 5:23.
18. This benediction is appropriated from Eph. 3:20–21.